The Complete Book
of
CAT HEALTH
AND CARE

by J. J. McCoy

A PERIGEE BOOK

For Joseph F. Morsello
and his unusual cat,
"Booger"

Perigee Books
are published by
G. P. Putnam's Sons
200 Madison Avenue
New York, New York 10016

Library of Congress Cataloging in Publication Data

McCoy, J. J. (Joseph J.), date.
       The complete book of cat health and care.

       Reprint. Originally published: New York: Putnam,
1968. With new foreword.
       Bibliography: p.
       Includes index.
       1. Cats. 2. Cats—Diseases. I. Title.
SF447.M345 1982   636.8'083   82-462
ISBN 0-399-50623-3 (pbk.)   AACR2

First Perigee printing, 1982
PRINTED IN THE UNITED STATES OF AMERICA

Contents

CONTENTS

PART III

CAT HEALTH   119

CONTENTS

CONTENTS

19. CARE OF THE PREGNANT CAT AND KITTENS 205

PART V

OLD AGE 217

20. CARE OF THE OLD CAT 219

Foreword

More people are keeping cats as house pets than ever before. And for many good reasons. One is that cats need less living space than do most dogs. Another is the cat's ability to adapt to an urban environment and even to a restricted life in a one-room apartment. A third reason is that many people, young and old, are discovering the unique qualities of *Felis catus*.

I do not consider the cat to be a domesticated animal as are dogs, horses, and other livestock. But the cat, its independent nature aside, does have an affinity for human beings. Moreover, this fascinating animal has managed to live in close association with human beings without undergoing any major changes in its basic behavior or a loss or dulling of its primitive instincts. However, modern civilization does put a strain on the lives of many cats, especially those that are forced to live in a limited or stressful environment or are wholly dependent upon their keepers for survival. Which brings us to the purpose of this book.

The Complete Book of Cat Health and Care is intended as a guide or manual on cat care for the cat owner or prospective owner. It is based on the knowledge that I have accumulated during my many years as an animal scientist, humane society officer, pet consultant, and cat owner. I hope that the transmission of the information set down in this book will help concerned cat owners to provide intelligent care for their pets and thus create a harmonious relationship between cat and owner.

A comment about the health and disease chapters in the book: the information provided in these chapters is not meant to be a substitute for the knowledge and services of a veterinarian. Nor is it intended to qualify the readers as a "cat doctor." The function of these chapters is to inform the cat owner—to aid him or her in distinguishing between a sick and healthy cat, to provide signposts along the cat's life, to point out the signs and symptoms of disease, and, most importantly, to provide clues as to when to take a cat to a veterinarian.

Finally, reading this book will not make you an expert on cats. But it can help you to become an expert on *your* cat. And that is a worthwhile goal.

J. J. McCoy

Part One

EVOLUTION AND HISTORY
OF THE CAT

1. The Domestic Cat and Its Relatives

Aloof, mysterious, courageous and changeable—the domestic cat is a most unusual animal. It certainly is enigmatic in character and history, with an origin that seems lost in antiquity. We don't really know when the cat first decided to live with people. The word "decided" is used advisedly, because the cat—unlike the dog—is very selective in choosing its human friends.

Yet, despite its strong sense of independence and its sphinxlike attitude, the cat makes a wonderful pet, companionable and useful. This interesting feline has few equals as a rodent exterminator. While we do not usually associate cats with acts of heroism toward human beings, there are recorded cases where cats have actually saved people from injury or death. For instance, at the time of the great earthquake in Messina, Italy, in 1908, a pet cat felt the tremors, sensed an approaching catastrophe, alerted the household with loud cries and led the family to safety. Some cats have saved families from fire by crying out and warning the people who slept unaware of the danger. Other cats have prevented human beings from being fatally bitten by poisonous snakes by attacking and routing the reptiles before they could strike. In these and other acts of heroism, cats have shown that they are highly intelligent and capable of devotion to human beings.

Critics of the cat—or, if you will, cat-haters—often point out that cats are fickle creatures that will walk out on their owners when the situation is not to their satisfaction. This sweeping condemnation of

3

cats is unwarranted. True, cats are sensitive and fastidious animals, quick to respond to abuse or neglect. Some cats do move out of a house; however, there usually is a good reason for the animal's departure. In most cases, it is indifference, neglect or mistreatment that motivates the cat's exodus.

Unfortunately—and as a result of ignorance, fear or even hatred—many cats lead miserable lives. They are kept merely as animated mousetraps and receive little, if any, attention or affection from their owners. In a situation such as this, one can hardly blame the cat for leaving home.

On the other hand, when provided with a good home, intelligent care and adequate affection, a cat can be a very responsive and faithful pet. Many city, suburban and rural families have found this to be true. For them, the cat is a highly prized member of the household.

The cat is an exceptional animal and, despite its independence and aloofness, readily adapts to family life. But if your relationship with a cat is to be harmonious, a basic understanding of the animal's nature, habits and needs is obligatory. To obtain such an understanding—or achieve some kind of rapport with your cat—you will find a general résumé of the cat family a good starting point. In learning about the wild cats, we shall see that the domestic cat not only resembles them in anatomy and habits, but "thinks" and reacts as they do.

THE CAT FAMILY, OR *FELIDAE*

The cats, or *Felidae,* are distributed throughout the world, with the exception of Australia, New Zealand and a few other regions. In general, they are the most carnivorous of all the flesh-eating mammals. We might place them in the same relative position among quadrupeds as the hawks, eagles and falcons hold among birds. Their anatomical features are admirably suited for their role as hunters. All of the cats have lithe, muscular frames, with longish bodies and relatively short limbs. They excel in climbing and some species live or spend considerable time in trees.

The cats—with the exception of the cheetah—are not the fleetest of mammals. However, they move rapidly, covering ground in a series of zigzag leaps or bounds rather than by direct running. Usually, wild cats advance stealthily on their prey when within striking distance, then seize their victim with a mighty spring or pounce. Some cats utter a roar or yell when attacking, paralyzing their prey with fear.

Cats move noiselessly; their soft velvety foot pads deaden any sound. They have strong, curved claws which—except for the cheetah —can be retracted. The sharp claws are withdrawn by the use of special muscles and ligaments. When retracted, the claws rest in sheaths which prevent any accidental hooking into objects.

All of the cats have very acute senses of sight and hearing. Their eyes are adapted for seeing in the day and night. Although cats have a good sense of smell, this trait cannot compare with that of the dog. Since their sight and hearing are excellent, the cats use their lesser sense of smell as a secondary aid in hunting.

Actually, the *Felidae* agree in form and structure to such a degree that zoologists have not formally subdivided them. Therefore, the cats are considered members of a single family, although some of the odd types, such as the cheetah, jaguarundi and serval, might merit separation.

The wild cats are not gregarious, but exhibit a strong independence in their relationship with others of the species. It is true that lions are seen in groups or "prides." But even these large cats do not congregate in numbers approaching those of some other mammals, notably the large grazing animals, such as horses, deer and bison.

Even though zoologists have not formally classified the *Felidae* into subfamilies, tribes or races, the cats usually are placed in one of three arbitrary groups or classifications.

GREAT CATS

The great cats, or *Panthera,* are distinguished by their large size and ability to roar. In contrast, the intermediate and lesser cats can only scream, yowl, hiss, meow or purr. Also, the great cats live longer than the others, especially the lesser, or smaller, species. For example, lions often attain an age of forty or more years, whereas the domestic cat has an average life-span of twelve to fourteen years.

Lion (*Panthera Leo*)

The lion has been known since ancient times as the "king of the beasts." Large, majestic and agile, it once ranged over a wide territory. As late as 500 B.C., lions roamed over eastern Europe as far west as Italy, the Near East from Turkey to India, throughout Arabia and all of Africa from Gibraltar to the Cape of Good Hope. Today, the lion's range has been greatly reduced and this big cat is found only in southern Africa, Iran, Arabia and western India.

A massive cat, the lion is well-muscled, powerful and surprisingly agile for its size. The male has a heavy mane, unique among the *Felidae*, which covers the head and neck, extending down onto the chest and backward over the abdomen to the hind legs. There are also thick growths of hair on the elbows of the forelegs and a hairy tuft on the tip of the tail. The coat is predominantly a solid tawny or yellowish-brown color without spots, rosettes or stripes. Males sometimes reach an overall length of ten feet, measured from the nose to the tip of the tail. Although the lioness is maneless and smaller than than the male, she is nonetheless a powerful and ferocious cat, similar in appearance to the puma, or mountain lion, of the western hemisphere. The old saying that the female of the species is more dangerous than the male is aptly applied to the lioness.

The lion, unlike some of the other cats, does not live in jungles. It is strictly a hunter and dweller of the plains, veldts and savannahs. Despite its ferocity in the hunt and its loud, threatening roar, the lion is basically a retiring animal. It is true that the Romans amused themselves by staging fights between gladiators and lions in the Circus Maximus and other arenas; the slaughter of Christians by lions before Roman spectators was another barbarous use of the lion. However, the fact remains that lions rarely attack human beings and when they do, the reasons usually are starvation, pain and lack of mobility resulting from wounds, and an instinct to protect their young. Even the most timid animal will attack a human being when goaded or enraged beyond its tolerance. More than likely, the Romans resorted to abnormal and possibly inhumane treatment of their lions to make the animals ferocious and willing to attack human beings.

Grazing animals, such as the giraffe, zebra, gazelle and other deer-like creatures, constitute the prey of lions. But when game is scarce, the big cats will hunt rodents, small mammals and—when driven to desperation because of hunger—even grasshoppers and locusts. The teamwork of a pair of hunting lions is a most impressive sight. The male usually drives the game toward the lioness and she makes the kill. In general, lions are not wanton killers; they never kill for mere sport, but only for food or in self-defense. Both the male and female are excellent parents, rearing and guarding their cubs. Consequently, they lead busy lives supplying food for the young and teaching the cubs how to survive in a rough, highly competitive environment.

The lion is a regal animal and even in the sometimes limited and unsuitable quarters of zoos and menageries this great cat manages to maintain its royal bearing. Our domestic cat also has this majestic mien and in some of its attitudes and mannerisms reminds one of the lion.

Tiger (*P. tigris*)

The domestic cat displays some characteristics of another great cat, the tiger. This member of the *Felidae* is the largest, strongest and most ferocious of the felines. The name "tiger" stems from an Iranian word meaning pointed or arrowlike, and was bestowed on this great cat because of its sharpness and quickness in the hunt.

Originally an arctic mammal that ranged over eastern Siberia, the tiger is now found in Amur, Korea, China, Burma, India, Indochina, Malaya to Sumatra, Java, Bali, Iran, Afghanistan and the Caucasus. Tigers have been associated with dense jungles, but actually, this great cat prefers grassy plains, swamps and fringes of forests. These areas provide the tigers with excellent "command posts" from which to observe their primary prey: grazing animals. Although some tigers do inhabit jungles, most of them suffer from the heat and will seek cooler regions, especially areas near rivers, streams or other waterways.

Tigers have an average length of nine feet, although larger specimens have been reported. A few years ago, a fifteen-foot tiger was said to have been killed in India's Assam Province—a truly gigantic specimen. Nature has provided the tiger with excellent camouflage; its coat is a bright fawn color, with wide, transverse black stripes. Albinos, or white tigers, while rare, are not unknown. They have been reported in the region of Rewa, India, but it has not been definitely established that these light specimens are true genetic albinos.

The tiger lacks the deep, powerful roar of the lion, but does have a resonant, hollow voice. This great striped cat, like the lion, is a hunter of grazing animals, including deer (chital, barasingh and sambar), wild cattle (gaur), buffalo and domestic cattle (zebu). The tiger also feeds on langur monkeys, swine and porcupines. Usually a lone hunter, a tiger may travel as much as fifteen miles in search of prey. Dr. George Schaller, who studied tigers in the field in Kanha National Park in the highlands of central India, reported that an adult tiger may eat from forty to sixty pounds of meat at one meal.

Tigers stalk their victims, relying on hearing and sight, then make the kill with a final short rush, springing onto the prey. While feared by man and beast, the tiger is not an infallible hunter or always victorious. Buffalo and wild cattle—large in size and equipped with sharp horns—can deter a tiger from attacking by banding together and presenting a united front. Stories of tigers attacking and killing people are not always tall tales; these great cats will occasionally storm a remote village and kill human beings. And, of course, there have been instances where tigers in wild animal acts have turned on their trainers and severely mauled or killed them. All in all, it is generally agreed that the tiger is the most dangerous of the *Felidae*.

Leopard (*P. pardus*)

Another interesting relative of our domestic cat is the common leopard, smaller than the lion and tiger, but larger than any other spotted cat. Some leopards reach a length of seven and a half feet. This sleek cat once ranged from Europe to Japan and southward through all of Asia and Africa. Today, the leopard has been squeezed into a limited range in Africa and southern Asia.

Leopards have yellowish-tan or reddish-buff coats, with many dark spots which are always arranged in rosettelike patterns or groups. Melanistic, or black, leopards are by no means rare; however, no albinos have been reported. A distinguishing feature of the leopard is its eyes. They are quite unlike those of other cats. When contracted in bright light, the pupils appear circular in shape. Those of other cats are linear or straight.

African leopards inhabit the jungles and veldts from the Mediterranean Sea to the Cape. In Asia, leopards frequent both plains and jungles. One subspecies, the Mountain Leopard, lives in the mountainous regions of India. A first-rate climber, the leopard is extremely fast and agile as it hurtles down from its perch hidden in the foliage of a tree. It usually preys upon large and small mammals, occasionally attacking man. The leopard roars, as do the tiger and lion, but with less volume than either of the other two great cats.

Snow leopard (*P. uncia*)

The snow leopard, sometimes called the "ounce," is a relatively rare cat, ranging from the mountainous regions of central Asia (north of the Himalaya mountains to the steppes), eastward to the Altai mountains in Siberia and on into Amur and Sakhalin Island. It is similar in appearance to the common leopard.

Especially adapted for life in a cold climate, the snow leopard is well-protected with a thick coat of pale yellowish-gray fur. The coat is clearly marked with large, dark rosettes. Snow leopards attain a length of seven and a half feet. They prey mainly on wild goats and sheep and rarely attack human beings.

Jaguar (*P. onca*)

The spotted jaguar is the only great cat native to the western hemisphere. It is found in southern California, parts of Arizona and New Mexico, Mexico, Central America and parts of South America as far south as Patagonia. The jaguar is the largest and most powerful of American cats. A yellowish-gray coat, vividly marked with black spots surrounded by black rings, distinguishes the jaguar. The rings and spots are in horizontal parallel lines on both flanks. Occasionally, an albino jaguar is seen in the Amazon jungles.

Jaguars are expert tree climbers, but are also at home on the plains and semidesert regions of the southwestern United States. They hunt animals, alligators, turtles, shellfish and—when other game is scarce —insects. South American jaguars are fond of the fat capybara, a huge guinea piglike rodent that lives along rivers and streams and sometimes weighs as much as 250 pounds. The jaguar's powerful forelegs—armed with razorsharp claws—can fell a victim with a single swipe or blow.

INTERMEDIATE CATS

The wild cats in this group are smaller than the great cats, but resemble them in general appearance. They lack the ability to roar, vocalizing instead with yells, screams or loud hisses.

Puma (*Profelis concolor*)

The puma, or American mountain lion, is a large cat resembling the true lioness, *Panthera leo*. It is also known as the cougar, catamount and painter. In colonial times, the puma ranged widely over North America, as far east as Pennsylvania, New York and the New England states. Although its range today is greatly diminished, the puma is still found from Alaska south to Tierra del Fuego, and from western Florida to Texas, Colorado, California and the North Pacific coast states. Occasionally there are reports of pumas being seen in some of the North Atlantic states; however, the majority of eastern pumas are restricted to Florida.

Pumas may reach an overall length of seven and a half feet; they are well-muscled cats, rather stocky when compared to a leopard or jaguar. The coat of the puma may be reddish-brown or reddish-gray, with light gray or solid white on the underparts of the body. This cat does not roar, but emits a combination of whistles and hisses and—upon occasion—a piercing scream reminiscent of the shriek of a frightened horse or woman. A stealthy hunter, the puma preys upon small mammals and birds. When its customary prey is scarce, a puma will attack and kill young, sick and old sheep and cattle.

As a result of its occasional forays on livestock, the puma—like the wolf and coyote—has been ruthlessly hunted. Actually, more livestock is lost because of droughts, blizzards and disease than by the hunting of pumas. Nevertheless, heavy trapping and hunting pressures have diminished the numbers of this American cat. The Florida puma (*Felis concolor coryi*), a subspecies, numbering about two to three hundred, is fully protected by law.

When obtained very young, pumas can be tamed and kept as pets, although they are not for the average person (see Chapter 7).

Clouded leopard (*P. nebulosa*)

The clouded leopard is almost the same size as the common leopard, but has some unusual distinguishing anatomical features—an elongated head, very long tail and long teeth. The basic body color is gray or grayish-yellow, with large and somewhat angular dark patches outlined in black. There are also two bands or stripes on the face, extending backward from the eyes and corners of the mouth. The underparts of the body are whitish, the legs are spotted and the exceptionally thick tail is marked with irregular rings.

An arboreal cat, spending most of its time in trees, the clouded leopard is found in southeastern Asia, from Bhutan in the Himalayas through Assam, Burma, Indochina, the island of Formosa

(Taiwan), the Malay Peninsula and the islands of Sumatra, Borneo and Java. Little is known about the hunting habits of this leopard, other than the fact that it preys primarily on birds.

SMALLER OR LESSER CATS

The third arbitrary grouping of the *Felidae* includes a variety of types which have necessitated further classification into subgroups. Some of the cats in these groupings appear to be miniature replicas of the great cats. Others vary somewhat in anatomy, general appearance and habits. When it comes to precise knowledge about the cats in these subgroups, there are gaps and incomplete data. It is not known just how many varieties of lesser cats exist in Asia, Africa and South America. However, a few of the lesser cats have been objects of considerable study; some have even been tamed and kept as pets.

Ocelot (*Felis pardalis*)

The ocelot is an attractive wild cat native to the southern United States, Central and South America. It is beautifully marked, with no two individuals having exactly the same pattern. The basic coat colors are gray, tawny yellow, reddish-gray or orange, with brown splotches or stripes enclosed by black borders. The splotches run down the back, across each shoulder and then backward to the tail. Ocelots have ringed tails, spots on the lower parts of all four legs and spotted underparts superimposed on a whitish or grayish background. Ocelot colors and spotches vary in different regions. For example, ocelots living in forests have dark splotches, while those inhabiting open areas or plains have lighter markings. These variations are nature's camouflage—the dark splotches blend with the shadows in forests and lighter marking fade into the background of sand and rocks on the plains and deserts.

The average ocelot is about twice the size of a large house cat, although some specimens are as large as a small Indian leopard. A tree dweller and skilled hunter, the ocelot preys on any small animals and birds it can catch. The adult is a remarkable jumper, often leaping seven or eight feet into the air from a set position on all four feet. It is a nocturnal cat and is particularly alert and active after dark. The ocelot, unlike its relative the domestic cat, loves water and is an accomplished swimmer.

Ocelots are becoming more and more popular as pets in the United

States and other countries. However, while these interesting cats are easily tamed and can adapt to living conditions in cities and suburbs, they are not suitable for the average person or family. (See Chapter 7 for the selection, habits, care and management of ocelots.)

Margay (F. tigrina)

Another South American wild cat that has been kept as a pet is the margay. When fully matured, the margay is about the size of a large house cat. Its basic coat color is champagne, orange or dark orange, with dark spots or stripes. Margay and ocelot kittens are very similar in size and appearance, and it is often difficult to distinguish one from the other.

Also a tree dweller, the margay is a strong and agile cat. It, too, is an excellent jumper and can leap many times its own length; margays can spring in any direction—upward, forward or backward—with ease. The front paws are unusually large when compared to those of the house cat. Margays use their paws to catch and hold small mammals and birds, much in the same way that a house cat cuffs and grips a mouse or bird. Although easily frightened, the margay makes a good pet for those persons with patience and understanding of this unique cat.

Lynxes

The lynxes make up a subgroup of the lesser cats. There are four distinct types of lynxes, all different in general appearance from other members of the *Felidae*. Lynxes have small heads, long hind legs, tufted or plumed ears, short, stubby tails, heavy bodies and hairy feet. They are widely distributed in the northern and temperate regions of the Old and New Worlds.

Canadian lynx (*Lynx lynx*). A familiar lynx of North America is the Canadian, or northern, lynx. It is a large, stocky cat with reddish-gray coat, sometimes spotted, especially in the young. The hair is long, the feet are furry and fluffy and the ears are tipped with long hairs or plumes. The lynx's hairy feet serve a useful purpose in enabling this cat to move freely and quickly over deep snow. Canadian lynxes often reach a length of four feet. This cat feeds on small mammals and birds. It occasionally ventures south of the Canadian border.

Bobcat (*L. rufa*). The bobcat is found throughout the United States and northern Mexico. It resembles the Canadian lynx but is smaller. Also called the bay lynx, this cat has a rusty-red or dark brown coat. Like the Canadian lynx, the bobcat adult and young may have spots. Bobcats are expert climbers and feed on small mammals and birds.

Although bobcats have been captured as kittens and tamed, they are generally unreliable pets. When angered, the bobcat can be a very dangerous animal, one that will not hesitate to attack a human being. Bobcats can and do interbreed with domestic cats, but offspring rarely survive beyond the kitten stage.

Caracal (*L. caracal*). The slender caracal is a lynx found throughout Africa, mainly in the arid regions, and in parts of India. It has a reddish-brown coat and very long ears that terminate in dark plumes which often hang down like tassels. The inside of the ears is white, the outside black. Caracals possess great speed and are capable of running down a fleet gazelle. This strange cat also catches birds, leaping high to slap its prey down in midair.

Jungle cat (*L. chaus*). A fourth member of the lynx group is known as the jungle cat. This lynx ranges from the Caucasus in western Asia, through the Near East, including Iran and India, to the eastern part of North Africa. It is also found in Ceylon and Burma. Despite its name, the jungle cat prefers open woodlands and cultivated fields.

Typically lynxlike in appearance, the jungle cat has an ash gray or gray-brown body, with plumes of longer hair on the tips of its ears. Jungle cats feed on small mammals and birds. As in the case of other lynxes, the jungle cat will interbreed with domestic cats. Because of this, it is believed to have played an important part in the evolution and development of the domestic cats, particularly the Abyssinian breed.

Wild Tabby Cats

Another group of cats considered to have played a role in the development of the domestic varieties is one that includes the tabby cats. Chief among these are the Kaffir cat (*Felis lybica*), African wild cat (*F. ocreata*) and European wild cat (*F. silvestria*). The first two species are definitely believed to have been involved in the development of the domestic cats, while the third—because of its shyness—may or may not have been a contributor to the evolution of the domestic varieties. All of the wild tabby cats have a striking resemblance to domestic tabbies. They are yellowish-gray, banded and varied with black markings.

Three other wild cats are highly distinctive and have more or less been placed in a separate category in the *Felidae*. Although feline in appearance and habits, they possess certain variations that make them something of a puzzle.

Serval (*Leptailurus*)

The serval is a long-legged, ewe-necked cat of equatorial Africa. An inhabitant of the veldts and savannahs, it hunts birds, small mammals and lizards. The serval's long neck enables this odd cat to see over the tall grasses. Also, its upright ears and keen hearing help to detect the presence of unseen prey. The serval hunts by day or night, utilizing its unique anatomical equipment. The basic coat color is yellowish-gray to bright orange, with black spots on the body, lower parts of the legs and flanks. The upper parts of the legs have broad bands or stripes.

Jaguarundi (*Herpailurus*)

Another catlike animal with questionable status among the *Felidae* is the jaguarundi, a strange mammal of Central and South America. It is a long-bodied animal, with short legs, long tail and rather small, round head fitted with round ears. The coat color is brown or gray, dark on the top of the body, light underneath and liberally sprinkled with silver hairs. The jaguarundi is a tree climber and feeds on mammals and birds. It is a common specimen in zoos.

Cheetah (*Acinonyx*)

Despite its catlike appearance, the cheetah merits a special place among the *Felidae*. Two anatomical differences set the cheetah apart from what we might call the true cats: a very high skull and claws that are only slightly retractile.

An inhabitant of central Africa and India, the cheetah often reaches a length of seven feet. It has a rather deep body, long tail and yellowish-brown fur that is thickly sprinkled with black spots. However, the arrangement of the spots is different from that on the jaguar or leopard. The cheetah's spots are separate, distinct and round, while the spots of the leopard are grouped in rosettes, and those of the jaguar are ringed. Cheetahs are sight hunters, and they have dark spots or shadows under the eyes which help reduce the glare from the sun when the animal is hunting on deserts and plains.

The beauty of the cheetah, along with its great speed and tractability, have made this catlike creature a popular pet and working animal since ancient times. Some cheetahs have been clocked at sixty miles an hour—so fast that they can run down a blackbuck, an exceptionally fast antelope.

Young cheetahs are frequently trained to hunt alongside their owners or keepers. Usually, the training period ranges from four to six months. Hand-raised cheetahs are docile and quite manageable. When taken out to hunt, the animals are hooded in much the same fashion as a hunting falcon. Once the prey is sighted, the hood is removed and the cheetah released. The cheetah turns on a burst of speed and simply outruns its prey, knocking it down with a blow from a powerful paw and then sinking its teeth into the victim.

THE DOMESTIC CAT (*FELIS CATUS*)

Although the preceding brief discussion of the various members of the cat family may seem superfluous to some, the discerning cat owner—or prospective owner—will readily see the value of the comparisons when it comes to understanding the domestic cat. There is no question that the domestic cat is a diminutive and complex mixture of all the *Felidae*. It has the majestic bearing of the lion, stealth of the tiger, agility of the jaguar and leopard, tree-climbing ability of the margay and ocelot, and the hunting prowess common to all the wild cats. And it is both a ferocious and docile animal. In the words of Joseph Méry, nineteenth-century French poet and librettist: "God made the cat in order to give man the pleasurable sense of having caressed the tiger."

The domestic cat appears in many colors, combinations of colors, sizes and shapes, although never spotted. Generally, the cat is small, well-muscled and geared for stalking and pouncing on its prey. It usually hunts alone, depending entirely upon stealth and agility to ambush its victims. The cat, like the ocelot and margay, can leap into the air and swat down a bird or butterfly. Like the cheetah, it can outrun many small mammals. Its jaws are short and powerful, especially adapted for seizing and holding prey. Yet, despite ferocity in the hunt, most cats make docile pets.

The cat, however, is less sociable than the dog. Perhaps this trait stems from the cat's habit of hunting alone. Most dogs, of course, hunt in packs and have learned to extend their teamwork to include human beings. Not so in the case of the cat; it is an individualistic animal, yet one that has an affinity with man. To put it succinctly: the cat is less obvious in its relations and friendship with people.

2. The Origin and Domestication of Cats

EVOLUTION

The complete stages in the evolution of the cats into their present forms have not yet been accurately determined by zoologists and paleontologists, although several theories have been offered. While scientists do not agree as to the exact origin of cats, they are in accordance with the fact that the felines have highly specialized skills which have enabled them to survive, and that the roots of their family tree extend back to prehistoric times.

It is possible that the cat, like many other mammals, evolved from a small insect-eating mammal known as the *Tupaia* (pronounced too-pie), which lived during the Paleocene epoch, some seventy-five million years ago. This prehistoric mammal was a tree dweller and resembled a squirrel, with eyes on the sides of its face. Its vision was poor but it had a highly developed sense of smell.

In the Eocene epoch, about forty million years ago, there appeared a descendant of the tupaia known as *Miacis*. This was an arboreal animal, a tree dweller with a long, slender body. *Miacis* was not a highly evolved animal, physically or mentally. It was a very primitive hunter and meat eater of the tropical forests of its epoch. Despite its relative insignificance at the time, *Miacis* was the rootstock of modern cats, dogs, weasels, bears, civets, hyenas and raccoons.

In the course of evolving these descendants nature produced many

17

types and forms, some of which might be considered evolutionary experiments. Various species, types and varieties descending from *Miacis* failed to adapt and soon became extinct. However, one group of mammals remained more or less like *Miacis,* their ancestor. These were the civets (*Viverridae*), the small catlike mammals of the Old World. The civets of today are not very different from *Miacis*. They are small, long-bodied animals with pointed, foxlike heads. Civets inhabit Africa, the southernmost regions of Europe, and the Orient. They are known for their contribution to the perfume industry: an exudate from the anal glands, called "civet," is used as a base for the more expensive perfumes.

The civets made their appearance in the Oligocene epoch (which followed the Eocene) some twenty million years ago. In the same epoch, the first cats appeared. The cats, however, did not go through intermediate stages of evolution from *Miacis* to their Oligocene forms, but seem to have just suddenly appeared on the scene. This type of appearance of a form or species is called saltation.

Perhaps the animal closest to a primitive cat is an odd mammal called the fossa (*Cryptoprocta ferox*). It is native to Madagascar and resembles the genet, a spotted animal related to the civets. The fossa may grow to a length of six feet, most of which consists of the tail. It has a foxlike head, retractile claws (five on each foot), teeth which combine the structures of those of the cat and civet, and a very disagreeable disposition. Unlike the cats, which walk on their toes, the fossa walks plantigrade, or on the soles of its feet. Despite its rather nasty disposition, the fossa can be tamed and is regarded by scientists as a very close relative of our domestic and wild cats.

In the saltation of the cats, two types appeared—*Dinictis* and *Hoplophoneus*. Although both were catlike in appearance, there were some major differences. *Hoplophoneus* was a large animal with unusually long canine teeth. *Smilodon,* the saber-tooth tiger, was a descendant of *Hoplophoneus*. *Smilodon* was a large, slow-moving cat equipped with long canine teeth for destroying its prey. Since its victims were unusually large, slow-moving mammals like itself, *Smilodon's* lack of speed was not a handicap. This prehistoric cat's teeth often reached a length of six inches and were set in jaws that opened to a 90-degree angle. When the large mammals which provided *Smilodon* with food became extinct, this great cat was unable to catch the smaller and speedier mammals, and so it, too, soon disappeared. All that remains today of this interesting cat are bones and reconstructed skeletons, which may be seen in some museums of natural history.

Dinictis, the other catlike animal of the Oligocene, proved to be more adaptable and eventually produced our modern cats. *Dinictis* was smaller than *Hoplophoneus* and was faster and more agile, both on the ground and in the trees. Furthermore, it was endowed with intelligence to match its speed. The descendants of *Dinictis* were apparently so well adapted for survival that nature made no attempt to improve upon them. Cats today, except for a few minor variations, are astonishingly similar to those of the prehistoric *Dinictis* group.

There is little doubt that domestic cats descend from more than one species of wild cat. The jungle cat probably helped produce some varieties, as did the Kaffir cat. Both of these cats have markings like our common tabby cats, and both mate readily with domestic cats to produce fertile hybrids. It is very probable that still other wild species were involved in producing some of the domestic types. This multiple ancestry is known as polyphyletic origin.

Charles Darwin held the above opinion as to the origin of the cat. In his great work, *The Variation of Animals and Plants Under Domestication,* Darwin described the process by which wild descendants of domesticated cats revert to the habits and appearance of their various ancestors.

DOMESTICATION

The cat is a relative newcomer to the ranks of man's domestic animals. What records we have of their early domestication date back only 5,000 years. The dog, on the other hand, is believed to have been domesticated at least 20,000 years ago, possibly longer. Sheep were domesticated by New Stone Age people nearly 11,000 years ago, and cattle have been working for man for nearly 8,000 years.

Our earliest reliable record of the cat's domestication is derived from ancient Egypt. Various papyri, tomb carvings and other artifacts of the Egyptians show the importance of the cat as a pet and animal of worship. Scholars who have translated Sanskrit writings tell us that cats were important also to the ancient Hindus. It is likely that other ancient peoples adopted cats as pets and working animals, but no records have been left of this. It is possible that New Stone Age men brought kittens home and trained them as pets and hunters. Today African and Australian aborigines, people not far removed from the New Stone Age, are fond of animals and often tame them. If cats were kept by Stone Age people at all, they were merely tamed and not domesticated.

THE CAT IN ANCIENT EGYPT

The cat enjoyed an unusual position among the animals in ancient Egypt. It was a pet, hunter and object of worship. As a pet, the cat was prized by both pharaoh and peasant. The cat's prowess as a rodent catcher must certainly have endeared it to the Egyptian farmers. The fertile Nile valley was the agricultural center of ancient Egypt, and New Stone Age people, among them the Fayumis and Merimdeans, migrated from Asia, settled there and engaged in agriculture and livestock breeding. Their grain crops attracted all kinds of insects and rodents to the fields and granaries. If the rats and mice of ancient Egypt were as voracious as those of today, the Egyptian grain farmers must have suffered severe damage to their crops before they put cats to hunting in the granaries and fields. When cats went to work, the rats and mice were quickly routed.

Egyptian hunters also utilized the cat's abilities. The cat, or Mu, as the Egyptians called it, was often trained to catch birds and other small mammals on the ground and in the trees. It was also trained to retrieve ducks from water, as depicted in ancient Egyptian drawings and papyri.

The cat played an important role in Egyptian religion. It was regarded as a sacred animal and was entitled to worship and protection. The cat symbolized both good and evil and was regarded as a god of fertility. It was also carried into battle by Egyptian warriors as a good-luck token. Some of the Egyptian gods and goddesses were depicted as possessing catlike traits and features. Ra, the sun god, was closely identified with the male cat. When the spirit moved him, Ra was supposed to assume the body of a cat. Bast, or Pasht, the cat goddess, was usually depicted with a cat's head. The popularity of Bast is shown by the large number of images of her—from life-size statues or paintings to tiny figures on earrings found in Egyptian tombs and mastabas. Archeological discoveries show that the Egyptians paid homage to Bast in the ancient city of Bubastis, to which hundreds of thousands of pilgrims traveled for the elaborate ceremonies held in honor of the goddess.

The sacred cats of Egypt were kept in various temples. When they died, they were embalmed and interred in tombs beside the mummies of Egyptian nobles. Amulets, bracelets and other trinkets fashioned in the image of the cat have also been found in the tombs. Charles Darwin, in *The Variation of Animals and Plants Under Domestication,* mentioned cat mummies brought to England by British archeologists. The University of Pennsylvania's museum also contains cat mummies, all carefully wrapped, in its Egyptian collection.

Darwin considered cat mummies to be of three species—*F. caligulata, F. Bubastes* and *F. chaus.* The first two species are extinct; the latter may have been the jungle cat, *L. chaus.* The modern Abyssinian cat probably descended from the *F. chaus* described by Darwin; at least it resembles the statues of most of the sacred cats of ancient Egypt.

THE CAT IS ADOPTED BY OTHER COUNTRIES

Greeks and other travelers in ancient Egypt were impressed by the domestic and practical qualities of Egyptian cats. The high esteem in which all Egyptians, from peasant to noble, held their cats inspired the famous Greek historian and traveler Herodotus to include the animals in his anecdotal and encyclopedic *Histories.* Book II of his work describes Egyptian customs and beliefs, in which the cat played an important role.

Such was the high regard and affection accorded the family cat that when a pet died, according to Herodotus, the family went into mourning for the lost animal. Each member of the family shaved off his eyebrows as a mourning symbol. Herodotus also mentions that cats were valued so highly that when a fire broke out, a family was more concerned about saving the cat than about extinguishing the fire. Undoubtedly, Herodotus' accounts and descriptions of the cat prompted the importation of felines into Greece.

Other travelers to Egypt brought back not only stories about the Egyptian cats, but some of the animals themselves. Phoenician sailors secured Egyptian cats and sold or traded them in countries along the Mediterranean. People in Rome, Greece and other southern countries which were plagued with rats and mice imported them in large numbers to exterminate the rodents. Later they began to develop their own varieties, and as the fame of the cat spread, more countries adopted the small felines as pets and hunters.

Oddly enough, the Bible makes no mention of cats, other than lions and leopards. Yet one wonders whether Noah didn't include the cat when he took aboard the Ark specimens of all the birds and beasts. The omission of the cat from the Bible is the more curious if we consider that the Hebrews were not only contemporaries of the cat-worshipping Egyptians, but even lived among them. It is possible that the authors of the Scriptures dismissed the cat because it was an animal used in alien religious rites; *i.e.,* a sacred animal worshipped by the Egyptians. While the Mosaic law lists a number of birds and animals as "unclean," the cat does not even rate mention. On the other hand, the cat is mentioned in the Talmud, which may have been written about the same time as Genesis. In the Talmud, the cat is called, quite appropriately, the "pouncer," and reference is there made to its prowess as a hunter and its adaptability as a pet.

At any rate, by the fifth century A.D., the Persians and other Asiatic peoples were keeping cats as pets and rodent killers. Roman invaders are generally credited with introducing cats into the British Isles, although there is some evidence that cats were there before the Roman invasion. Regardless of when they arrived, cats were numerous and popular in Britain by the ninth century. By the year 1000 cats had gained favor as pets and hunters in China and Japan. Although Egyptian cats formed the basic stock in many countries, native species were also tamed and varieties developed in other lands. The *huang pao* cat of China, for example, is quite distinct from the sleek Mu of Egypt; the same is true of the Maine Coon Cat of New England.

In some of the more enlightened countries, the cat was given some measure of protection. Wales, Switzerland, Saxony and other regions of Europe enacted laws or issued proclamations protecting cats, and, prior to the Middle Ages, cat killers faced a stiff fine and possible imprisonment. An old Welsh law stipulated that the owner of a slain cat was to be compensated in the form of enough wheat to cover the cat's body from nose to tail when the animal was held up by the tail, with its nose touching the ground. Wheat, of course, was a precious commodity and the amount prescribed in the Welsh fine or penalty was not always easy to obtain or surrender.

Unhappily, the cat fell into disfavor during the Dark Ages and these were years of torture and persecution for the once popular felines. Protective laws meant nothing to the gangs of cat haters that roamed the streets and alleys in search of victims. What was the reason for the wholesale slaughter of cats? Ignorance and superstition were the major factors.

Since the time of the pharaohs, when Egyptians worshipped the cat goddess Bast, men had regarded the cat as a creature endowed with supernatural powers. The Egyptians considered Mu to be a symbol of both good and evil, but in the Dark Ages, ignorant and superstitious people associated the cat exclusively with witchcraft and other evils.

In the fourteenth century, old or eccentric women were accused of being witches and of assuming the form of black cats that ventured forth at night to spread mischief and evil. Consequently, both witches and cats were dragged before ecclesiastical courts and summarily condemned to torture and death. Black cats were especially singled out as symbols of bad luck and evil, and these unfortunate animals were usually killed on sight.

The thoughtless and wanton destruction of cats produced an unexpected sequel—plagues affecting man and animal spread throughout England and Europe. One of the worst, the dreaded bubonic plague, was carried by rats. Thousands of people and animals died from this disease in the British Isles and on the Continent.

Since vast numbers of cats had been killed in the infamous cat hunts in England and Europe, the rats had enjoyed a population explosion. The increase in the number of rats, carriers of organisms that caused bubonic plague, or "Black Death" as it was often called, produced a corresponding increase in the number of cases of the plague. Although the science of bacteriology was as yet unborn, some people began to suspect that the rats had something to do with the spread of the Black Death. Happily—because they were notorious rat killers—cats gradually came back into favor.

CATS IN THE NEW WORLD

Prior to the arrival of European and English settlers, only wild cats were found in the Americas. The North American Indians were familiar, of course, with the puma, lynx, ocelot, bobcat and jaguar, but did not attempt to tame them. The various tribes respected the hunting prowess of the native wild cats and used carvings and drawings of them as clan totems. Some Indians were called or known by the names of the various wild cats.

South American Indians kept jaguars, ocelots and margays as pets, capturing these felines as youngsters. Most of the South American tribes had a high regard for the powerful jaguar. Among various Central and South American Indians, the jaguar—along with the brilliantly colored quetzal bird—was accorded a place as a supernatural animal. The Incas of Peru worshipped a cat god with jaguar-like features during the Chavin culture, which flourished from 1200 to 400 B.C.

However, it was the English, Dutch, French and Spanish colonists who introduced the domestic cat to the New World. Even though there is no direct record of cats being aboard any of Columbus' ships, it is quite probable that some cats came over in the *Niña, Pinta* and *Santa María*. Cats were frequently taken to sea, in spite of the fact that superstitious mariners believed that shipwreck or other calamities would result from a cat's gamboling on the deck. Another belief of the times was that when a cat washed its face on shipboard, a storm was sure to follow.

Once in America, the immigrant cats quickly proved their worth. The fledgling colonies abounded in all kinds of rodents and small mammals that became pests. The cats were kept busy hunting and killing the rats, mice and other animals that ate or damaged the precious grain crops.

History is hazy as to just what kind of cats the colonists brought to the New World, but there definitely were both long- and short-haired varieties. Few of the colonists were cat fanciers, at least in the matter of breeding or pedigrees, and they cared little about a cat's ancestry. So long as the animal performed the all-important task of keeping down the rodents it was valued simply as a useful animal. It was only later, in the eighteenth and nineteenth centuries, that cats became more than rat catchers to Americans.

When the wagon trains pushed westward in the early part of the nineteenth century, many families took along their cats. French voyageurs on the Mississippi and Missouri rivers also carried cats northward and westward on their barges and in their canoes. Indian tribes, pestered with rats and other vermin in their teepees and lodges, heard about the value of cats as rodent exterminators and so, although scarce, cats were traded to the Indians for beaver, fox and otter pelts.

Western mining and lumbering towns were overrun with rodents, and cats were in great demand. Even the poorest specimen brought a high price, and some cats were sold to miners for as much as fifty dollars each. Cat "dealers" earned a good living from stealing cats in the East and shipping them to the West.

As cats became more and more popular for various reasons, breeders began to experiment. Various types of cats were mated, producing offspring with different colors, sizes and dispositions. Different strains, based on color and length of coat, were developed. However, selective breeding notwithstanding, the cat changed very little in anatomy and general appearance; it remained the same basic feline of ancient times. Cat fanciers did not develop nearly as many different varieties as did dog breeders. Furthermore, no attempt was made to breed abnormal features, such as the short legs and long body of the dachshund or the bowlegs and flat face of the bulldog. Instead, cat breeders concentrated on color and length of the coat, so that today we have two major groups of cats: long- and short-haired, with various colors and color combinations.

MODERN DOMESTIC CATS

Selective breeding, while it hasn't altered the basic anatomy or nature of domestic cats, has produced some striking breeds.

LONG-HAIRED CATS:

There are twenty color varieties of long-haired cats recognized as "official."

Blacks

Jet black is the desirable color for cats in this group. Tints of brown or a grayish, singed color on the coat are regarded as faults by show standards. The black coat must also be free of white or silver streaks or ticking. Black long-haired cats should have copper or orange eyes.

Blues

The so-called blue cats are not actually blue, but more of a mauve color. A blue cat, to meet show standards, should be a uniform "blue" throughout. There are different shades of blue, but they may not appear on the same individual. These cats are also required to have deep orange or copper-colored eyes.

Tortoiseshells

A tortoiseshell cat has three colors, displaying distinct splotches of red, black and cream. Male tortoiseshells are extremely rare and when discovered are usually sterile. However, there are exceptions. A famous male tortoiseshell cat (Torti-Man of Gallus) sired nineteen litters, but none of the kittens was a male tortoiseshell. In fact, not even one of the kittens was a tortoiseshell!

Tortoiseshell and Whites

The tortoiseshell and white cat is a four-color feline with a coat of red, black, cream and white. It is also known as a "calico" cat. The tortoiseshell and white, unlike the plain tortoiseshell, does not have a rarity of males.

Creams

Cream-colored cats often appear in tortoiseshell litters. The accepted standards for this cat are a full cream coat, without any shadings or markings. The eyes should be copper-colored.

Blue-creams

Blue-cream cats have coats splotched with blue and cream, the splotches being more or less intermingled. The eyes must be copper or orange to meet show standards.

Tabbies

Tabby cats have a solid coat color marked with black bands or stripes. These cats are classified according to three basic types: those with narrow stripes, those with medium stripes and those with blotches. Silver tabbies should have green eyes. Red tabbies must have copper eyes and brown tabbies should have hazel or copper eyes.

Chinchillas

The chinchilla long-haired cat is an aristocratic feline. The undercoat is pure white, that on the back, flanks, head, ears and tail is tipped with black. The black tipping gives the chinchilla's coat an overall appearance of sparkling silver. The eyes should be emerald or blue-green.

Shaded or Clouded Silvers

Another common long-haired breed is the shaded silver. The coloring should be unmarked silverish, gradually shading on the sides of the body, face and tail. This cat is darker than the chinchilla. The eyes should be green or blue-green. Kittens are usually marked with tabby bars and stripes, which fade and disappear as the cat matures.

Whites

White long-haired cats must be pure white, without any markings or shadings in the coat. Show standards call for deep blue eyes.

Smokes

A long-haired smoke cat is a handsome animal. Its light silverish undercoat is tipped with black. The ruff (collar), flanks and ear tufts are pale and silvery when contrasted with the rest of this cat's body. The eyes should be copper or orange.

Reds

The red long-haired cat should have a deep, rich red color with no markings. Its eyes must be a deep copper color.

Himalayan

The Himalayan is a long-haired cat with Siamese markings—seal, blue or lilac points. It is a result of selective color breeding. The eyes should be deep blue.

Maine Coon Cat

The Maine Coon Cat may be of several colors; however, the most common specimens are brown with tiger markings. While the Maine cat has long hair, it lacks the thickness and density of what we might call the true longhairs. Maine cats have a ruff or collar of fur around their necks, as do other long-haired cats, but it is not as thick or prominent as those of others.

There are various tales about how the Maine Coon Cat evolved. One story, which has never been substantiated, is that a Captain Coon brought a male and female cat from the Orient and started this particular strain. Another tale is that the doomed French queen Marie Antoinette sent six of her Persian cats to a hideout in Maine. These French cat refugees are supposed to have mated with native tabby cats to produce the Maine Coon Cat. Some "Down Easters" swear that the Maine cat is a cross between a cat and raccoon, but this is nonsense, of course, since cats and raccoons cannot interbreed. Regardless of its origin, the Maine cat is alert, rugged, able to withstand considerable cold, and is a skilled hunter.

SHORT-HAIRED CATS:

The cats in the short-haired group are the most popular as house pets, especially the variety known as the domestic shorthair.

Abyssinian

The Abyssinian is a trim, short-haired cat which probably originated in Abyssinia (present-day Ethiopia). It is graceful, with a slender body, long tail, pointed head and sharp-cut ears. The coat is distinct, quite unlike that of any other short-haired cat. It is russet, with the texture of rabbit fur, and has ticking, or series of black dots, on the tips of the hairs. Abyssinians have green, hazel or yellow eyes. They are extremely alert cats and, as previously mentioned, resemble the sacred cats of ancient Egypt.

Siamese

The origin of the Siamese has never been satisfactorily pinpointed, although several theories have been advanced. One that is generally accepted is that this breed was developed from sacred cats of Burma that mated with Annamese cats three to four hundred years ago.

A Siamese cat is distinctive in appearance: well-muscled, medium-sized, with a long, narrow head. The ears are set widely apart at the base and taper to sharp points. In contrast to the rest of its body, the tail is short. Some Siamese cats have kinked or crooked tails.

Siamese kittens are born an off-white color. As they mature, the coat turns to cream or fawn with seal-brown points (mask, ears, legs and tail) in the variety known as the Seal Point. Another variety has a grayish-white coat with "blue" points and is known as the Blue Point Siamese. There are other coat variations of red, frost and lilac points. The eyes of all Siamese are blue and slanted, somewhat like those of the Husky or Malamute dog.

These interesting felines are very vocal and often complain loudly when left alone. They become quite attached to people and follow a person with a doglike devotion. The Siamese makes a good house pet and is an excellent mouser.

Burmese

A somewhat rarer breed that closely resembles the Siamese in both general appearance and disposition is the Burmese, a breed developed in Burma. However, the coat of the Burmese is darker than that of the Siamese. It is a rich sable brown and has clearly defined points. The coat is much shorter and is very close to the cat's body. While the Siamese has blue, slanted eyes, those of the Burmese are round and golden.

The Burmese show cat is medium-sized, with a long, lithe body, legs in proportion to the body, and small, oval-shaped feet. Burmese cats are affectionate and intelligent, traits which make them good house pets. They are also skilled hunters and will keep a house clear of rodents.

Manx

The Manx is a tailless cat from the Isle of Man and is another domestic cat whose origin is uncertain. One theory is that they are descendants of tailless Spanish cats that swam ashore to the Isle of Man when the Spanish Armada met disaster near England. Another story is that the tailless cats were of Asian origin and were brought west by Spanish sailors. Whatever their origin, Manx cats are unique in other ways besides lacking tails. The hind legs are very long, and the front legs are short; thus this cat waddles and hops along instead of walking or running as do other felines. It has a very round rump (the English refer to it as a "Rumpy"). Its coat is soft and can be of any color. For showing, all of the longhair colors are allowed, but eye colors must contrast with the coats.

Both the lack of a tail and the long hind legs are inherited characteristics. The true Manx is completely tailless, with a mere hollow where the tail would normally protrude. Cats with short, stubby tails are not true Manx cats. Pure Manxes are in danger of extinction. Ordinary shorthairs brought to the Isle of Man have interbred with them to produce litters of kittens with tails or stumps. In an attempt to restore the true Manx, the government has established an experimental Manx cat-breeding farm.

Russian Blue

The Russian Blue is supposed to be a native of northern Russia. It has a long, slender body with long legs and very small feet. A wedge-shaped head on a long neck (but not as long a neck as that of the wild serval) sets the Russian Blue apart from other short-haired varieties.

Actually the Russian Blue—like other so-called blue cats—is not a true blue color, but more of a mauve, although it does appear bluish when observed in certain lights. The common eye color is green. The fur of the Russian Blue is fine-textured, very similar to that of seals. These cats are very active and skilled hunters of rodents. Unfortunately, they are not very common.

Domestic Shorthair

The most common and best known of all cats is the Domestic Shorthair, which, to its discredit, has often been called the "alley cat." It is an excellent house cat and has no peer as a rodent exterminator. Despite its mixed ancestry, the Domestic Shorthair is eligible to compete in cat shows and has its own standards. Also, it is possible for a Domestic Shorthair to win the coveted award of Best of Show in an all-breed cat competition.

The Domestic Shorthairs come in all sizes, shapes and colors. Those recognized by the various cat associations include reds, tabbies, tortoiseshells, blacks, whites and black-and-whites. In general, to meet show standards, a Domestic Shorthair must have the following features:

1. Broad head, with medium-sized ears that are rounded at the tips and set wide (but not too wide) at the base.
2. Close-coupled, powerful body, with a good depth of chest.
3. A tail that is not too long or too short, but in proportion to the body, heavy at the base and tapering to an abrupt tip.
4. A coat that is clearly short; in-between lengths are not allowed.
5. Contrasting coat and eye color according to standards set for long-haired cats.

Rex Cat

The Rex cat is a mutation bred from short-haired varieties. It is a slim feline with soft fur that lacks guard hairs; the coat is curly or wavy. The Rex, like other animal mutations, does not resemble any particular one of its progenitors. Rex cats have colorations similar to those of the Manx, with eyes that are almond-shaped and colors that depend on the coat color.

Havana Brown

The Havana Brown cat has a rich mahogany color and chartreuse eyes. Its coat is medium-length and rather smooth. The ears are round-tipped, with very little hair inside or out. Havana Browns have medium-length bodies that are firm and well-muscled.

Part Two

CAT CARE

3. The Cat as a Pet

The large number of cats kept in homes is the best endorsement of felines as pets. They are a unique combination of house pet and work animal, with qualities that enable them to fit into city, suburban and country situations.

First of all, the domestic cat is relatively small and does not require a great deal of space. It is a basically clean and fastidious animal that quickly learns to use a sanitary pan or box. This habit is an important factor in city apartments and houses where the cat is kept confined. Also, cats do not need the vigorous exercise or frequent outings required by the average dog. In fact, most city cats can get all the exercise they desire right in the apartment or house; running, jumping, playing and stalking toys (and mice) can be performed in one room. True, a city cat may live a more artificial life than its country cousin, especially if it does not go outdoors. But confinement to an apartment or house should not be considered inhumane or unfair to a cat and should not deter you from obtaining a feline pet. Modern cities—with their heavy traffic, air pollution and other human and animal hazards—are no places in which to allow a cat to roam at large. You will find that a cat can thrive and be contented in a one-room apartment as long as it receives proper care and affection.

WHY A CAT FOR A PET?

The most important consideration in keeping a cat may best be stated as a question: Why do you want a cat? There are, of course, various answers to this question. For instance, you may simply like cats and want one for a pet. If so, you belong to the majority of cat owners who keep cats just because they like these interesting animals and their companionship. Or you may have a rodent problem and want a cat to rid the premises of rats and mice. Again, you may wish a cat for its beauty, aloofness and intelligence, as opposed to the more slavish qualities of a dog or other pet. And it's quite possible that you don't actually know why you want a cat, but are somehow intrigued by the animal. Regardless of the reason you want a cat, it's something to think about, for it will have a great deal to do with your relationship with the cat.

The next important step in considering a cat is that you select the *right* cat—one that will suit your particular needs and fit into the family situation. Cats as a group are intelligent, good company, neat, clean, companionable and entertaining, but individuals vary in temperament and ability to adjust to people and certain living conditions. The combination of the right cat and intelligent care can result in a harmonious and rewarding relationship. Conversely, the wrong cat— even with good care—may well prove incompatible, and the result is an unhappy experience for both cat and owner. The selection of your cat, then, should be made only after considering all the factors involved in keeping the pet and family compatible and happy. Before we discuss the specific techniques or hints for picking a suitable and healthy cat, it would be wise to consider some other factors which will or should have a bearing on your final choice.

CHILDREN, DOGS AND CATS

As the author of a syndicated pet column, I constantly receive letters from parents of young children in which I am asked if it is all right to bring a cat into the home. I am well aware that most humane societies and some animal authorities answer such queries with an unequivocal "No!" However, I do not agree. I contend that any decision depends upon the child, the parents and the cat. In my experience, cats and children are not necessarily incompatible—at least not irrevocably so.

The main argument against mixing cats and small children is that youngsters often abuse the animals. This can be true. Some small children seem to have an innate cruelty toward cats and other pets. Others are simply too young to differentiate between a cat and stuffed toy, and still others mistreat cats because they have not been taught otherwise.

Therefore, if you have young children and want a cat, you will have to shoulder the extra responsibilities that go with the situation. It will be necessary to take proper safety precautions for both cat and children, starting the first day the cat enters the home. A child needs to be taught that a kitten or cat is a living creature, not a toy. Young kittens cannot stand or long survive severe maulings. You will have to be on the lookout to prevent rough handling, kicking or hoisting the cat by the tail. The overly aggressive child who insists on mistreating a cat will, of course, get bitten or scratched.

Kindness to the cat can be taught; however, here again, it all depends on the child and the parents. The child should be shown how properly to lift and hold a kitten or cat. Firmly discourage any abuse to the animal and, whenever possible, allow the child to help with some of the easy chores in caring for the cat.

Remember that children imitate their elders. If a tot sees an older brother or sister—or parent—mistreating the cat, the chances are he or she will do the same. My advice is to put kindness into action by treating the cat kindly at all times. When a child learns respect for the cat, a lasting friendship is possible.

If you have very small children and are unable or unwilling to take the necessary time to supervise the cat and children, my advice is to postpone getting a cat until the children are able to understand that they are not to mistreat the animal. Or, if you still insist on having a cat, then at least get one that is five or six months of age or older and able to get out of the way of the children.

Another question that arises in the matter of children and cats is the old wives' tale about a cat sucking the breath of young children or babies. Such action on the part of a cat has never been demonstrated, at least to my knowledge. It would be very difficult, if not impossible, for a cat to accomplish this feat. A cat, to suck the breath from a child, would have to adjust its mouth in such a manner as to cause a vacuum. Anatomically, the cat cannot do this. Also, to suffocate a child completely, a cat would have to cut off breathing through the child's nose. Clever and agile as cats are, they cannot manage this trick. However, *it is possible for a cat to lie on top of the child's face and cause suffocation.* But that can be prevented by placing a strong net over a baby's crib or by keeping the cat out of the nursery. It is true that cats will curl up close to a baby, but their intent is not to harm. In my own experience with cats and children, I have found that cats cuddle up to a child for warmth and will lick a child's— especially a young baby's—face because of milk or other food that may cling to it.

Another consideration that should not be overlooked before obtaining a cat is the matter of the home containing a dog. This is not to imply that because you have a dog, you can't have a cat. But the situation will—in most cases—be analogous to that of cats and children: until the cat and dog have accepted each other or arrived at a truce, you will have to keep a sharp watch for altercations. If you have had the dog for any length of time, you should be able to gauge its probable reaction to a cat, or at least know whether to expect a "hot" or "cold" war between the dog and new cat. At any rate, the presence of a dog in the house will have a definite bearing on the kind of cat to bring home—that is, a kitten or older cat.

WHICH CAT FOR YOU?

You may already have made up your mind as to which kind of cat you want. If not, then the following hints should be helpful in making a choice.

PUREBRED OR ORDINARY HOUSE CAT?

Which shall it be—a purebred longhair or shorthair, or a plain house cat? Actually, there is little difference in the care of a purebred and a house cat. Both require attention. Furthermore, the domestic or ordinary house cat will respond with just as much affection and loyalty as the fanciest purebred. Your choice depends more or less upon your personal preference and financial situation, and upon whether you intend to breed purebred cats and show them.

There are some advantages in owning a purebred cat. The breeders spend considerable time, money and effort in developing their particular breeds. You profit from the breeder's investment, because the cats are usually well taken care of, and kittens from a purebred dealer usually are in better health than those obtained elsewhere. Another, and important, advantage is that when you get a purebred cat, you have standards by which to judge it. For example, when you buy a purebred Siamese kitten you know that it will grow up to look like a Siamese cat. This is not true of the ordinary house cat which, when mature, may turn out to be quite different in appearance from what you expected.

The purebred cat will cost considerably more than a house cat. It may be that you will have to pay nothing for your ordinary cat. The cost of a purebred cat will depend upon its breed and pedigree. Purebred cats, when purchased from reliable breeders, are worth their price. Most breeders are reputable individuals with high standards for breeding, sanitation, health and honest business practices. You are reasonably sure of getting your money's worth when you deal with them.

KITTEN OR MATURE CAT?

Whether you should get a kitten or mature cat depends upon your situation. If you want a hunter to eliminate rodents immediately, a mature cat, preferably a short-haired variety, is best. If you are looking for a family pet, and you are in a position to give it the attention it needs, then get a kitten. Raising a kitten is a great deal of fun and you will learn much about cats in the process. However, if you work all day, you will be better off with an older cat.

MALE OR FEMALE?

Your choice between a male and a female should be based on facts, not superstition or misinformation. There are naturally pros and cons on both sides. The usual objections to a female are the problems raised by her estrous cycle, or heat periods, and the disposition of her litter of kittens, should she be mated.

The promiscuous breeding of cats has created a serious problem in this country. Hundreds of thousands of unwanted kittens are born every year. Allowing a female cat to roam around, mating and producing litter after litter, is unintelligent cat ownership. But it happens again and again. Female cats, even when not mated, can be troublesome in city apartments. A female in heat can be very vocal and active, much to the annoyance of neighbors.

If you and your family have your hearts set on a female, all is not hopeless, however. The female can be spayed—an operation involving the removal of her ovaries. A spayed female has no heat periods and cannot breed, so produces no unwanted kittens.

On the other hand, male cats can also present some problems. The male is sexually active throughout the year, and has a constant urge to roam about in search of females in heat. Also, the urine of mature tomcats has a strong odor. When a female in heat is scented, the tomcat sprays urine about the house and premises. The strong odor serves to attract the female. While the tom's urine may be attractive to a female in heat, it is unpleasant to most people and may cause complaints in a city apartment house. Fortunately, the tom's desire to roam and to spray urine can be eliminated by altering, or castrating, it (neutering). The operation consists of removing the testicles—a simple and safe procedure. Male cats are usually altered when they are from six to eight months old.

LONG- OR SHORT-HAIRED CAT?

Should you get a long- or short-haired cat? Here, again, the choice is primarily a matter of preference, influenced only slightly by the situation. As a rule, short-haired cats are better ratters. But long-haired cats are usually more docile. Short-haired cats need a minimum of grooming, while long-haired ones require frequent grooming. If there are small children around, do not choose a long-haired cat, as you will constantly be removing candy, chewing gum and other sticky substances from its coat.

In choosing a cat, whether long- or short-haired, an allergic sensitivity on the part of some member of the family should be taken into account. Especially when kept in warm apartments, both long- and short-haired cats continually shed hairs which might be a source of irritation to a person sensitive to animal hair. It is now possible, however, for people allergic to cat hair to be desensitized, and many such persons are now enjoying a pet cat.

WHERE TO GET A CAT

When you have decided what kind of cat you want, take your time and shop around for the right cat for your situation.

BREEDERS

Many cat breeders advertise in the local newspapers. Their advertisements sometimes appear near the pet column, if the newspaper carries one. More often, however, the breeders list their cats for sale in the classified section, under the heading *Pets and Livestock*. You will also find breeder advertisements in periodicals devoted to pets, such as *All Pets Magazine, Pet Digest, Cats Magazine* and *Pet Fair*. Whenever possible, select a breeder within a short distance from your home. Should you have to return the cat or need further information, there will be less travel and expense involved.

PET SHOPS

Many pet shops sell purebred cats as well as ordinary house cats. In general, purebred cats bought in a pet shop cost less than those purchased from a breeder. But let the buyer beware. Many of these bargain purebreds are the runts of a litter, poor show prospects or are deformed or sickly. It stands to reason that a breeder will not sell his best purebred cats to a pet shop, as this would be poor business. It is wise, therefore, to proceed with caution when considering the purchase of a purebred cat in a pet shop, particularly if you want to breed or show cats.

HUMANE SOCIETIES

Occasionally, purebred cats can be found in humane society shelters, but most of them are older cats. The humane society shelter, however, is the best source for procuring an ordinary house cat. Most shelters have both kittens and mature cats for adoption.

Other sources of house cats are friends, neighbors and, as already stated, pet shops. A word of caution—exercise the same care in selecting your house cat as you would in choosing a more expensive purebred, especially at a pet shop.

WHAT TO LOOK FOR WHEN SELECTING A CAT

Regardless of where you get your cat, keep the following hints in mind.

When you first enter a pet shop, cattery or shelter, note its appearance and sanitary condition. Is it clean and free of odors? Are the cats and their cages in good condition? If either cats or cages are soiled and neglected, it would be wise to seek another source.

Don't base your selection of a kitten or cat entirely upon a "cute expression or appealing look." While that can be a factor in choosing a cat, it should not be the sole criterion. A cat chosen on that basis alone may prove to be a problem. Select a kitten or cat that is alert and playful. Avoid the very shy kitten or cat, particularly if there are small children in the family. Such a pet will require careful handling and will not submit to being mauled.

Examine the cat's eyes for redness, sores or discharge. A discharge from the eyes may be a sign of feline pneumonitis or other serious cat disease.

The cat's nose should also be free of discharge. A warm or hot nose, however, does not necessarily mean that the cat is ill.

Inspect the cat's ears for cleanliness. Look for sores and parasites. Does the cat keep shaking its head or scratching at its ears? If so, there is a possibility that it has ear mites or an infection.

Pay close attention to the condition of the cat's coat. Run your hand through the hair. It should be soft and glossy and free of mats and tufts. Avoid a cat with heavily matted hair, dry skin or dandruff. These are signs of neglect. Older cats with matted hair may even have to be anesthetized before the hair can be combed or the matted parts cut or plucked out.

The cat's rectal region should come under scrutiny. Look for signs of diarrhea, which is sometimes visible in the form of dried excrement adhering to the anal region. Diarrhea is a symptom of some disorder. Look for signs of worms, either in the excrement or in the anal region. Tapeworm segments often cling to the anal hairs and may be seen as small, brown kernel-like objects.

If you see any excrement in the cages or pens, note whether it is well-formed or loose. Find out when the cat was last wormed.

Examine the cat for fleas, lice and ticks. A complete discussion of these parasites will be found in Chapter 13.

Check for possible deformities in the legs and feet. Watch for bowed legs, which may be the result of nutritional deficiencies.

Many white cats with blue eyes are deaf. If you are interested in buying a blue-eyed white cat, make some hearing tests. Stand behind the cat where it cannot see you and snap your fingers or make some other noise. If it fails to respond, the chances are it is deaf.

If you buy a purebred cat, make certain that you obtain an application for registration or, in the case of a cat already registered, a transfer form, in both cases signed by the breeder. These papers are important in the event you wish to register the cat in one of the purebred cat associations or clubs. (See Appendix for list of cat organizations.)

Regardless of where you obtain your cat, request a two-week trial period. The cat may be incubating a disease. If so, it will usually show up within the two-week period. Make arrangements in advance to return the cat should sickness develop. Insist upon this important condition. Also insist that the sale be conditional upon a veterinary examination certifying the animal to be in good health. This examination should be made on the day of purchase or as soon thereafter as possible.

BRINGING THE CAT HOME

It will be easier for you, your family and, most important, the cat, if you plan in advance for the cat's arrival.

SLEEPING QUARTERS

There is not much point in choosing a definite sleeping place for an older cat in advance. Most older cats choose their own beds and all your labor may be for nothing. Keep in mind, however, that cats like to sleep above the level of the floor or ground. You might set up a convenient shelf for the cat to use as a perch. Otherwise, it will climb up on chairs, couches and other elevated places.

Young kittens will sleep in baskets or boxes or in one of the commercial cat beds available in pet shops or pet supply stores. If you plan to use one of the latter, prepare it ahead of time, although there is no guarantee that the cat will use it.

FOOD AND WATER PANS

The cat will need pans for food and water. There are all kinds of pans and dishes available, ranging from bright-colored plastic dishes to shiny stainless steel pans. Most of them are satisfactory and durable. To be serviceable, a food or water pan should be unbreakable, not too large, and easy to clean. Plastic dishes, unless you provide a metal ring or stand, will tip over easily, as will lightweight aluminum pans. Low earthenware crocks are excellent for water, since they are heavy and keep water reasonably cool in hot weather. Water and food pans should be no more than two inches high; the deeper the pan, the more easily it will tip over should the cat try to put its paws on the rim.

TOYS

Young kittens and most older cats enjoy playing with toys. A few simple toys, such as a hard rubber ball, catnip mouse, Ping-Pong ball, and a spool on a string will help keep the cat contented. Have these available before the cat arrives. Kittens and cats will get plenty of fun and exercise out of batting a Ping-Pong ball around the floor. A swinging toy, such as a spool on a string tied to a chair rung, will also give the cat hours of fun. Make sure the toys are safe—avoid soft rubber and sponge toys. In general, any toy the cat can break or chew up should be avoided.

Many toys are sold in the pet shops and pet supply stores. They range from gaily painted balls to more elaborate gadgets. Some of them are expensive and some are dangerous. Select your cat's toys with care.

You can rig up an exercise area in a very small space. Cats love to crawl through tunnels; cardboard boxes with holes cut in each end, terra-cotta drainpipes or other pipes with large diameters make excellent ones. A cat can sharpen its claws or rub off any material adhering to them on a scratching post. This device may also prevent wear and tear on your furniture and rugs. With some forethought and ingenuity, you can create an interesting and healthy playground for your cat, and it need not be expensive.

COLLAR AND LEASH

It is a good idea to equip your cat with some identification attached to a safe collar. (See Chapter 6, Collars.) It is better to wait until you have had the cat a week or so before fitting it with a collar. You can also get a leash later on, should you plan to train the cat to walk with you.

SANITARY PAN

Cats are meticulously clean animals. They will not voluntarily soil their beds or immediate surroundings, but you will have to provide your pet with a proper place in which to relieve itself. You cannot blame it for soiling the house if you fail to make the necessary provisions. A sanitary pan is a necessity if your cat is confined to the house or apartment, but you ought to keep one handy for the cat that goes outdoors, too. The country or suburban cat may not want to go outside in bad weather.

The permanent sanitary pan or box should be sturdy and waterproof, and preferably made of stainless steel or aluminum. It should be sufficiently large to permit the cat to turn around in it. A good sanitary pan or box should be durable, easy to clean, and have a depth of two inches. Cat pans are available in pet shops and pet supply stores, which also carry disposable sanitary pans constructed from treated cardboard.

Decide in advance where you wish to place the sanitary pan, and do not move it after the cat starts to use it. Moving it from place to place will confuse the cat, and the animal may stop using it.

You will need some kind of absorbent litter for the pan. Sawdust, bird gravel, sand, peat moss, shredded newspapers, shavings or one of the commercial litters (usually clay particles treated with a deodorant) may be used. Sand, gravel or a commercial litter are best for long-haired cats.

INTRODUCING THE CAT TO THE FAMILY

Resist the temptation to surprise the children or other members of the family by suddenly bringing home a kitten or cat. To do so will cause difficulty for the cat and for anyone who may be afraid of it. Announce the fact that you are getting a cat before you bring it home.

TRANSPORTING THE CAT HOME

The trip from the breeder, pet shop or humane shelter can be a trying experience for the kitten or cat. Cats are very nervous animals, and you should make the trip home as easy on your pet as possible. Most pet shops, breeders and humane societies provide some kind of box in which to carry the cat home. Or you can go prepared with a cardboard box, a basket with a lid or a commercial cat carrier. Be sure that the carrier you use has adequate space and plenty of air holes. Baskets usually have enough space between the reeds to permit the cat to breathe easily. Cardboard boxes should have air holes punched in the sides. The holes should not be too large, or else the cat may get a paw through and perhaps even gnaw its way out of the box. The commercial carriers are provided with screens or air holes.

Many animals become carsick when riding in a car for the first time. Some are never able to ride without becoming sick. Cover the bottom of the box or carrier with newspaper, and place some shredded newspaper on top of that. When bringing the cat home in a car, place the box or carrier on the floor. If you are not alone, your companion can hold the box on the seat. Words of reassurance during the trip home will help the cat immeasurably. It is not advisable to open the carrier while en route in the car, since the cat may leap out. Keep the cat in the carrier until you are home.

WHEN THE CAT MEETS THE FAMILY

The cat's first day in its new home is a crucial time. It must adjust to a new world of sights, sounds, people and smells. How well it adapts to its new environment depends upon how it is handled the first day. If mishandled, it may become permanently shy and nervous.

Naturally, everyone will want to hold the new cat, but go slowly. It is better not to lift or handle a mature cat until it has had time to explore the house and get acquainted with its new family. If you have brought home a new kitten and there are children in the family, strongly emphasize the correct way to lift and hold a young kitten. If the kitten is mishandled, mauled or dropped, both it and the children may be hurt. Proper handling means fewer scratches for the children and less injury and fright for the pet.

Children and adults alike should be taught to place one hand under the cat's chest, grasping the forelegs gently but firmly with the fingers, and at the same time support the hind quarters with the other hand. The hind legs should not dangle. Lifting the cat by the scruff of the neck is not advisable except under certain conditions. (See Chapter 15, Handling the Injured Cat.)

FEAR OF CATS

Many people, both children and adults, are afraid of cats. This fear is called ailurophobia. Should there be such a person in your household, be considerate and understanding of his fear and do not force the cat upon him. This will only aggravate the condition and alienate the person and cat. The causes of ailurophobia are varied. Fear of cats often stems from the ignorance of parents who warn children to beware of all cats. Sometimes it is the result of some unpleasant experience with a cat. Regardless of the reason, always permit the cat and the person who fears it to get used to each other gradually.

THE CAT'S FIRST DAY AT HOME

Let the cat take its time in adjusting to the new environment. Try to avoid anything that might confuse it. Give it some warm milk, and then let it alone for a while. It will feel lonely and may cry, especially if it is a young kitten. But unless it is sick or injured, the cat will soon get over its loneliness and bewilderment. Too much petting and handling the first day will only make matters worse. First let the cat investigate the house, and then confine it to one room with its sanitary pan, bed and toys. Later, as it becomes more used to the new home, you can begin administering the more comprehensive care outlined in Chapter 6.

4. The Cat's Body: How It Functions

The cat, as we learned in Chapter 1, is a unique animal in many ways. Despite this fact, there is not too much difference between his body and those of other higher animals, including man. The cat has all the vital organs found in most other mammals: heart, lungs, spleen, liver, pancreas, intestines, bladder, and so on. Although there are variations in the functions of some of its internal organs, skeletal and muscular systems, the cat's anatomy and physiology in general closely resemble those of other animals.

A knowledge of the cat's body and how it functions is important to every cat owner and will prove helpful in the pet's daily care. It will also be useful in giving the veterinarian the information he needs, especially when you consult him by telephone and he is unable to examine your cat in person.

HAIR

The outermost part of the cat's body is the hair. Good condition of the hair is vital to a cat's well-being. First of all, the hair serves as an insulator against heat and cold. It also protects the cat against insect bites, stings, thorns and other dangers or annoyances. Children and adults often ask why a cat's hair stands up when it sees a dog. The raising of the hair is a protective device given the cat by nature.

When the animal is frightened, its hairs, which normally lie at an angle to the skin, immediately stand upright and the cat assumes a wary position. The back arches, tail hairs bristle so that the tail looks like a thick bottle brush, and the animal's muscles and nerves are tensed for flight. In this position, the cat hopes that its ferocious appearance will frighten away any would-be attacker.

Cats shed their hair according to climatic conditions and their state of health. During the shedding process, the old hair is replaced by new. Nature arranges shedding of hair in such a way as to keep the cat in a more or less uniform coat throughout the year. Excessive shedding, caused by poor diet, disease, parasites or overheated environment, defeats nature's attempts to keep the cat's hair uniform. Therefore, it is important that your cat's hair be kept in good condition. (See Chapter 14, for skin and hair ailments.)

SKIN

The cat's skin is made up of two layers, the outer *epidermis* and the inner *dermis*. The epidermis actually consists of four sublayers, with the innermost one providing for the regeneration of skin cells.

While the cat's skin is waterproof, it is not impermeable—that is, certain oils and medicines can be absorbed through the skin. This fact should be kept in mind when you use insecticides or medicines on the cat's skin. A toxic substance may be fatal to a cat when absorbed through the skin.

The cat's skin contains sweat glands. The cat also has sweat glands in the pads of its feet. Little is known about how much the sweat glands in the foot pads affect the regulation of the body temperature. But the sweat glands in the skin do help regulate the body temperature, although not quite in the way people's sweat glands do. The cat is cooled by a radiation of heat rather than by the inner cooling caused by the activity of human sweat glands.

Cats also have sebaceous glands in the skin. These are connected with the hair follicles and contain a secretion known as *sebum,* an oily substance that solidifies when exposed to air. It coats the cat's hairs, thus protecting and making them glossy and pliable. In a healthy state, the cat's skin is always elastic and pliable, with the ability to regenerate at a rapid rate.

SKELETON

The cat's skeleton is not so different from that of man as one might suppose. Even though the cat has more bones (230 to man's 206), many are identical to those in the human being.

Although the cat is a quadruped, with a skeletal structure adapted for walking on all fours, if you stand a cat on its hind legs or crouch down on all fours yourself, you will note an astonishing similarity between its skeletal structure and your own.

The variations between the cat's skeleton and man's are really minor. The cat has thirteen ribs and man twelve. Unlike man, most cats have no clavicles or collarbones. Their forelegs are attached directly to the shoulder bone, or scapula, as are man's arms. All cats except the Manx have tailbones. Man has coccygeal vertebrae, but they are vestigial bones and serve no function now. Whereas man has four or five of these coccygeal vertebrae, the cat has from eighteen to twenty-three. Human beings have well-developed opposable thumbs, while the cat has dewclaws instead, which serve none of the purposes of real opposable thumbs.

While it is not necessary to know all 230 bones in the cat's skeleton, it is useful to know some of the major ones. The body of the skeleton consists of the skull, ribs and spinal column (consisting of the atlas, the axis, and the cervical, thoracic, lumbar and coccygeal vertebrae). The skull is attached to the vertebral column at the atlas. The front, or fore, leg consists of the shoulder blade (scapula), humerus, radius, ulna, carpus (wrist), metacarpus and digits. The hind leg consists of femur, tibia, fibula, tarsus (hock), metatarsus and digits.

The cat's skeleton is a strong framework, and under normal conditions provides adequate protection for the vital organs. Unfortunately, many domestic cats are exposed to conditions which endanger skeletal structure. In the motor vehicle accidents that kill or injure many cats every year, some part of the cat's skeleton is usually cracked or broken. The bones most frequently broken are the ribs, bones of the fore and hind legs and the pelvis. (See Chapter 15, First Aid for Fractures.)

Finally, the skeleton allows for freedom of movement. Cats do not run like dogs or most other animals, which (except the pacing horse, camel and giraffe) have a one-two-three-four movement of the feet. The cat moves in a manner similar to a pacing horse—first the front and hind legs on one side move forward, then those on the other side.

MUSCULAR SYSTEM

The cat's muscles are tough and well coordinated and help to make the cat an agile hunter. Basically, the cat's muscles are geared for walking, running, leaping and twisting. Cats are extremely nimble because of their unusual musculature.

Most people are familiar with the old saying that a cat "always lands on its feet." This is almost true. Not all cats are able to land on their feet under certain conditions, but most manage to do so after a fall. The cat's muscular control and skeletal flexibility enable it to right its body with incredible speed. Slow-motion pictures of a cat falling through the air show that it rights itself by a series of twisting motions, while rotating on the axis of its body. But under some conditions cats fail to right themselves and are killed or injured by a fall.

NERVOUS SYSTEM

The cat's nervous system is not unlike that of the dog. However, the cat is generally regarded as a more nervous animal, with a highly developed nervous system which makes it a superb hunter.

Essentially, the cat's nervous system consists of the peripheral and central systems. The peripheral system is made up of sensory fibers and motor neurons, which are gathered together in sheaves or bundles called nerves. The central system has segregated neurons and lies within the skull and spinal cavities. It is composed of the brain and spinal cord. The brain has an important role in complex behavior, since it controls learning, motivation, perception, etc. The spinal cord functions as a conductor to and from the brain and as an agent in reflex actions.

The cat's brain, like that of man and the dog, is divided into two major parts—the *cerebrum,* or front section, and the *cerebellum,* or lower section. The cerebrum is the base of all conscious and rational actions. The cat's cerebrum is small compared to the rest of the brain. The cerebellum is the center for controlling equilibrium and coordinating equilibrium with the cerebral motor cortex. In a cat, it is a highly developed area of the brain.

Its intricate nervous system serves to make the cat an unusually alert animal, particularly in the area of reflex actions. Surprise a cat by suddenly coming up behind it and making a noise and watch it react with lightning speed. It will whirl around, leap upward or sideways or dash off with blinding speed. These fast reflexes play a large part in making the cat a magnificent hunter.

SENSES

The cat's senses, with the possible exception of that of smell, are unusually keen.

SMELL

Cats have small noses. Their olfactory nerves are not as sensitive as those of dogs and some other animals. This is not to say that the cat has a poor sense of smell; it is quite adequate. Cats can scent people, animals and objects at a considerable distance, but they do not rely as completely upon their sense of smell when hunting as some other animals do.

Most cats are sensitive to odors and dislike most of the same ones that human beings dislike. This is important to remember when cleaning the cat's sanitary pan or when spraying or dusting the animal with insecticides. Cats have a particular fondness for certain odors, particularly that of catnip (*Nepeta cataria*), a strong-scented plant of the mint family.

Just how catnip affects cats is not known. Some authorities believe its odor acts as an aphrodisiac, stimulating the cat sexually, and also as a tranquilizer. These reactions seem to be paradoxical, but experiments have proved both. Regardless of just what reactions catnip produces in the cat, it is certain that they are pleasant. Give your cat a few leaves of the plant and it will go into ecstasies, rolling on the leaves, purring and growling. These antics leave no doubt that the plant triggers something enjoyable. Catnip is harmless and you can give your cat as much of this "feline snuff" as it wants.

TASTE

Cats, as any person who owns one will tell you, have very definite likes and dislikes when it comes to taste. Give a cat distasteful food and it will not only refuse to eat it, but probably paw the unwanted item out of the pan. Generally, cats will not eat anything which offends their sense of smell.

The cat's tongue is the primary taste organ. It contains sensitive areas or "taste buds," which react to chemical stimuli to produce sensations of acidity, sweetness, bitterness, saltiness, etc. While many cats prefer the familiar tastes of meat and fish, it is not unusual to find cats with exotic tastes, which include food items such as olives, candy or tomato sauce.

SIGHT

Cats have exceptional eyesight. They have excellent vision in the early evening after sundown, and at night can see better than human beings. The cat, after all, hunts day and night, and nature has given it eyes that can see in light and darkness. Most cats can see ultraviolet rays and other kinds of light invisible to human beings. They also have an optic faculty known as "eyeshine," or *tapetum lucidum.* This phenomenon is apparent at night when the headlights of a car or flashlight are focused on a cat's eyes. A glow is produced which is caused by the light reflecting from a layer of cells at the back of its eyes. Human beings do not have this faculty, although other animals do.

The cat's eyes are not complicated organs, but are strong and durable. The eyes appear as large, round globes or orbs with a transparent covering known as the *cornea.* Around the cornea is a ring or band of white, shiny tissue called the *sclera.* In the lower part of a cat's eye is what might be called a third eyelid, the *nictitating membrane,* which serves as protection for the eye. It is a valuable diagnostic aid in detecting disease or parasites. Intestinal disorders and internal parasites often cause the nictitating membrane to stretch upward across the middle part of the eye.

Next, in the center of the eye, is the *pupil.* The pupil, actually a hole in the eye, can expand or contract, depending upon the amount of light needed for sight in varying circumstances. The pupils also contract or expand when certain drugs are administered and when the brain is injured or diseased. The pupils of cats' eyes, with the exception of those of the leopard, contract into linear slits when exposed to bright light. When the light is reduced the pupils expand. The colored part of the eye which surrounds the pupil is called the *iris.* The colors vary in different species and in individuals.

In back of the pupil is the *lens,* which sometimes develops a cataract when a cat is advanced in years. It is composed of strong, crystal-like, fibrous tissues. Light rays entering the lens are bent to allow any image to rest on a very sensitive area known as the *retina.* The retina is that part of the eye which receives light and images. It is well-lined with nerves, which transmit the impressions or images to the brain by way of the *optic nerve.* As far as scientists have been able to determine, cats are more or less color-blind. They see only various shades of gray.

HEARING

Cats are exceedingly sensitive to sound and can hear noises too faint for the human ear. It is probable that the cat has a keener sense of hearing than most dogs, since it depends more upon sight and hearing, when hunting, than upon its sense of smell.

Cats, like all four-legged animals, have cupped outer ears which serve as conductors of sound, in much the same way as a radar antenna or artificial ear trumpet does. When listening, the cat will turn its head this way and that, reacting to sound by pricking its ears or tipping them forward or backward. The sound is directed downward through the outer ear canal, which is fitted with small knobs or protuberances.

The outer ear tapers and becomes smaller as it nears the skull, then turns upward and ends in a delicate membrane known as the *drum.* This is the only hearing mechanism located in the outer part of the ear. The rest is protected within the cat's skull.

On the inner side of the eardrum are three small, delicate bones, the *hammer, anvil,* and *stirrup.* These descriptive names indicate somewhat the shape of the respective bones, whose function it is to transmit sounds into a section of the inner ear known as the *cochlea,* a snail-shaped canal containing the *auditory nerve.* This nerve relays the sound messages to the brain. Near the cochlea are three horseshoe-shaped tubes known as the *semicircular canals.* They contain fluids which help the cat maintain its excellent sense of balance.

In the middle ear is another tube known as the *Eustachian tube,* which connects the ear with the throat. Its main purpose appears to be that of equalizing pressures. Without this safety device the eardrum would be ruptured when subjected to great pressure. Man has a similar tube connecting his ears and throat. When we fly in an airplane, drive through a tunnel under a riverbed or ascend rapidly in an elevator, we feel the pressure in our ears. Swallowing relieves the pressure. The same phenomenon occurs in the cat. When any pressure is exerted on its ears, it swallows and sticks out its tongue.

TOUCH AND FEEL

Cats are very sensitive to touch and sometimes react violently to it. For example, they do not like to have anything adhere to their skins and will go through all kinds of gyrations to remove it. The feel of water, especially on the feet and face, annoys most cats except the ocelot. When a cat accidentally steps into water or other liquid, it will immediately leap out of it, shake each foot carefully, and then lick each paw to remove the offensive liquid.

The cat's whiskers, or *vibrissae,* provide it with an additional feeler. At the roots of the whiskers are nerve bulbs which connect with the nerves of the lips and send messages to the brain. By means of its whiskers, the cat detects objects before they come into direct contact with its body, and the animal is thus able to feel its way in the dark.

Since the cat has a sensitive nervous system, it dislikes being touched on various parts of its body. Its whiskers are very sensitive and it will object when they are touched or pulled. Some cats become violently angry and bite and claw when touched, while others can be handled and petted at will. Sensitivity to touch varies, and one has to learn about and respect the individual cat's tolerance to touch.

RESPIRATORY SYSTEM

The cat's respiratory system is similar to that of other mammals. The lungs are on each side of the chest. They function along with the blood in transferring oxygen and carbon dioxide and, to a certain extent, aid in regulating the body temperature. (The cat's normal temperature range is 101 to 102 degrees F.)

All mammals have a partition which divides the chest cavity and separates the lungs. In the cat this membrane is very thin, and often presents a problem when the cat sustains chest injuries. If the chest cavity on one side is torn or crushed, allowing air to enter, both lungs collapse. Human beings have a strong membranous partition, and when one lung collapses the other does not necessarily deflate.

The cat breathes through its nose and mouth. A tube extends from the throat into the cat's chest and branches into two other tubes known as *bronchial tubes,* one of which is connected to each lung. The bronchial tubes may become inflamed from injury or disease. They branch into smaller tubes (bronchioles) and finally into air sacs. Each air sac is enclosed by a network of blood capillaries which allow gases to escape or be absorbed.

CIRCULATORY SYSTEM

The cat is a warm-blooded animal with an intricate circulatory system.

HEART AND BLOOD VESSELS

The cat's body is nourished by blood, which supplies food to the body cells and also collects and carries waste materials to the organs of excretion. The core of this complex system is the four-chambered heart, situated in the cat's chest.

Impure blood is carried to the heart by the *anterior* and *posterior vena cavas,* two large veins. The heart contracts in a squeezing motion, forcing the blood into two large arteries, the *anterior* and *posterior aortas,* one of which leads to the lungs, while the other divides and circulates the blood through the body. In the lungs, the blood releases carbon dioxide, picks up oxygen and circulates again to the heart, where it is pumped throughout the cat's body to distribute oxygen and pick up waste materials.

BLOOD

Blood is composed of cells suspended in a special fluid called *plasma.* In the plasma float the red cells, which contain a chemical known as *hemoglobin,* which functions in oxygen distribution. If your cat has a serious cut and the blood flow is bright red and pumping out, it is arterial blood carrying much oxygen. If the blood oozing from a wound is dark and bluish, it is venous and contains little oxygen.

The blood also contains white *corpuscles* which vary in size and number. Under a microscope these usually appear as small, spherical bodies, but they may change shape. Their function is to surround impurities and microbes that may enter the body. Another constituent

of blood is the *platelets,* small oval bodies which play a part in causing the blood to clot or coagulate.

The spleen is a long, narrow organ, purplish in color, situated behind the stomach. The cat has a rather small spleen, with an average
length of three or four inches. Its functions are to store blood and to
destroy old blood cells. The capillaries in the spleen are very large,
and rupture of this organ may cause severe hemorrhaging and possibly death. Although the spleen itself acts as a filter, there are other
filtering agents or devices. Lymph nodes are scattered along the blood
route. Their function is to purify the blood by destroying bacteria,
viruses and other alien matter. Lymph, the fluid discharged by the
lymph glands, does not circulate through the cat's body by pressure,
but by muscular activity, intestinal action and peristalsis.

DIGESTIVE SYSTEM

The cat's digestive system consists of the mouth, teeth, esophagus,
stomach, pylorus, small intestine, large intestine, liver, pancreas and
rectum. All of these organs help to produce or process the nourishment distributed by the blood.

MOUTH

The cat's mouth is the doorway to its digestive system. Its lips are
mainly used to hold food and to retain mouth secretions. The tongue
is rough and covered with small hooklike appendages of several
shapes and is used to lap up liquids. Cats also use the tongue in keeping themselves clean. If you allow a cat to lick your hand, you will
notice that the tongue feels like a soft file or rasp.

TEETH

Cats have twenty-eight teeth. However, the cat develops two sets
of teeth. The first, or milk teeth, appear early in kittenhood and fall
out when the roots have been partially absorbed by the body—when
the cat is about five to seven months old. New, or second, teeth grow
in quickly and their appearance may be accompanied by fever and
loss of weight.

A simple formula will show the number and arrangement of the various kinds of teeth found in the cat's mouth (an initial indicates the type of tooth, a number indicates how many of that type there are, and a horizontal line differentiates between the upper and lower jaw). The mature cat's dental arrangement is as follows:

Incisors   I $\dfrac{3\text{-}3}{3\text{-}3}$ (six incisors in upper jaw and six in lower)

Next to the last incisor, moving toward the back of the mouth, on each side of the upper and lower jaws are the canine teeth. There are two in the upper jaw and two in the lower.

Canine   C $\dfrac{1\text{-}1}{1\text{-}1}$

Behind the canine teeth are the premolars. There are four premolars in the upper jaw and four in the lower.

Premolar   P $\dfrac{2\text{-}2}{2\text{-}2}$

Finally, there are the molar or grinding teeth. There are two in the upper jaw and two in the lower.

Molar   M $\dfrac{1\text{-}1}{1\text{-}1}$

Assembling the cat's total dental formula, we have:

I $\dfrac{3\text{-}3}{3\text{-}3}$:   C $\dfrac{1\text{-}1}{1\text{-}1}$:   P $\dfrac{2\text{-}2}{2\text{-}2}$:   M $\dfrac{1\text{-}1}{1\text{-}1}$

Healthy teeth are important to the cat's digestion and well-being. Unfortunately, many cats are fed the wrong kind of food, which often injures the teeth. Also, as the cat ages, tartar forms on the teeth and must be removed if the animal is to maintain the full use of its teeth.

That part of the tooth visible above the gums is called the crown. The part below the gums is known as the root. At least half of each canine tooth grows below the gumline. The roots of all teeth are strong and deeply imbedded. The crown and neck of each tooth are covered with enamel, which protects the buried part of the tooth made of dentine. The roots have no enamel. Inside each tooth is the pulp, which houses the nerves and blood vessels. Cats often have tooth trouble involving the nerves and pulp, although they rarely develop cavities.

ESOPHAGUS

The esophagus, or gullet, is a strong, elastic tube which carries the food from the mouth to the stomach. It is rarely subject to disease, although it may become infested with esophageal worms.

STOMACH

The cat's stomach has elastic walls which stretch to accommodate varying amounts of food. Some digestion takes place in the stomach, where acid liquids help to digest proteins and fats.

INTESTINES

The contents of the stomach enter the *duodenum,* a thick section of the small intestine. A valve or sphincter muscle at the bottom of the stomach, called the *pylorus,* controls the flow into the duodenum. Bile, manufactured by the liver and stored in the gall bladder, flows into the duodenum as needed and breaks down fat into tiny globules. Also entering the duodenum is a digestive enzyme manufactured by the pancreas. The small intestine itself secretes substances which first convert starches into dextrin, then break them down into glucose. In general, the digestive system transforms carbohydrates into a usable form and reduces fats and proteins to their component elements (fatty acids and amino acids). All are then carried by the blood to the various parts of the cat's body.

LIVER

The liver is the largest organ in the cat's body. It is situated in front of the stomach on the right side of the body just back of the diaphragm. The liver has many functions, among them secretion of bile, manufacture of urea, destruction of bacteria and regulation of sugar utilization.

PANCREAS

In addition to producing enzymes, the pancreas regulates the body's ability to utilize blood sugar. It cooperates with the liver in this function. The pancreas is located near the stomach. In it are tiny bodies called the *Isles of Langerhans,* whose purpose is to manufacture insulin, the lack of which results in a condition known as diabetes.

EXCRETION OF WASTES

After the food has passed through the small intestine, it is deposited in the large intestine, where large amounts of water which it may contain are absorbed. A heavy bacterial action also takes place in the large intestine, which breaks down waste and unassimilated material until it is excreted through the rectum and anus.

URINARY SYSTEM

The important organs of the cat's urinary system are the kidneys, ureters, bladder and urethra. Liquids are filtered through the kidneys (one on each side of the body, near the lumbar region), then liquid wastes are sent through the ureters to the bladder. The urethra, a tube connecting with the bladder and exterior of the body, discharges the liquid wastes. Diseases of the urinary system are more common in older cats, but young cats may also have urinary troubles associated with disease or injury.

REPRODUCTIVE SYSTEM

Cats are fertile animals and the female may produce three litters of kittens a year, which is one reason for the large number of stray cats.

FEMALE REPRODUCTIVE ORGANS

The external parts of the female's reproductive system consist of the vagina and vulva. The vulva are the lips of the vagina, located just below the anus. The vagina connects the outer and inner parts of the reproductive system, and serves as the passageway for the tom-cat's penis in copulation.

The inner reproductive organs include the ovaries, cervix, uterus and Fallopian tubes. The two ovaries are located in the front part of the abdomen just behind the kidneys. Eggs or ova are formed within the ovaries. When the female is mated, ova descend through two Fallopian tubes into the Y-shaped uterus. There they are fertilized, and the kittens develop.

Female cats have an estrous cycle, or heat period, during which time they can conceive when mated. If the female is not mated, however, estrus will be repeated periodically until she is mated. (See Chapter 17 on Heat Period or Estrus of the Female.)

MALE REPRODUCTIVE ORGANS

The reproductive organs of the tomcat consists of the testicles, prostate gland, scrotum and penis. The testicles are suspended in the baglike scrotum outside the cat's body. Most tomcats have two testicles, although some have only one, and a few have none at all. The testicles manufacture the sperm and also secrete the hormone *testosterone*. The prostate gland provides the seminal fluid, and the penis is the organ by which copulation is effected and sperm ejaculated into the female's vagina.

INTELLIGENCE

The cat is an intelligent animal, capable of learning and retaining what is learned. It can also exercise a certain degree of reason in solving problems which confront it.

Anyone who has ever owned a cat or watched one at work will admit its high intelligence. Consider the cat as it watches a mouse hole. Though a lover of ease and comfort, the cat will lie in wait for hours in the cold. Before it takes up its vigil at the mouse hole, it will examine the room or whole building to determine whether the mouse has another hole. It doesn't fancy wasting time at one hole, only to have the mouse slip out another. Surely this kind of reasoning requires high intelligence.

This intelligence is common to all breeds of cats. Many years ago, in the Dublin Zoological Gardens, a lioness was tormented by rats. The zoo keepers placed a small terrier in the cage. At first, the lioness resented the dog. But she was impressed when the terrier caught a rat, tossed it into the air and caught it again with a death-dealing snap. She swiftly came to the conclusion that the dog was a valuable partner and was not to be harmed. When the dog finally nestled up to her side, she folded a huge paw about him, and there he rested, alert to pounce on any rat that dared to disturb the lioness.

Although it is not always easy to teach cats to perform on command, they can learn certain tricks, but the process requires infinite patience. This fact should not be taken to mean that the cat is stupid —far from it. It is quick to learn when its welfare is involved. It is simply too aloof and independent to be brought under the same control as the dog.

TEMPERAMENT

Make no mistake about it—cats are temperamental animals. Some of them are moody, aggressive, nervous and quick to resent any hurt or neglect. On the other hand, many cats are docile, even-tempered and respond to affection and gentle handling.

ANGER

Cats are quick to anger, and when they are angered, they assume a ferocious pose. Watch a cat attacked by a dog. The cat rapidly reacts by arching its back, while the hair on its body and tail stand on end, and it snarls and spits. All these signs denote fear as well as anger. The cat then drops into a crouch, body extended, with the tail, or just its tip, lashing from side to side. As the cat prepares to attack, the ears are pressed back onto the head, the mouth is partly open, with lips drawn back and teeth exposed; the forefeet are firmly planted, with claws extended. Then the cat snarls angrily and attacks.

AFFECTION

The cat, when expressing affection, is all gentleness. It stands upright with back slightly arched and tail held up, stiff and straight. Its ears are erect and pointed, the mouth remains closed and the cat purrs contentedly as it rubs against your leg. When in an affectionate mood, the cat's claws are retracted.

COURAGE

Cats are very courageous animals, often attacking animals twice their size, especially when their young are threatened. Some years ago, a cat was playing with her kittens in a barnyard. Suddenly, a red-tailed hawk darted down and snatched up one of the kittens. It beat its wings furiously in an effort to gain altitude with its prey. But the mother cat quickly sprang at the hawk, and he was obliged to drop the kitten. A battle ensued. The hawk gave the cat a terrible mauling with its powerful wings, beak and talons. Although torn and lacerated, the mother cat refused to give up and finally managed to rip the hawk's wings off. Unable to fly away, the hawk then became the prey and was soon killed by the infuriated cat.

Once she had dispatched the hawk, the mother cat ran over to her kittens, and calmly proceeded to lick the wounds of the injured one. Paying no attention to her own gaping wounds, she licked her kitten and purred in great contentment. There are any number of similar true stories that testify to the great courage of the cat.

5. *Nutrition*

Proper nutrition is important to your cat's health and well-being. Cats confined entirely indoors are wholly dependent upon their owners for food, and are the ones most likely to develop nutritional deficiencies. Those that roam outdoors usually supplement their diets with rats, mice, other mammals and birds. A basic knowledge of cat nutrition will help you properly feed your pet.

THE ESSENTIAL NUTRIENTS

Your cat needs certain essential nutrients in its daily diet. Its nutritional requirements are not too different from your own. The cat's daily diet should include proteins, fats, carbohydrates, vitamins and minerals.

PROTEINS

Proteins are vital to the growth and repair of the body. They are biological compounds consisting of various combinations of amino acids. Approximately twenty amino acids, in various combinations, mingle to form the different proteins. The cat requires more protein than does the dog. Proteins are found in all kinds of meat, especially muscle meat and fillets of fish.

FATS

The importance of fat in the cat's daily diet has also been demonstrated in nutritional tests. Fat is a source of energy and heat and is composed of certain essential fatty acids. Fatty acids perform other functions besides regulating body heat and providing energy. They are also responsible for the condition of the cat's skin and hair. An absence of the essential fatty acids has a marked effect on the cat's nervous system and resistance to disease, particularly skin diseases. Recent tests on fats and oils have revealed that the addition of poly-unsaturated vegetable oils (processed from whole soybeans) contributes to a healthier skin, glossier fur and a general longer "prime of life."

The essential fatty acids are found in fish, meats and fowl. Vegetable oils are added to the high-quality canned cat foods. The fat content of dry cat foods is open to question, since it is difficult to stabilize or retain fats added to dry foods. You can see to it that your cat gets enough fat by feeding it meat, fish, fowl and canned cat food.

CARBOHYDRATES

Carbohydrates are also a source of energy. They are present as sugars in green plants and vegetables (usually introduced into prepared cat foods in the form of cereals). Cats have difficulty in digesting raw carbohydrates. Therefore, starchy foods such as vegetables and cereals should be cooked.

MINERALS

Another group of important nutrients essential for proper growth of the cat are minerals. Calcium and phosphorus assist in the production and preservation of sound teeth and bones, as well as blood. Iron, copper and cobalt are needed for red blood cells. Iodine helps to prevent goiter. Still other minerals—often called "trace elements" —are required by the cat in minute quantities.

VITAMINS

Vitamins are food constituents necessary for the normal nutrition of the cat.

Vitamin A

A deficiency of vitamin A causes poor appetite and emaciation. Insufficient amounts of this vitamin can also cause weak hind legs, inflamed lungs, inflammation of the eyes (especially the nictitating membrane) and impairment of the hearing and nervous systems. An acute shortage of vitamin A may even result in death. The absorption of vitamin A is helped by fat. Vitamin A is found in high concentration in fish liver oils (*e.g.,* cod-liver oil) and in leafy green vegetables, as well as in carrots and sweet potatoes.

Vitamin B_1 (Thiamine)

An insufficient supply of vitamin B_1 can lead to poor appetite, vomiting, faulty coordination, abnormal reflexes, heart disorders and convulsions. Certain kinds of fish, such as carp and herring, are deficient in thiamine. It is found in high concentrations in the outer shells or coats of grains, in yeasts and in lesser concentrations in meats.

Vitamin B_2 (Riboflavin)

A lack of vitamin B_2 results in poor appetite, emaciation, hair loss, impaired nervous function and anemia. Cats manufacture riboflavin in the intestines from carbohydrates. Most cat foods contain cereals to provide carbohydrates and bulk.

Folic acid

Another of the vitamin B complex is folic acid. Its absence or deficiency causes anemia and a reduction in the white corpuscles. Since folic acid is widely distributed in plant and animal tissues, a diet containing both meat and vegetables would insure an adequate supply of this essential nutrient.

Vitamin B_6 (Pyridoxine)

Pyridoxine helps to prevent emaciation, convulsions, anemia, kidney disease, stunted growth and unwanted deposits of iron in the liver. It is found in yeast, liver and vegetables.

Vitamin C (Ascorbic acid)

Cats manufacture their own vitamin C, which helps to stabilize fats and promote their use in the body.

Vitamin D

Vitamin D is the well-known antirickets vitamin. It is essential for the efficient utilization of calcium; both calcium and vitamin D are important for strong bone and teeth structure. Pregnant cats should receive supplementary amounts of vitamin D. However, supplemental feeding of vitamin D should be given only with the advice of a veterinarian, since overdoses may cause loss of appetite, diarrhea, demineralization of the bones and, possibly, accumulations of calcium in the kidneys. Vitamin D is present in various foods, but the best source for cats is fish-liver oils.

Vitamin E

An antisterility factor, vitamin E promotes breeding ability, production of healthy kittens and a high red blood cell count. It also aids in the stabilization of fats. A deficiency of this vitamin in cats may result in a painful disease known as *steatitis*. Vitamin E is found in wheat germ and other cereals.

Niacin (Nicotinic acid)

Supplemental niacin has been found to maintain firm, healthy tongues, mouths and gums. (The absence of niacin or its deficiency in dogs causes a condition known as "black tongue.") Niacin or nicotinic acid is found in yeast and meats.

CAT NUTRITION IS STILL UNDER STUDY

While considerable information about the nutritional needs of cats has been amassed by animal nutritionists and biochemists, research in this area still goes on. Fundamentally, it centers around the following questions: (1) Which basic food ingredients—and in what combination or proportion—will provide a balanced, nutritive diet for cats? (2) What supplements are necessary; *i.e.,* vitamins, minerals or foodstuffs? and (3) Which diets do cats *prefer* when it comes to taste, palatability, smell and texture? To learn more about the nutritional requirements of cats, nutritionists, food technologists, biochemists and other scientists constantly work on analyzing and developing various cat food formulas.

FEEDING YOUR CAT

Before discussing the various cat foods and amounts to feed, it is well to mention some generalizations about feeding cats. First, forget about feeding your cat in terms of your own needs or tastes. Your foods and preferences should not be imposed on the cat. It is true that some cats develop a taste for unusual or exotic foods, but fancy, elaborate or gourmet diets are not necessary. Plain, wholesome and proven cat foods (not necessarily prepared) are best for your pet.

SUITABLE FRESH FOODS

While the cat is regarded as a carnivorous animal, the variety of foods which it will eat is surprising.

Vegetables

Many cats like vegetables. Since vegetables contain starch, or carbohydrates, they should be cooked before feeding to the cat. Strained spinach, string beans, carrots and tomatoes are often relished by cats. You may find that your cat likes other vegetables as well.

Meats

The cat, as a carnivorous animal, should have fresh meat every day. However, meat should not constitute the sole diet. Even though it is rich in proteins, meat is deficient in other nutritional factors, mainly calcium. Therefore, meat should form part of the daily food ration.

There is no need to cook the cat's meat (except pork); it can safely be fed raw. Most cats, however, prefer warm meat, so it is best to warm the meat to room temperature before feeding to the cat.

Here is a list of suitable meats, although your cat may not like all of them:

Liver (beef, sheep and chicken)

Kidneys (beef, lamb and *cooked* pork)

Hearts (all kinds)

Muscle Meat (beef, lamb, sheep, horse and chicken)

Fish (the whole fish, including protein-rich fillets, liver, glands and bones—the fish should be cooked and the bones ground, if possible, for complete digestibility, as well as for the calcium and phosphorous content)

Glandular Organs (brains, tripe, spleen, etc.)

Meats to Avoid: cured and spiced meats, such as ham, bologna, salami, etc.

Some cats are finicky eaters and may acquire a taste only for liver and kidneys. Discourage this one-sided appetite. While high in vitamins, these two organs are not a balanced diet for your cat, and when fed solely on liver or kidneys, a cat can develop nutritional deficiencies. Also, a steady or exclusive diet of liver tends to produce a soft bowel movement, possibly diarrhea. Liver and kidneys are nutritious when fed in combination with other foods.

Milk

Many people just assume that all cats are crazy about milk. Milk is unquestionably a nutritious food, but not all cats like or tolerate it. Milk can act as a cathartic, causing diarrhea in both kittens and older cats. You will have to judge for yourself as to whether your cat can tolerate milk. If your pet likes milk, but has trouble with loose bowel movements because of it, then try diluting the milk with water, or substitute skim milk, powdered or whole.

Eggs

Eggs are a source of nourishment, but they are not necessary as a daily staple in your cat's diet. Some cats—like dogs—have difficulty digesting the whites of eggs. Also, egg white contains a substance that interferes with the action of *trypsin,* an enzyme produced in the pancreas. An occasional egg—with the white removed—may be fed to vary the cat's diet. Hardboil the egg for easier digestion.

Potatoes

Even though they are high in carbohydrates, potatoes may be used as a variation in the cat's diet. A small portion of mashed potatoes, liberally seasoned with plain meat gravy, is often relished by cats.

PREPARED CAT FOODS

The cat owner who prefers the ready-mixed or prepared cat foods will find many types and brands on the market. Some are of high quality and provide a nearly balanced diet for cats; others are of low quality and need considerable supplementation to provide the cat with even the minimum daily nutritional requirements.

Canned Cat Foods

Cat food manufacturers now provide a wide variety of canned foods that are geared to the tastes of even the most particular feline. Your cat can have a choice of canned chicken, meat, liver or fish combined with cereals, or, if the cat prefers, just plain meat or fish.

Canned cat foods are easy to store and serving them involves nothing more than opening the can and placing the food in the cat's dish. The unused portion of the food should be left in the can and kept in the refrigerator until the next meal. Whichever type or formula of canned food you and your cat decide upon, my advice is to procure a high-quality product from one of the leading pet food manufacturers, since keen competition among top cat food manufacturers forces them to produce well-balanced diets. There are, as I mentioned before, many brands of cat foods; however, the cheaper ones are pale and inadequate imitations of the better grades. Many of them are "padded" with cereal or other fillers and contain little meat or fish. (A few years ago, a small dog-and-cat-food manufacturer in Pennsylvania was found to be using sawdust as a filler for his canned pet foods!)

Since some people have misgivings based on misinformation about feeding cats an all-fish diet (canned or fresh), I think the matter should be clarified. First, fish is a very nutritious food for cats (and human beings, for that matter). Its protein is of a high quality and the carbohydrate content is low. In addition to the protein, fish contains unsaturated fats, which have been found valuable in preventing deposits of cholesterol on artery walls. There is another element which the cat receives from a ration of fish that it may not get from another source: iodine.

Some veterinarians and cat authorities advise against feeding cats an all-fish diet, some even say feed no fish at all. One fact behind these admonitions is that fish is high in minerals, especially calcium, and these may contribute to the formation of uroliths, or stones, in the urinary tract. Actually, fish is not as high in calcium as some other foods. For example, the United States Department of Agriculture Handbook Number 8, *Composition of Foods,* gives the following calcium content of 100 grams of fish and other foods:

Milk	118 milligrams of calcium
Liver	8 mgs
Kidney	11 mgs
Raw mackerel	10 mgs
Raw codfish	10 mgs
Canned tuna	8 mgs

Thus, if we are to rule out fish as a cat food because of a high calcium content, then we will have to eliminate the foods mentioned in the list, and others which are as high or higher than fish in their calcium content. Canned salmon does contain a considerable amount of calcium, but the mineral is all in the bones. When the bones are removed, salmon has about the same calcium content as tuna.

The exact cause of urinary stones is unknown, although the retention of urine seems to be a major factor. This would indicate that any abnormal condition, such as disease, injury or thickening of tissues (which sometimes results from the castration of male cats), would allow mineral and other sediment in the retained urine to form into stones. Another theory about the formation of urinary stones is that they result from a disorder of calcium metabolism. A Canadian physician has shown that a lack of vitamin C is largely responsible for the formation of kidney stones in human beings. Since cats manufacture their own vitamin C, they should have no problem from stones formed by a possible lack of this vitamin.

Another reason for not feeding an all-fish diet to the cat is that, when fed over long periods of time, fish produces serious nutritional deficiencies. Experiments have been conducted in which cats have been fed an all-fish diet over a period of several weeks. After two weeks, according to the nutritionists making the study, the cats lost weight, displayed a marked decrease in muscle tone, developed dry, dull coats and scaly, sore skins. Severe nervous disorder symptoms also appeared in the cats. Eventually the cats lost their sense of balance and had impaired vision. Autopsy findings on these cats showed degenerative organic deficiency diseases.

Some canned all-fish foods, especially the poor-quality grades, are deficient in vitamin E, the nutrient that helps stabilize fats. The canned fish foods with little or no vitamin E contribute to a deficiency disease known as *steatitis*. Cats afflicted with steatitis have sore areas on their backs and abdomens, fever and poor appetites. It is a painful disease, one in which a heavy yellow fat accumulates in the normal fat layers of the cat's body, just under the skin. Cat food manufacturers, as a result of the steatitis problem, have added vitamin E, usually in the form of *alpha-tocopheral* (an alcohol which has the properties of vitamin E, derived from the oil of wheat germ or produced synthetically). However, even after the fortification of all-fish foods with vitamin E, some cats still develop nutritional deficiencies.

All of this is not to say that you should never feed your cat fish. What it does imply is that cats should be fed fish in moderation or at least supplemented with the other required nutrients, just as wild cats which prey upon fish supplement their diet with meat, organs and vegetable matter such as grass, which contain—among other elements —vitamins A, E and C. I see no reason to deprive cats of a food that is not only nutritious when fed judiciously, but one which they love.

Dry Cat Foods

There are various dry cat foods on the market today. These foods are made in different shapes, sizes and colors (some are a brilliant red, green or yellow, but the colors are wasted on the cat, of course, since it can't tell one from another). The dry foods usually contain cereals, bone meal, vitamins and minerals and are flavored with beef, lamb, chicken, fish, liver or even cheese (many cats love cheese). These dry foods are prepared and processed in a manner similar to that used for dog biscuits, milk bones or kibble.

High-quality dry cat foods are wholesome and nutritious, but not all cats like them. Thus, the dry foods have not enjoyed the popularity of canned cat foods or fresh foods. Nevertheless, dry foods have some extra advantages, aside from their nutritive value. They can be used as snacks or tidbits for those cats that like them. The hard wafers or biscuits also help remove or keep down accumulations of tartar on a cat's teeth, especially the animal fed exclusively on soft foods. And, if you must be away from home for a long period of time and are afraid the cat's regular food will spoil when left out in large quantities, a large ration of dry cat food can be substituted without the problem of spoilage. There's the possibility that your cat may refuse to eat the dry food, but at least you will have provided food. The choice of whether to eat or not to eat is strictly up to the cat.

BONES

The question arises as to whether cats should be given bones and— as in the case of dogs—there are differences of opinion on the matter. It is true that most cats do not seem to have the same enthusiasm for bones that dogs do. Cats gnaw on bones, of course, but they do so with a more businesslike attitude and less gusto than dogs. The average dog treats a bone as a *pièce de résistance,* a delectable food-object that should be gnawed, worried, tossed about, and buried for future enjoyment. The cat simply works on a bone until it extracts the marrow and then walks away and forgets it. This applies to the bones of mammals.

Cats will completely eat fowl bones, and owners are usually warned against giving them chicken, duck, turkey or other fowl bones. The reason is that these bones splinter and the sharp edges can perforate a cat's stomach or intestines. Some steak and most chop bones have sharp edges and present the same hazard.

Upon several occasions, when I have written in my pet column warning about feeding fowl bones to cats, I have received letters telling me that cats kill and eat birds, bones and all, without harmful effects, and aren't chicken, duck and turkey bones hollow like those of other birds?

The answer, of course, is yes. But there is one major difference between the bones of wild birds killed and eaten by the cat and those from roasted, broiled or cooked poultry. Raw bird bones are supple and resilient. Cooked fowl bones lose all of their juices and become very brittle, splintering into sharp pieces when the cat goes to work on them. Therefore, I consider the difference between cooked and raw fowl bones an important distinction. Feed fowl meat to the cat, but toss the bones into the garbage pail.

WATER

We usually think of water as a thirst quencher. However, it has a more important function. It aids in the transportation of proteins and other nutrients to various parts of the cat's body. Since most of the cat's body is composed of water, the animal needs a constant supply of fresh water to help maintain the body's water balance. See that your cat has an ample supply of cool, fresh water available at all times.

VITAMIN AND MINERAL SUPPLEMENTS

What about adding vitamin and mineral supplements to the cat's daily diet? Here, again, we have an area of cat nutrition that has two schools of thought. Some nutritionists believe that cats fed a balanced diet do not need extra vitamins (except in special cases), while others argue that we never can be sure the cat is getting the right amount of the important vitamins and minerals in its diet. I belong to the former school of thought and advocate vitamin and mineral supplements only in certain cases.

Pregnant cats certainly should receive a vitamin and mineral compound. Also, since some mother cats may develop *eclampsia* (see Chapter 19 for a discussion of this postnatal condition), they should be given extra calcium. Kittens that are being weaned also should receive vitamins, such as *Oleum Percomorphum* or other compounds containing vitamins A and D. Sick cats or those with vitamin and mineral deficiencies should, of course, be given supplements as prescribed by the veterinarian.

Except when prescribed by a veterinarian, vitamin and mineral compounds should be fed according to the manufacturer's directions. It is just as dangerous to overdose a cat with vitamins and minerals as it is to permit a deficiency. An oversupply of vitamins may also cause severe nutritional disturbances in a cat. Your safest course is to have the veterinarian prescribe the kind and amount of vitamin and mineral supplements for your cat.

FEEDING REGIME

While it is true that the house cat's wild relatives can't have their meals with regularity (if prey is scarce or they miss a kill, wild cats have to go hungry until another opportunity presents itself), domestic cats have become creatures of habit, especially in the matter of meals. They want to be fed more or less at the same time every day.

Kittens at Weaning Age

When kittens are about four weeks of age, the mother cat will start to wean them for two good reasons: her milk supply slows down, and the kittens develop sharp teeth. You can aid in the weaning process by feeding the kittens small quantities of lukewarm milk twice a day. If whole milk seems to cause diarrhea, dilute it with an equal part of skimmed milk. It is best to feed kittens in individual pans or saucers, thus assuring the weaker kittens a chance of getting a meal.

Four to Eight Weeks of Age

Feed a high-quality canned cat food four times a day at the rate of a large teaspoonful of the cat food and two teaspoonsful of evaporated milk and water (mixed half and half) at room temperature. Also, provide about a half jar of beef or liver baby food—or an equal amount of finely scraped or ground beef, horsemeat or liver—once a day. Add one drop of *Oleum Percomorphum* or other vitamin A and D compound to the meat.

Gradually increase the amount of food and vitamin supplement. The vitamins can be increased at the rate of another drop each week: *e.g.,* at four weeks of age, one drop; five weeks of age, two drops and so on until the eight-week-old kitten is receiving four drops of vitamins daily. The amount of food can be increased according to what the kitten will eat at one meal. Nobody can give you the exact amount to feed your kitten or cat; you will have to experiment and be the judge as to how much your cat eats. When the kitten is four months old, you can reduce the number of feedings to three a day.

Five to Seven Months of Age

In this age period, the young cat's baby teeth have been or are being replaced by the second or permanent teeth. And by seven months of age, the number of feedings can be cut down to two a day, with the quantities increased according to the cat's appetite. If you are feeding a high-quality cat food, it no longer will be necessary to provide a vitamin and mineral supplement.

Eight Months and Over

At eight months of age, your cat can be regarded as almost mature and fed a good-quality cat food twice a day. Some cats eat only one meal a day, but this is something you will have to determine from observations of your cat's feeding habits. You can add variety to your cat's diet by feeding some dry food or fresh foods mentioned in the section on the various kinds of foodstuffs.

Pregnant Cats

The pregnant or nursing cat requires a special diet and this is covered in detail in Chapter 19.

Altered Males

When not given adequate chance to exercise, altered males may put on excess weight. Feed sparingly, but with a high-quality food. Avoid foods with a high carbohydrate content.

Spayed Females

Spayed females, like altered males, may also gain weight rapidly, especially as they grow older. Avoid starchy foods.

Aged Cats

The old cat needs fewer calories because of its general slowing down in activity. Special attention should be paid to the nutritional needs of the old cat. (See Chapter 20, Care of the Old Cat.)

Sick or Convalescent Cats

Feed the sick or convalescent cat according to your veterinarian's directions. (See Chapter 16, Home Care of the Sick or Injured Cat.)

GRASS

Why do cats eat grass? Is the habit harmful? Nobody knows the exact reason that cats eat grass, although it is quite obvious that grass acts as an emetic, causing the animal to vomit. Perhaps this is nature's way of helping the cat get rid of hair balls and other indigestible matter. Grass-eating is not harmful, *provided the grass contains no poisonous sprays or other chemicals*. You might feed apartment-bound cats a weekly ration of clean, freshly cut grass. Or you can sow grass seed in a window box and let the cat nibble on the shoots when they come up. You'll have to replenish the grass seed from time to time, of course.

GENERAL FEEDING HINTS

Feed the cat in the same place and at the same time every day.

Serve all food at room temperature—70 to 72 degrees F.

Avoid sudden changes in the cat's diet, especially with young kittens. Introduce new foods gradually to prevent digestive upsets.

Do not feed spiced foods, even though the cat may have a taste for them.

If the cat is eating its regular meals with no leavings, a tidbit now and then will do no harm. But skip the snacks if the cat is passing up the regular meal in favor of tidbits.

If a cat refuses more than two successive meals, keep the animal under observation. It may be ill or supplementing its diet by catching rats or mice, thus reducing its desire for its regular food. You'll have to decide what is happening when your cat begins to skip meals, and act accordingly. If you are positive that the cat is not doing any hunting, then a trip to the veterinarian is in order.

Place a rubber mat or newspaper under the cat's food pan if you are fussy about the kitchen floor. Remember that cats like to drag their food out of a pan or dish and eat it from the floor—which is a more natural way for them to eat, of course.

Cats eat slowly, so don't hurry your pet's meal. Leave the food out for an hour; if the cat doesn't eat it all by that time, remove it.

Avoid feeding the cat cooked fowl bones, which are brittle, or sharp-edged steak or chop bones.

Permit your cat to eat in peace. Keep young children and other pets away from the cat at feeding time.

Avoid overfeeding, particularly in the case of the altered male, spayed female and aged cat.

Keep a pan or crock of fresh, cool water available at all times.

All foods, with the exception of fish, pork and starchy vegetables, can be fed raw.

Remember that fish is very nutritious, but supplement it with other foods.

Finally, study your cat's eating habits and adjust the diet accordingly. Observe your pet from day to day; you can obtain a good idea of whether the cat is getting enough of the right kind of food by the animal's general appearance. When properly fed, your cat should be sleek, not fat. The coat and skin should be soft and pliable. And —most important—the cat should have a contented look that comes from good food and care.

6. Care and Training

Unfortunately for cats, too many people have the mistaken idea that all the care a cat needs is to be given a saucer of milk and be put outdoors at night. This was the standard care given most cats years ago and it is still meted out to cats in city, suburbs and rural areas today. Needless to say, it's the lazy owner's way of taking care of a cat. While cats require relatively little care compared to some other pets, they do need something more than a handout of milk and a push outside. When given this primitive care, a cat can't be blamed for turning into a tramp or so-called alley cat.

The intelligent and thoughtful cat owner will provide his cat with care that befits the dignity and contributions of the pet. Proper food, water, snug sleeping quarters, affection, grooming and medical attention—these are the obligations of cat ownership. They are little enough in return for all the fun, loyalty, service and companionship which the cat offers the person or family with whom it lives.

GROOMING

Cats are fastidious creatures and keep themselves clean. However, there are times when the cat needs a helping hand in getting a complete grooming. This is especially true of the long-haired varieties. Grooming, which includes brushing and combing as often as necessary, not only improves the cat's appearance, but makes the animal feel better. Grooming may be an easy or difficult chore, depending on the condition of the cat's coat. Dead hair must be removed and snarls or mats picked or combed out. Burrs, chewing gum and other sticky substances will have to be removed with care. Long-haired cats will need more work than shorthairs.

Start grooming your cat early in kittenhood, so that it becomes accustomed to being handled. If you permit the cat to grow up without handling, you will have a struggle when the time comes for grooming. Rough treatment or too heavy a hand with the brush and comb will irritate the cat and make it unwilling to be groomed the next time. Work quietly and gently.

Expensive or fancy grooming tools are not necessary. A stiff brush, metal comb with close-set teeth, a smoothing glove or cloth, a pair of tweezers and blunt-end scissors are all that are required for a good grooming job. Place the cat on a table or high bench. Brush and comb the cat both with and against the lie of the hairs. If the hair is matted, gently pick apart the mats or snarls with the tweezers. Should you be unable to separate the mats by combing or plucking, they will have to be clipped off. Gently pull the matted hair away from the cat's skin, insert the blunt-end scissors between the skin and matted hair and snip. After combing and brushing, use the smoothing glove or cloth and rub the cat's fur with the lie of the hair to bring out the gloss.

BATHING

Sometimes cats get so dirty or greasy that only a bath will make them clean. They get grease and oil on their coats by crawling under cars or trucks or into other dirty areas. In such cases ordinary grooming is not enough.

Remember that the average house cat dislikes being wet and bathing it will be a chore. No matter how gentle the cat usually is, it is going to resist. Whether the bath turns out to be successful or a free-for-all fight between you and the cat depends on how you go about it. Be sure to prepare everything in advance. A laundry tub, kitchen or bathroom sink or large galvanized tub are the best receptacles in which to bathe a cat. The bathtub has disadvantages. It is large and so low that you have to bend over it; furthermore, the cat may panic at the sight of so much water. You will need a rubber mat or rough towel to place in the bottom of the tub or basin you elect to use, and also a large towel for drying the cat. A shampoo containing at least

20 percent coconut oil will be satisfactory for lathering the cat. Avoid medicated or caustic soaps.

Don't make a circus out of the bath. Keep children out of the room. The cat's abhorrence of water is enough for it to contend with without the additional strain caused by a noisy audience. When you are ready to bathe the cat, put three or four inches of water in the basin or tub. Be sure the rubber mat or rough towel lies smooth on the bottom to give the cat a foothold and prevent it from slipping and falling into the water.

Next, spread Vaseline or eye ointment around the cat's eyes, as a protection against soap. Place the cat in the tub or basin feet first. If it struggles or is very excited, lift it by the scruff of the neck, supporting the hind quarters with one hand. When the cat is in the tub, hold it there for a few minutes, meanwhile speaking to it gently and reassuringly. Work slowly and gently. Try pouring some water no warmer than 80 degrees F. over the cat's body. If it reacts violently to this technique, wrap a towel soaked in water around the cat. Hold the animal firmly as you do this, leaving its head out of the towel.

Once the cat is thoroughly wet, you are ready to lather its coat. Work some coconut oil shampoo into the hair, and leave it there for a few minutes to loosen the dirt or grease. Talk reassuringly to the cat while waiting. After you have worked up a good lather, rinse the soap from the hair by working the fingers of one hand through the hair while pouring warm water over the cat with the other. One soaping and rinsing are usually sufficient unless the coat is very greasy or oily; then it may be necessary to repeat the soaping and rinsing several times.

The cat must be thoroughly dried. Use a rough towel and rub the coat vigorously, making sure that the hair next to the skin is dried. If the cat is bathed in winter, be certain to pick a sunny day. Or, better still, bathe the cat at night and keep it indoors until morning. In that way, you can be sure that it is thoroughly dry before it goes outside. Young kittens should be bathed only when absolutely necessary. Normally, kittens and cats in good health suffer no ill effects from a bath, but there always is a danger of their being chilled. Pay particular attention to the drying process.

Bathing usually loosens hair. After you have thoroughly dried the cat, comb out any loose hair. If any mats or snarls remain, comb them out or snip them off.

REMOVING PAINT

Cats occasionally brush against freshly painted surfaces. Before it has dried, paint can be removed with a cloth dipped in turpentine. Try to prevent the turpentine from coming into contact with the cat's skin.

Hair on which paint has dried and hardened will have to be clipped off. This measure often results in a ragged coat, but this will last only for a short time, as the coat will soon grow out. It is very important to get paint off a cat's coat. Some paints, especially those containing lead and Paris green, are toxic. The cat will constantly lick the painted area and may swallow some of the poison.

Sometimes small areas of dried paint can be softened with linseed oil. Soak the areas with the oil, allowing it to remain for a few minutes. Then carefully try to loosen the painted hairs with your fingers, meanwhile rubbing the oil into the snarled tuft. After the paint is softened, wipe the area with a cloth, then comb or brush it.

REMOVING OTHER STICKY SUBSTANCES

Cats often walk on newly tarred or sun-softened macadam roads and pick up small balls of tar on their feet. These can be removed with kerosene. Kerosene, however, is a skin irritant and must be washed off after it has dissolved the tar. Use shampoo and water to remove the kerosene. Tar will discolor the hair, but will not harm the cat. Lard rubbed into the tarry hair regions will also loosen the tar, which can then be rubbed off with a rough towel. This method has had good results.

Grease and chewing gum may be removed with kerosene or acetate (nail polish remover). Be sure to wash off the dissolving agents as quickly as possible. You may have to repeat the process several times.

SHEDDING HAIR

All cats living indoors shed hair the year round, but some shed more than others depending upon various factors, including the amount of light available, dryness of the skin, humidity, heat and cold. In its natural state, a cat sheds according to the seasonal light pattern. As the days get longer, the hair stops growing and begins to fall out, and new hair replaces the old. When the days get shorter, the new coat grows faster and less hair is shed. Thus, cats living indoors in artificial light shed some hair all year, but usually more heavily in spring. Regular combing will help prevent the hair from falling and accumulating on rugs, furniture and clothes.

CARE OF THE CLAWS

The cat's nails are appendages of the skin. Each has a hard outer covering, with blood vessels and nerves inside. Cats use their nails or claws as defense weapons, as well as for catching and holding food. The nails are attached to the toes and are retractible in all cats except the cheetah.

Cats that live indoors most of the time should have their claws trimmed at regular intervals. Young kittens have needle-sharp claws which can be caught or snagged in rugs, furniture and other places. If a kitten has a weak bone structure, a trapped claw may cause a broken bone should the kitten twist its leg in trying to free itself. Older cats also sometimes get their claws caught in rugs, chairs and curtains.

Provide a scratching post for the kitten or cat. A cedar post with the bark left on makes a good one. Most pet shops and pet supply stores sell scratching posts. To make one yourself, simply fasten a four-foot cedar or other rough-barked post onto a heavy wooden base (¾-inch plywood at least a foot square will suffice). If a post with rough bark is not available, cover a post at least three inches in diameter with carpet and attach it to a base. A catnip mouse fastened to a spring imbedded in the top of the post will provide additional exercise for the cat. If you have the space and want to be naturalistic, you can set up a tree branch or piece of driftwood in a room. This will make not only an excellent scratching post, but also a perch for the cat.

TRIMMING

If you intend to trim a cat's claws yourself, obtain a pair of regular nail clippers from a pet shop. Ordinary scissors can be used, but they are not as handy as the nail clippers. Hold the cat in your lap. If the animal is nervous or struggles, put it into a cat bag or wrap it in a towel, leaving the forefeet out. It isn't necessary to trim the nails on the hind feet, although they can be filed down with a sandpaper file.

When ready to trim the nails, grasp the toe firmly with your thumb under the pad on the bottom of the toe and your forefinger on the fur on top of the toe, just to the rear of the first toe joint. Exert pressure until the claw is unsheathed. Ordinarily, this does not hurt the cat. When the nail is exposed, clip off only the tip. Each nail has a blood line, or "quick," usually seen as a pink portion of the nail about one-third of the way down from the tip. Avoid cutting into the quick. It is better to remove only the tips of the nails, and then file them with sandpaper, than to remove too much and injure the quick. If you should happen to cut into the quick, the nail will bleed. Apply an antiseptic powder such as BFI, place a gauze compress or clean folded handkerchief over the nail and hold the paw up for a few minutes. This will usually stop the bleeding. A styptic pencil can also be used to stem the flow of blood.

DECLAWING

Some cats constantly claw the rugs and furniture in spite of the provision of scratching posts or other gadgets, often causing considerable damage. If your cat is incorrigible in this respect, you can have its front claws removed by surgery. The operation is called an onychectomy. It is not disfiguring and does not disable the cat. The animal still can climb and fight, although not quite as well as before. One main argument in favor of declawing is that it allows many people to keep cats that otherwise would have to be disposed of. Declawed cats quickly recover from the operation. Consult your veterinarian about having your cat's claws removed if the animal is damaging your rugs and furniture and you cannot get it to use a scratching post or log.

CARE OF THE MOUTH AND TEETH

A cat's teeth do not usually need much attention until the animal is about a year old, although kittens sometimes have trouble when cutting new teeth. Dirty or infected teeth in the older cat often cause unpleasant mouth odors and may lead to gingivitis, a disease of the gums. Infected or broken teeth also interfere with the proper mastication of food. They should be brought to the attention of the veterinarian.

It isn't necessary to brush the cat's teeth, but an occasional massaging of the gums with salt water will help to reduce mouth odors and check the growth of bacteria. Tartar forms on the older cat's teeth, usually near the gum line. It keeps building up and ultimately must be removed. This can be a difficult task, since some cats object so violently that they have to be anesthetized. It is better to let the veterinarian do the job; he has the proper facilities and knowhow.

CARE OF THE EYES

Unless diseased or injured, the cat's eyes need little care. Once in a while hair around and near the eyes curls upward or downward, and gets into the eyes. When this happens, remove the hair by clipping. Use blunt-end scissors and work carefully. Occasionally, cats' eyes become inflamed from smoke or soot, from getting small particles such as seeds in the eye, or from a flick from a weed, piece of brush or other flexible object. Wash the eyes with warm water to remove any foreign material, then apply an ointment such as Neomycin ophthalmic ointment inside lower lid.

If a speck of dust, dirt or small seed gets into the cat's eye, you will have to remove it. Take a clean handkerchief, roll one corner to form a probe and carefully remove the speck. You may need a second person to hold the cat while you work. Or you can put it into a cat bag. (See Chapter 15, Handling the Injured Cat.) After removing the particle, wash the eye with warm water. Use an eyedropper and place a few drops of water in the corner of the eye. When the cat blinks, it will distribute the water. Apply an eye ointment to the inflamed eye. Should you be unable to remove the foreign object take the cat to the veterinarian. (See Chapter 11 for more serious eye conditions and their treatment.)

CARE OF THE EARS

Examine your cat's ears during the grooming session, using a bright light or a flashlight to look down into the ear canal. Cats often are troubled by dirt, insects and excessive wax in their ears.

Ear mites are a common cause of ear troubles in the cat and the damage caused by these pests is not to be underestimated. (See Chapter 13, Ear Mites.) The diagnosis and treatment of ear mites are best left to the veterinarian.

An accumulation of wax in the ears can also be a source of irritation to a cat. It is not difficult to remove wax, although it should be remembered that the cat's ears are sensitive to touch and that rough handling or probing too deeply into the ear canal may cause serious damage. To remove excessive wax, first put the cat in a bag or wrap it in a towel. Next, soften the wax with light mineral oil or glycerin. Warm the oil by standing the bottle in hot water. A temperature of 80 or 90 degrees F. is satisfactory. Use an eyedropper and place a few drops of the warm oil in each ear, permitting it to remain for a few minutes.

After the oil has had time to soften the wax, gently remove the wax with a cotton swab. Again, don't probe too deeply into the ear; you may puncture the eardrum. Repeat the cleaning as needed. Several applications of oil may be required to soften the wax. Do not use soap and water in the ears.

More serious ear conditions, such an cankers and hematomas, are discussed in Chapter 11, Ear Troubles.

EXERCISE

Although cats need exercise, most of them manage to get sufficient activity in limited spaces. The fact that most apartment house cats remain so trim and agile may be a source of wonder to the uninitiated. But observe your cat as it plays with a toy. First, it stalks the toy, crouching and crawling toward it, then it tenses itself for the attack, and with a lightning-fast spring, leaps on the toy, clutching it in its claws. The cat then bats or pushes the toy around the floor. A cat may play at this game for hours, using various muscles and keeping itself in excellent physical condition.

Suburban and country cats that wander outside need little exercise equipment, but the city cat needs various toys. City cats can also be trained to walk on leashes. While this is a restricted form of exercise, it does get the confined cat out of doors.

You can also construct an outdoor cage or pen if you have adequate space. Or you can make an exercise "sun porch" and attach it to a window. In warm weather the cat can go in and out at will, yet be perfectly safe within the enclosure. The sun porch is easy to make. It is simply a wire mesh box attached to an open window. The size depends on the window opening, width of sill and available supports. When finished, the sun porch resembles a window green-house, only it is made of wire mesh.

TRAINING THE CAT

The cat is usually very independent and cannot be forced to do anything against its will. It cannot be coaxed, cajoled or threatened into sitting down, walking, meowing or playing. Cats do enjoy play-ing, but will not always play when you want them to. We might say that the cat makes all the decisions, as far as work or play is con-cerned. On the other hand, if you study your cat and learn to know its moods, you may possibly train it to shake hands, roll over on its back and perform other simple tricks—but, at best, you will need a great deal of patience.

Cats are intelligent and learn many things by themselves. Some of them have learned to go outside and come in through special doors cut for them in walls or doors. Others retrieve balls, toys and other thrown objects. But don't expect too much from your cat; it is too independent to jump through hoops on command. If your cat does surprisingly perform a trick upon command, you should of course be sure to give it a reward, such as a word of praise or a tidbit. But this does not guarantee that it will perform the trick again.

THE SANITARY PAN

It is not difficult to train the cat to use a sanitary pan. Actually, the cat itself learns to use it. Place the pan in an easily accessible place. The cat may already have picked a spot. If so, move the pan accordingly. But avoid moving the pan about the room or from room to room once the cat has become accustomed to one location.

Use an absorbent litter (sand, peat moss, peanut hulls, etc.) and cover the bottom of the pan with this litter to a depth of about two inches. Since the cat instinctively cover up its excreta with its paws, it will look for a place where it can do this. The pan with the litter meets its requirements and as a rule you can expect your cat to use the pan almost from the start.

It is important to keep the pan clean. You can sometimes merely remove the soiled part of the litter and replace it with new. Or it is possible that all the litter will have to be thrown out. Wash the pan at least once a week with hot water and an odorless detergent. Under no circumstances should you wash the pan with any compound containing *phenol,* which is highly toxic to cats. Nor should you spray the pan with any aromatic spray, or you may find the cat abandoning the pan and finding some other place to relieve itself.

Occasionally, a cat refuses to use a pan. Try to learn the reason and correct the situation. Sometimes the pan is placed in too public a spot or children are permitted to interfere with the cat when it wants to use the pan. Female cats in heat sometimes will not use the pan and have to be confined to one room with newspapers spread about. Finally, a sick cat may be unable to use the pan and newspapers will have to be spread on the floor.

You may have heard of cats that use the toilet. This is not a tall story. Cats can and do learn to balance themselves on the toilet seat. Some cats prefer to use the bathtub, but the owner can easily discourage this practice by keeping a few inches of water in the tub for a few days. After the cat leaps into the tub and wets its feet a few times it will abandon the idea of using the tub as a toilet.

Suburban and country cats usually present no problem when it comes to housebreaking. Simply let the cat outdoors and it will find a place to do its business. Some people cut a special opening in a wall or door of the house, thus allowing the cat to go in and out of the house at will. A hinged flap over such a hole will keep out rain and cold.

THE COLLAR AND LEASH

If you want to train your cat to a leash, you will have to start when it is a kitten.

Collars

A collar can be a dangerous accessory unless certain safety precautions are taken. Even if you do not want to train your cat to walk on a leash, you may have to keep some identification tag on it. Some communities require that all cats be properly tagged for identification; otherwise they are picked up as strays.

The danger lies in the possibility that a cat may get its collar caught in a fence or other obstacle and be strangled to death. It is possible to provide the cat with a safe collar, however. It should not be too large, or the cat may get its foot or mouth caught in the collar. On the other hand, if the collar is too tight, the cat may choke to death.

The best kind of collar to use on your cat is one that stretches. All-elastic and other safety collars are available in pet shops and pet supply houses. If your cat must wear a collar when outdoors, see to it that a proper identification tag is firmly attached.

Harness

Cats that are not allowed outside except when taken out for an airing can be fitted with a harness instead of a collar. Pet ocelots are usually walked by the use of a harness and lead. The harness should fit snugly, but not too tightly. It is a good idea to pad the straps that go across the chest to help prevent chafing.

Bells

Some cat owners attach small bells to the cat's collar as a warning to birds. The bells are not always effective since many young birds do not heed them and grown birds are seldom caught by cats. Also, some cats learn to stalk birds so stealthily that the bells do not sound the alarm until the cat springs, and it is then too late.

Leash

A leather leash with a swivel hook is best. Before you attach the leash to the collar, let the cat sniff it and make sure it is harmless. After the cat has been permitted to examine the leash, snap the hook onto the ring on the collar and try to lead the cat. It is doubtful that you will be able to get the cat to walk at your side. Although some cats do this, most of them wander back and forth. The most you can hope for at first is that the cat will not balk. If it does balk, be patient and don't jerk the leash. Give the cat plenty of opportunity to stop and sniff, and in time it will learn to walk when you do.

TRAINING THE CAT TO BEHAVE

Since cats are highly individualistic, each cat owner will find that special problems will arise. By learning all you can about your cat's habits you will be in the best position to cope with various behavior problems.

Jumping Up on Furniture

Cats like to jump up on tables, especially when food is being prepared. They see nothing wrong in this action, of course, since they like high perches, but you cannot have your cat jumping up on the table at mealtimes. Pushing the cat down each time it jumps up will not in most cases break the habit. A firmer approach is necessary. Put it in another room or outdoors at mealtimes or when food is being prepared, or discourage it by making a loud noise (which all cats dislike) by striking the table with a rolled-up newspaper. Should your cat insist upon climbing onto a stuffed chair or couch, you can discourage it by placing a mousetrap under some newspapers. When the cat leaps on the newspapers, it will set the trap off. The noise will frighten the cat without harming it. These examples may suggest other ideas or techniques for breaking your cat of bad habits.

Getting into Bed with Children

Many cats like to sleep with children, and some of them will leap into a baby's crib, because they like the baby and because they want to be kept warm. It is better to discourage the cat from sleeping with children, not so much because it will harm them, but because it may carry dirt, insects and disease. The best way to keep the cat from joining the children at bedtime is to put it in another room.

Clawing the Rugs and Furniture

Most cats will claw rugs and furniture. You will have to discourage yours by providing substitutes. (See Care of the Claws earlier in this chapter.) There are sprays on the market that are supposed to stop cats from going on or near furniture. They have strong odors discernible to cats but not to people. They are not always reliable but I suggest you give them a trial if your other remedies have failed.

CATS AND SAFETY

Under the complex conditions of modern living, especially in the cities, some hazards to the cat must be expected. But if you exercise intelligent control of your cat and are prepared for emergencies, many dangers can be eliminated or minimized.

TRAVELING WITH THE CAT

When you take a cat out in an automobile always put it in a safe carrier. You can use one of the commercial cat carriers or a strong cardboard box. Make sure there are enough air holes in the sides of the box and that it is tied securely with strong cord. Never let the cat loose in the car, particularly if it is nervous about riding. Serious accidents have been caused by frightened cats suddenly leaping upon the driver.

MOVING TO A NEW HOME

Cats become very attached to places. When moving, place the cat in a safe carrier or box *before* the moving men arrive; otherwise, it may become frightened and run away, and you will have a difficult time catching it.

When you arrive at the new home, keep the cat confined to the house for a few days. Many cats have returned to their old homes, some traveling many miles. The cat's homing instinct is a strong one, so take precautions and keep it inside until it has accepted the new surroundings. Your veterinarian can provide tranquilizers to calm the cat's nerves before, during and after moving, if this is necessary.

HIGH PLACES

City cats can and do fall from roofs, open windows, fire escapes and other high places. Although the cat has a remarkable ability to land on its feet, a fall from ten or twelve stories can prove fatal. Avoid playing with a cat on a roof, near an open window or on the fire escape, unless these places have wire or screen protections. Cats like to sit on windowsills and watch the world go by. This is a harmless pastime when the window is closed. When the window is open, protect the cat by a strong screen or wire mesh over the window.

INACCESSIBLE PLACES

Cats often wander into places inaccessible to people and are often unable to extricate themselves. Mother cats often give birth to their kittens inside partitions, above cellar or attic beams and in other hard-to-reach places. When your cat is expecting kittens, keep an eye on her to see that she does not hide the kittens. If the kittens are born inside a partition or some other inaccessible place, they may die of starvation when the mother weans them and they are unable to find their way out.

Cats often become stranded in trees, atop telephone poles and in other such places. Rescuing the cat may be a difficult task and it is better to leave this job to experienced persons. Call your local humane society or the police. They have experienced men and special equipment. You may be severely bitten and scratched in the process of rescuing a frightened cat.

COLLARS

If you must put a collar on your cat, make it an elastic one. (See Collars, earlier in this chapter.)

TIN CANS AND JARS

Empty tin cans and jars can be deathtraps for cats. A cat searching for food may stick its head into an empty can or jar and be unable to get it out. Flatten all tin cans before placing them in the trash barrel. Put empty jars in a metal pail and cover with a tight lid.

POISONS

Poisonings, accidental and intentional, take the lives of many cats. You can prevent accidental poisonings by keeping all insecticides, paints and rodenticides locked up. Antidotes for most poisons are not likely to be on hand. Dangerous drugs and medicines should also be kept in a safe place, away from cats and children. (See Chapter 15, Poisoning.)

ELECTRICITY

Cats can be killed by electric shocks. Lamp and other electrical cords, particularly those extending along the floor, are potential hazards. Some floor lamps are easily overturned by a cat playing with a cord. This presents a fire hazard, as well as a possible source of electric shock to the cat.

You will have to take some protective measures in the case of the cat that insists on chewing on telephone and electric cords. One method that has proved satisfactory is to purchase plastic retractor coils (available in most hardware stores) and cover lamp and telephone wires with them. Another trick is to coat the cords with powdered alum or bitter aloe solution. These substances are harmless to the cat, but are very distasteful and may prevent further chewing on electric or telephone cords.

If your cat should get a shock from nibbling on an electric cord, *unplug the cord from the outlet before touching the cat.* (See Chapter 15 for first aid in case of electric shock.)

TRIPPING OVER THE CAT

Cats get underfoot and may cause falls and injuries to themselves and people. Before carrying heavy objects, hot liquids or other dangerous loads, put the cat in another room or, if you live in the country or suburbs, put it out of doors. A hungry cat is more apt to get underfoot and trip you (another reason that your cat should be fed regularly).

DRAWERS, BOXES AND TRUNKS

Cats sometimes get trapped in drawers, boxes and trunks when someone closes them, not knowing a cat is inside. If your cat is missing, search all the drawers, boxes and trunks on the premises. You may find Puss curled up asleep in one of them.

CHRISTMAS TREES

Christmas trees with electric lights are dangerous. Cats may leap onto them and knock them over if the trees are not securely anchored, and an overturned tree with electric lights is a fire hazard. Also, cats may become seriously ill from eating Christmas tree ornaments such as tinsel and balls.

FIREPLACES

Open fireplaces are sources of danger when a cat is around. Be sure the fireplace has a screen.

KEROSENE LAMPS AND CANDLES

Kerosene lamps and candles present another hazard to cats. Keep an eye on the cat when they are lighted, especially if moths or bugs are flying around the flames. If you leave the room, extinguish the lamp or candles—or take the cat out with you.

RIBBONS

My advice is to forgo putting ribbons around the cat's neck. They are easily caught on snags, and when pulled tight the cat may be strangled or at least panicked.

CATS AND OTHER PETS

Cats can get along with other pets, even dogs, when proper supervision is exercised.

DOGS

You may expect various reactions when bringing a cat into a home that contains a dog or vice versa. The animal that was in the home first may resent the newcomer, and may attack or torment the new cat or dog. More than the "pecking order" is involved in these cases. One must consider prior rights to the house territory, jealousy over attentions shown the new animal, competition for food, sex differences and other behavioral factors.

On the other hand, the first animal may readily and eagerly accept the newcomer. In fact, the older animal may be overjoyed that there is to be a companion, especially if he has been alone most of the day. Time will tell; you'll just have to wait and see how the animals take to each other.

Despite the belief that cats and dogs are natural enemies, many cats and dogs live together in harmony. Actually, the relationship between dogs and cats—as far as getting along together is concerned—is not clear. So far, there is no positive evidence that cat-and-dog fights are the sole result of natural enmity or natural law. Puppies and kittens can be very easily trained to live together in relative peace and friendship.

I strongly advise against forcing an introduction between a cat and dog. Allow the pets to make their own introductions in their own way and time, but under your supervision. It is foolish and dangerous to hold a struggling cat down to a dog so that Fido can "make friends" with the cat (and I have seen this advocated in some cat books). All three of you may well end up with severe scratches and bites. If necessary, keep the dog and cat in separate rooms until they both become used to each other's presence in the house.

There is no guarantee, however, that once the dog and cat have accepted each other peace and harmony will reign. Expect some tussles. Various factors will trigger a cat-and-dog fight; some stem from the nature of the animals, others may be caused by thoughtless people ("sic the cat!" is an all-too-common pastime). You must guard against unfavorable stimuli that may cause the dog and cat to tangle. Your main task is to prevent any excessive or fatal encounters.

CAGED BIRDS AND SMALL MAMMALS

Keep all pet birds and small mammals in strong cages that cannot be knocked over or opened by the cat. Hang birdcages from the ceiling or wall. Put strong locks on hamster, gerbil or guinea pig cages. Other safety precautions will undoubtedly occur to you as you study the cat-and-other-pet situation in your home.

AQUARIUMS AND TERRARIUMS

Since fish, frogs, toads, snakes and other reptiles will attract the cat's attention, place strong glass over the aquarium and wire mesh over the terrarium to prevent Puss from fishing or hunting.

Regardless of the kind of cat you own, the basic rules of good care should be routinely observed. The proper management and care of your cat are largely a matter of watchful supervisory habits. Beware of slipping into the easiest way. Bad habits are easy to acquire and difficult to eliminate. Take good care of your cat from the very first day the animal arrives in your home. See to its basic needs and give it plenty of affection. When you do so, you will be well on your way toward becoming the happy owner of a contented cat.

7. Care of Wild or Unusual Cats

WILD CATS AS PETS

The trend toward keeping wild or unusual cats as pets has gained considerable momentum over the past few years. Lions, cheetahs, pumas, lynxes, jaguarundis, margays and ocelots are some of the exotic cats now being kept in the United States and abroad. In the United States, the larger cats are more popular on the West Coast.

Various wild cats have been kept as pets since ancient times, so the idea is not new. History, however, does not reveal just how well these wild cats adapted to life as more or less captive pets. In modern times, we have numerous accounts of keeping greater and lesser wild cats as pets, the most famous story being that of Elsa the lioness, in Joy Adamson's book *Born Free*. Another lion that achieved considerable fame and notoriety in the United States was Leo, a great cat that shook up a community. There will be more about Leo and his status as a pet in the next chapter, which deals with cats in the community and laws governing them.

Since they are only slightly larger than big tomcats, ocelots and margays are the most popular and practical of the wild cats for city and suburban homes, provided there are no ordinances prohibiting them.

Almost everyone is impressed when he sees an ocelot or margay being walked on a leash down the main street of a city. Unquestionably, both of these cats are strikingly beautiful animals, but—and this is a fact to remember—they are not suitable pets for the average person or family. One needs plenty of patience, understanding and time to learn to live with an ocelot or margay. Unfortunately, a number of persons—mostly those who have obtained one of these cats out of curiosity or as a status symbol—have learned the hard way that they have made mistakes. Faddists, status seekers and those with little true interest in the animals soon discover that there is a vast difference between a "tiger in the tank" and an ocelot or margay in the house.

Even though a number of ocelots and margays bought as pets end up in zoos and menageries, there is a hard core of dedicated persons who have a genuine interest in and love for these cats. Many of them belong to the Long Island Ocelot Club in Amagansett, New York, which, despite its name, is neither a local organization nor restricted to ocelots; serious owners of any of the unusual or exotic cats may become members. This organization, under the guidance of its president, Catherine Cisin, has done much to promote the intelligent care of ocelots and other wild cats kept as pets. I have met Mrs. Cisin and other members of the club and have found them to be extremely well-informed on all aspects of their unusual cats; in fact, some members have contributed valuable data on the habits and care of wild cats kept in environments less confining than those of zoos, game farms and menageries. Furthermore, the Long Island Ocelot Club does not go in for competitions or commercialism, believing instead that ocelots and other wild cats are *private* pets that should not be exploited or used to impress or startle friends or strangers. I might add that I heartily subscribe to these sentiments.

Unless you are willing to expend plenty of patience, tact, ingenuity, devotion, determination and time, don't get an ocelot or other wild cat for a pet. While ocelots and margays look like oversized house cats, their care entails a lot more knowledge and work than that of the average domestic short- or long-haired feline. If you think that I may be overstressing the difficulties in keeping wild cats as pets, I suggest you communicate with anyone who has, or has kept, an ocelot, margay or other wild cat. My intention is not to discourage *everyone* from obtaining and keeping one of these cats, but only those who, because of unsuitable temperament, inadequate facilities, lack of time and little dedication, will find themselves in a situation that can be very unpleasant for both cat and owner.

Since ocelots and margays are the most common of the wild cats

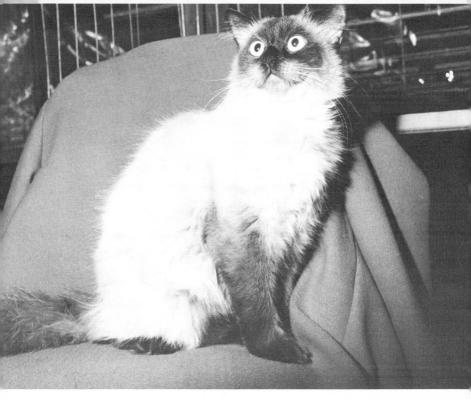

Himalayan

Abyssinian

Siamese

Burmese

Domestic Shorthair

Manx

Russian Blue

Rex

Ocelot. It is presently classified as a peripheral animal, but could become endangered by excessive killing or capture in certain areas.

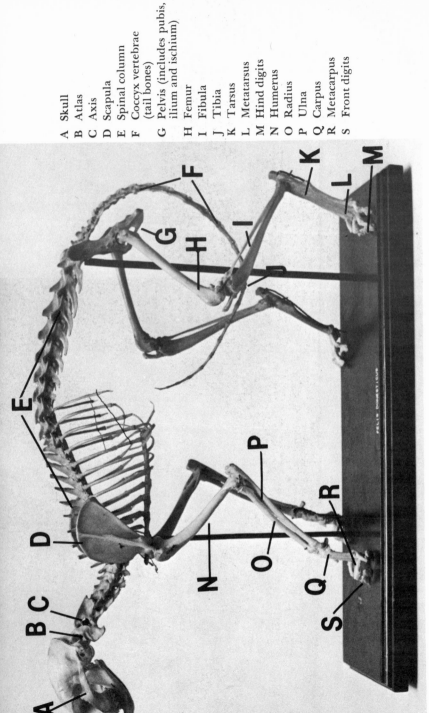

A Skull
B Atlas
C Axis
D Scapula
E Spinal column
F Coccyx vertebrae
   (tail bones)
G Pelvis (includes pubis,
   ilium and ischium)
H Femur
I Fibula
J Tibia
K Tarsus
L Metatarsus
M Hind digits
N Humerus
O Radius
P Ulna
Q Carpus
R Metacarpus
S Front digits

MAJOR BONES IN THE CAT SKELETON (most often involved in accidents)

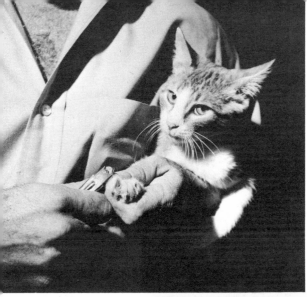

Nail clipping. Restrain the cat on your lap or under an arm. Press on the toe to unsheath claw, then clip carefully. Avoid cutting into the "quick."

The long-haired cat needs a daily grooming. Start grooming early in kittenhood and the daily session will be much easier.

A cat can get enough exercise in the house or apartment—there's no need to risk the dangers of city or suburban streets.

A cat carrier is the safest way to transport a cat.

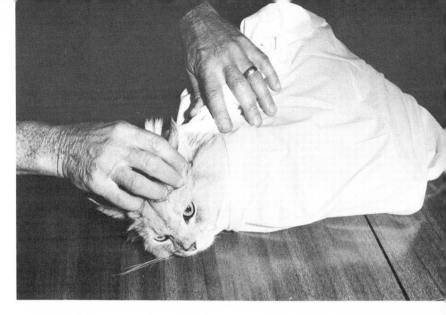

The cat bag proves its worth when you have to medicate the cat's ears. It may also be used when defleaing the cat. Dust the cat with a safe insecticide, place the animal in the bag for a few minutes, then remove and comb out the excess powder and dead fleas.

The Elizabethan collar, which may be made out of stiff cardboard, prevents the cat from licking medicine or ripping bandages off its feet or legs.

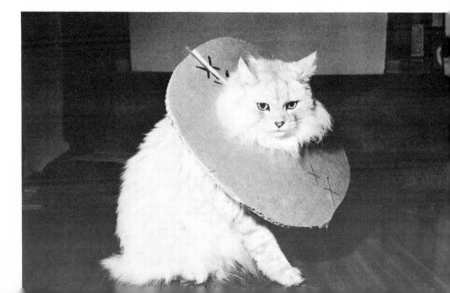

To administer a pill, hold the cat's upper jaw at the corners, tilt the head back, press the mouth open with your other hand, and drop the pill as far back as possible. Hold the mouth closed, and natural swallowing should follow.

To give the cat liquid medicines, insert a dropper or syringe into the side of the mouth. If the cat is cooperative pull the skin away from the teeth to form a pouch. When liquid has been poured in, hold the cat's mouth closed until it swallows.

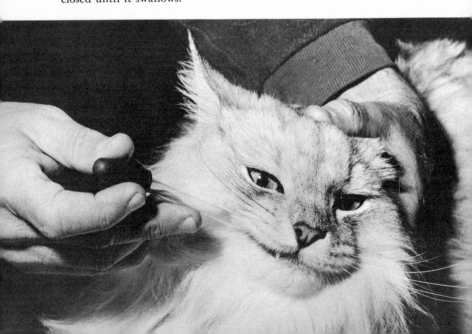

now being kept as pets, we will limit the discussion of care, training and health problems to these species.

ACQUIRING AN OCELOT OR MARGAY

The first fact you should understand in acquiring an ocelot or margay is that either one is an expensive pet. Prices range from $110.00 up, depending upon various factors, such as the available supply, importer, etc. There are few ocelot kittens born to adult pets in the United States; in fact, the successful breeding of these cats is still a difficult enterprise. Margay kittens born to domesticated or pet margays are almost nonexistent in the United States. The first margay kitten born to pet margays in the United States on November 27, 1966, in Cambridge, Massachusetts, was a notable event and caused quite a stir in the feline pet world. This rare feline "happening" was the size of a large mouse at birth.

You will have to order an ocelot or margay kitten from an importer (make sure of the person's or organization's reputation before engaging their services). Older ocelots and margays are sometimes available from persons who wish to part with their pets for some reason or other. The Long Island Ocelot Club, Amagansett, Long Island, New York 11930, publishes a newsletter in which are listed persons or dealers who have ocelots and margays for sale. My suggestion is that if you are genuinely interested in owning one of these cats you join the club (you don't have to attend the meetings) and benefit from the newsletter. You will also be able to correspond with or meet other members who have successfully raised these cats.

Another word of advice before you start the machinery working to obtain an ocelot or margay: check your state and local ordinances to see whether you are permitted to keep one of these cats. Many large cities prohibit them. New York City, for example, recently amended its Animal Section of the Health Code and now prohibits *any* wild animals, including ocelots and margays. Philadelphia, Pennsylvania, is considering outlawing certain wild animals, including ocelots, lions, margays, etc. My own community (which adopted a wild animal ordinance which I helped draft) does allow ocelots and margays to be kept as pets, provided the owner secures a special permit. At any rate, be sure to find out if you can keep a wild cat in your community. This precaution will save you not only money but disappointment and hard feelings if you find that you must get rid of your cat.

You should be prepared to wait some time for your ocelot or margay kitten to arrive from South America. Animal exporters usually ship cats that are three to five months old, since experience shows this is the best age range for the kittens to stand the ten- to twelve-hour air trip to New York City. (The cost of air freight has to be added to the price of the ocelot or margay.) Generally, the reputable animal exporters keep the ocelot and margay kittens several weeks before shipping them. They do this to see that the cats are in good health and ready for the trip. Despite their precautions, a number of ocelots and margays arrive in the United States in very poor health, suffering from nutritional deficiencies and infestations of internal parasites, such as roundworms, tapeworms, coccidia and giardia organisms. (See Chapter 12, Internal Parasites of Cats.) A number of new ocelot and margay owners have spent a long time nursing their pets back to good health. Unhappily, in some cases, the animals never recovered. Therefore, until better standards of care, medical treatment and shipment are set up between the exporter and importer, one just has to hope that he will receive a healthy cat.

Decide beforehand whether you want a margay or an ocelot. While these two cats are closely related, there are some notable differences. The ocelot will grow to a larger size than the margay; a mature ocelot will weigh from thirty to forty pounds, while margays at maturity will average twelve to fifteen pounds. Individuals within the species differ, of course. Margays have longer tails than do ocelots. Both cats have powerful forelegs, but those of the margay are more slender than those of the ocelot.

Until these cats are about ten months old, they behave somewhat like ordinary house cats. They play (albeit a bit rougher than a house cat), meow, hiss, spit and growl when angered or frightened. When full-grown, however, the similarity between either the ocelot or margay and the house cat comes to an abrupt end. Both wild cats develop into powerhouses of strong muscles and triggery nerves. They are extremely sensitive cats, quick to resent mistreatment or neglect. When treated with understanding and kindness, they make good pets for the right person.

Decide whether you want a male or female before you order your ocelot or margay. As a rule, the male is gentler than the female. Also, although both can be altered, the male seems to survive surgery better than the female.

CARE OF THE KITTEN

The ocelot or margay kitten needs plenty of understanding and care. Even ordinary domestic kittens separated from their mothers and littermates for the first time experience difficulty in adjusting to a new home. Consider how much more acute this problem is for the new ocelot or margay kitten, jungle-born and unused to man and his ways. When the baby ocelot or margay is taken from its mother, it is sent to an animal compound to await shipment, and it is there that it often learns either to love or to hate human beings.

Animal compounds, which are holding places for captured animals awaiting shipment to various countries as pets or display animals, are part of the animal importing and exporting business. Zoos, game farms and pet shops usually obtain their animals from compounds. The kind of treatment an ocelot or margay receives there has a great deal to do with determining its future health and behavior. Unfortunately, in many compounds animals do not get the best care. Many kittens are roughly handled, poorly fed and neglected. In such a case, you will have to undo all these evils and perhaps spend many hours nursing the ocelot or margay kitten back to health.

SLEEPING QUARTERS

Like the domestic cat, the margay or ocelot will select its own place to sleep. You may, if you wish, provide a box or bed.

TOYS

Ocelots and margays love to play with toys and will obtain sufficient exercise if provided with a variety of gadgets. Select the toys with care and supervise their use. Toys that "respond" to the cat are best. These include balls, tin cans (with edges crimped to prevent injury) and other hard, rolling and bouncing objects. Avoid soft rubber, plastic or cloth toys. The ocelot and margay have powerful canine teeth and grinders and can easily chew off and swallow pieces of rubber, cloth or plastic, which may become lodged in the stomach or intestines and cause serious trouble.

SWIMMING POOL

Ocelots, unlike margays, love water. You can let your ocelot swim and play in water in the bathtub or provide a special pool for it. It will spend many enjoyable minutes—hours, if you let it—swimming and chasing toys in the water. It also enjoys running in and out of a stream of water played from a hose. A word of caution: if the ocelot swims indoors on a cold day, keep it inside until it is thoroughly dried.

PLAYING WITH THE OCELOT OR MARGAY

Margays and ocelots are very playful, but are sometimes also very rough. The ocelot likes nothing better than to lie in ambush and charge or leap at you, wrapping itself around your leg and biting, not viciously but hard enough to be painful. The margay, on the other hand, prefers to leap upon you from heights. Both these habits should be nipped in the bud.

The margay and ocelot are hardy, and do not mind being lifted by the skin or tail. Some ocelots do not even object to being carried about by their thick tails. In contrast, a house cat, when picked up by the tail (which should never be done, of course), will yowl and curl up on your hand in a flash, sinking its teeth and claws into your flesh.

Try to curb the ocelot or margay kitten's tendency toward rough play by offering it substitute games. For example, ocelots and margays can be taught to retrieve balls and other thrown objects. To start the training, simply toss a ball. The kitten will immediately dash after it. When it reaches the ball, give the command "Fetch!" It will not bring it back to you the first time, but growl and play with the ball, knocking it this way and that. Eventually, however, the cat will bring the ball back to you and wait for you to throw it again. Have patience until the animal learns to bring you the ball. Each time, before you throw the ball, hold it up for the cat to see, say "Fetch!" and then toss it. If you repeat this routine over and over, the cat will soon get the idea and will dash back with the ball for you to toss it again.

TRAINING TO COME WHEN CALLED

Training the ocelot or margay to come when called will take time and patience. The technique used is similar to that for training dogs to come when called. Keep repeating the cat's name over and over again during the training session. When you place food on the floor, call the cat by name or give a whistle or other signal. You should also use the name or signal whenever playing with the cat. Expect some lapses or refusals to come when called. Ocelots and margays, like domestic varieties, do not always give blind obedience.

COLLAR OR HARNESS?

Some ocelot and margay owners use collars, others prefer a special harness. If you use a collar, it's best to have two of them: one for walking the cat, the other (the stretchable kind) to be kept on the cat as a permanent means of identification.

Regular dog harnesses are not satisfactory for an ocelot or margay, since it is not always possible to get a good fit and the straps often bind the animal's forelegs. The most comfortable harness for an ocelot or margay is a modified *martingale*—an idea borrowed from horse harnesses. It can be made by a shoemaker or, if you can find one, a harness maker. The modified martingale allows the cat freedom without binding and provides a maximum of control.

LEASHES

While heavy leather leashes are strong enough to hold an ocelot or margay, none are satisfactory because the cat will chew the leather. Secure a strong chain leash with a leather handle. The best type of clip or hook is the one known as the "blindman's" clip. It is opened by exerting pressure on a lever; it closes when the pressure is released after putting one end of a loop through the collar or harness ring. Keep extra clips or hooks on hand, since they may come in handy to lengthen leashes or fasten onto a chain.

WALKING THE OCELOT OR MARGAY ON THE LEASH

When ready to take the ocelot or margay out for a stroll, simply snap the leash onto the collar or harness and step to one side or slightly behind the cat. The cat may balk or try to get behind *you,* since it is against its instincts to allow anyone or anything to get behind it (the animal wants to keep everything under observation). But with patience, the cat can be taught to walk ahead of you.

The cat may fight the leash at first, but be patient, constantly reassuring the animal, and it will eventually become accustomed to the leash. Don't drag the cat along, but allow it to set its own pace. Avoid taking a margay or ocelot out in congested traffic areas. Cars, trucks, buses and crowds of people will confuse the animal. Take it for a peaceful walk in a secluded region, resisting the temptation to "show off the cat."

FEEDING

The ocelot and margay are, of course, basically carnivorous animals. They eat fish, birds, rodents, reptiles, and other small prey that is available. Keep these natural foods in mind when planning your cat's diet. While either of these cats can be fed the prepared cat foods, the animal should get some fresh meat each day. Beef hearts and chicken necks are especially relished by both cats. Boned fish and shrimp are also nutritious and tasty foods for the ocelot or margay. You may find that your cat will develop a taste for some vegetables; if so, then by all means include them as part of the diet.

Remember that margays and ocelots imported into the United States are usually malnourished, as well as heavily parasitized. Therefore, provide a high-quality vitamin and mineral supplement every day. The amount can be reduced when the kitten shows such obvious signs of general improvement as good appetite, glossy and pliable coat, healthy skin, bright eyes, alertness and weight gain. Some owners continue with the vitamin and mineral supplements in adult life; however, if you feed a balanced diet, the supplements can be eliminated—unless some condition indicates their need in the diet.

Ocelots and margays like to eat grass, which acts as an emetic, causing the cat to vomit and clear its stomach of hair and other accumulated matter. Cats kept indoors should be given a handful of grass as least once a week. Either crabgrass or domestic rye grass is satisfactory. Rye grass can be grown indoors in a flower box. But make certain that any grass fed to the cat is free from harmful insecticides or other chemicals. An ocelot in my locality died recently from eating grass that had been sprayed with chemicals.

GROOMING

Ocelots and margays, like other cats, keep themselves clean in ordinary circumstances, but there may be times when you will need to help. Groom the margay and ocelot as you would a short-haired cat. (See Chapter 6 for grooming instructions.)

BATHING

You will encounter no difficulty in bathing the ocelot, but the margay dislikes water and should be bathed only when absolutely necessary. In such cases, bathe the margay according to directions in Chapter 6.

CARE OF THE CLAWS

The claws of the margay and ocelot need to be trimmed regularly. If your cat keeps clawing the furniture or other objects—or uses its claws on people—you would be wise to have the animal declawed. (See Chapter 6.)

PARASITES

Ocelots and margays are susceptible to infestations of worms, coccidia and giardia organisms. Consult Chapter 12 for the life cycles, symptoms and eradication of these internal parasites. For the life cycles, control and eradication of fleas, lice and ticks, see Chapter 13.

HOUSE TRAINING

Margays and ocelots, like domestic cats, are naturally clean animals and will search for a suitable place to relieve themselves. See that your cat has a private toilet, consisting of a sanitary pan or tray containing one of the prepared litters or peat moss, shavings (but not sawdust) or sand. These cats prefer to be hidden when answering nature's calls, so you might place the sanitary pan behind some object. A few ocelot owners have trained their pets to use the toilet and the animals are adept at balancing themselves on the toilet seat. However, this is an unnecessary trick, although it probably does make a good conversation piece. An ordinary tray and litter are quite satisfactory for your ocelot or margay.

ENCLOSURES

There may be times when you don't want the ocelot or margay to have the freedom of the house or apartment—for instance, when you are entertaining small children or guests who are not cat enthusiasts. A cage made of wood and strong wire mesh (10, 11 or 12 gauge wire will do) will make a suitable place in which to isolate the cat. It should measure at least three feet wide, four feet long and three feet high. The cage should have a gate and lock that can't be opened by the cat.

OUTDOOR PENS

When the weather gets warm, an outdoor pen or cage will provide a safe place for the ocelot or margay. It may be constructed of wood and wire, or of wire alone. Whichever materials you use, be sure to make the pen large enough for you to walk into standing upright (10x6x6 feet will be satisfactory). If possible, the floor should be made of concrete or other nonporous material, thus allowing for flushing and easy cleaning.

DISEASES

Ocelots and margays are susceptible to all the diseases and ailments common to domestic cats. They are highly sensitive to the feline enteritis (panleukopenia) virus and intestinal diseases. (See *Part Three, Cat Health,* Chapters 9 through 14.) Your margay or ocelot should be vaccinated against feline enteritis; consult your veterinarian for the best inoculation program for your cat.

WILD OR UNUSUAL CATS IN HOMES
WITH CHILDREN

Since they are stronger than the house cats, margays and ocelots are well able to defend themselves against children who might try to mistreat them. Very young children can be hurt when one of these cats plays too roughly or uses its claws. I do not mean to imply that an ocelot or margay cannot be kept in a home with children. Whether you want to have one of these cats with your children depends on you, the children and the cat. Children must be taught—as in the case of domestic kittens and cats—that they are not to mistreat the ocelot or margay. Teach the children to respect the animal's prowess. Since it is smaller and not as strong as the ocelot, the margay usually makes a better pet in homes where there are young children. However, I have seen ocelots in homes with toddlers and there was no trouble at all—the parents had been wise enough to teach the children about the cats.

To repeat: margays and ocelots require special understanding and handling if there is to be a harmonious relationship between cat and owner. Furthermore, the acquisition and importation of these cats is becoming more difficult for Americans.

The margay and ocelot are regarded as peripheral mammals by wildlife authorities; that is, while not rare or endangered everywhere, their occurrence in certain areas is low and a cause for concern. Both the margay and the ocelot occur in northeast Mexico and south Texas and it is in these regions that they are peripheral. Both the Mexican and United States governments are interested in preserving these cats; thus, importation from these regions is not sanctioned. Poaching of these cats goes on in these regions, as well as in the more southern ranges. Needless to say, if you do think you are qualified to own a margay or ocelot—and state, federal or community laws do not prohibit your keeping a wild cat—you should legally obtain such a cat, demanding proof from the dealer or supplier that the margay or ocelot was not captured and exported contrary to any state, federal or national laws.

8. Your Cat and the Community

Intelligent cat ownership extends beyond daily care. It also involves responsibility for the cat's behavior in the home and community. Cats are an integral part of modern community life; however, whether they are a pleasure or nuisance depends largely on the owner and the community itself. Gone are the days when cats shifted for themselves without disturbing people or property. A continually growing human (and animal) population, lack of space, increased traffic and other hazards make it extremely unwise to allows cats to roam at large. Hard feelings, possibly legal actions, may arise from irresponsible management of pet cats. It behooves the cat owner, then, to see to it that his cat is kept under proper control.

LEGAL STATUS OF CATS

Unfortunately, the legal status of the cat is not always as clearly defined as that of dogs and livestock. A few states afford the cat protection by direct laws; others just fall back on anticruelty laws when there is any question of inhumane treatment of cats. Also, the cat does not always enjoy the status of being property, as do dogs. Nevertheless, under the unwritten or common law of many communities, sanctioned by long usage and acceptance, cats are considered pets and as such have both intrinsic and real value. Therefore, the theft of any pet—particularly in view of the federal Protection of Pets from Theft law (Public Law 8S-544) enacted in 1966—constitutes a crime.

It is true that the number of legal cases involving cats does not come anywhere near that involving dogs. But since cats, including wild or unusual varieties, are increasing in popularity as pets in cities and suburbs, we may expect a corresponding increase in legal difficulties resulting from cats biting or scratching people or damaging property.

LICENSES

Cat licensing, because of the large number of cats, their questionable status as property, and other factors, has not been attempted by state, city or county governments, except in a few instances. Five years ago, Kansas City, Missouri, tried to pass a law requiring the licensing of all owned cats. The proposal from the city council brought forth roars of disapproval from the cat-owning public. Under the proposed cat license ordinance, cats would be required to wear collars with a license tag attached; the fee for license and tag was to be three dollars. Cat owners pointed out the dangers of cat collars, as well as the illegality or invalidity of some other provisions of the ordinance. Consequently, the city quickly withdrew the ordinance and buried it.

The city of Point Comfort, Texas, does have a cat license law, which was passed over the protests of cat owners. While the law does not mention cats by name, it does state: *"Animal* for the purposes of this ordinance means *any* animal (male or female) which is or could be used and kept as a domestic pet." (One doesn't need to be an attorney to see some flaws in that definition!) The ordinance goes on to state that "No person shall own, keep or harbor *any* animal within the limits of the City of Point Comfort, Texas, unless such animal is licensed as herein provided"—the fee for said license is $1.00 for each male animal and $3.00 for females; spayed females (proof of spaying has to be submitted with the application for the license) are licensed at a fee of $1.50.

The Point Comfort law also requires all animals to be vaccinated against rabies when over six months of age. Furthermore, the vaccination shall have been administered by a veterinarian within one year preceding the date of application for a license. The fine upon conviction of any violation of this ordinance (which also covers other aspects of keeping animals in the city of Point Comfort) shall not exceed $100, and *each day's violation constitutes a separate offense!*

Now, this law is rather severe and, after a careful reading, seems open to considerable debate as to its validity in certain areas. According to a Point Comfort cat owner with whom I corresponded, the sessions prior to the passage of the law were charged with emotion and hard feelings. It appears that the problem of loose and stray dogs was the paramount issue and cause for the ordinance. But dog owners who felt that their pets were being discriminated against argued that if dogs were to be licensed, vaccinated and subject to seizure, then cats and other animals should be liable for the same treatment.

The point I want to make by citing this cat licensing law is that harsh, unfair pet laws can be avoided when owners assume the responsibilities that are inherent in keeping a cat or other animal in today's cities and suburbs. The community in which I live and serve as Chairman of the Board of Animal Regulation has no cat licensing law; to date, we have had no reason to consider such an ordinance, although we do have some irresponsible cat owners. In the matter of the control of pets in our community, we are using a general educational program, one in which we stress the need for responsible pet ownership and the need to control *all* pets.

ANTICRUELTY LAWS

Most states have anticruelty laws that include cats. Many of these states have used the "Bergh Law" as the basis for their anticruelty statutes. Henry Bergh was the humanitarian who founded the first humane society in the United States in 1866 (the ASPCA in New York City). Basically, the Bergh Law requires that all animals have adequate food, water and shelter and prohibits malicious abuse. Some states have enacted their own humane laws that go far beyond the basic requirements of the Bergh Law.

It should be remembered that anticruelty laws—which are usually enforced by humane societies aided by state, county and city officers —should not be confused with police powers for the preservation of the peace or abatement of a nuisance. A police officer or sheriff and his deputies can enforce both anticruelty and disturbance-of-the-peace laws. Humane societies are limited to the enforcement of anticruelty laws. Therefore, yowling cats in the backyard, unless the vocalizing is caused by physical pain, are strictly a matter for the police, not the local humane society.

ABANDONMENT

In most states, it is unlawful to abandon a cat. Fine and imprisonment or both may be the punishment, upon conviction, for abandoning a cat in an empty house, along a highway or other place. If you find that you must give up your cat and you can't give or sell the animal to some person or family, call your local humane society.

WILLFUL POISONING

The willful poisoning of cats is unlawful in some states; unfortunately, the practice is condoned in others, especially when cats are accused of molesting or killing poultry or game birds. Happily, many local communities outlaw the use of animal poisons for any reason. The poisons are certainly hazardous for children and other animals, including wildlife, and it may be that their inhumane and dangerous use will eventually be prohibited in all states.

TORTURING, ABUSING OR INHUMANE KILLING

Regrettably, many persons are either cat-haters or *ailurophobes* (those who have a pathologic fear of cats) and because of their hatred or fear of cats, purposely abuse, torture or kill the animals in various inhumane ways. Those states that have sound anticruelty laws provide stiff fines or sentences for such cruel practices. If it is necessary to kill a cat, the act should be done in a humane fashion, preferably by a police officer, humane society agent or veterinarian. Malicious children and thoughtless adults are also guilty of injuring or mutilating cats, and the number and kinds of horrors perpetrated on cats by such persons would not only appall, but disgust and enrage considerate cat owners. The hazard of injury, torture or death is one good reason for keeping your cat in the house or in a wire enclosure.

HIT-AND-RUN TRAFFIC ACCIDENTS

Again, many states have laws that provide a penalty for hitting an animal with a car, truck or other motor vehicle and leaving the scene. If you or any member of your family strikes a cat with a car, remember to do the following: (1) stop, (2) report the accident to a policeman, (3) if possible, try to locate the owner of the cat (although it may be a stray), (4) call or have someone else call the nearest humane society or veterinarian (very few veterinarians will come ot on an emergency call, but telephone one just the same) and (5) remain at the scene of the accident until the matter is well in hand.

YOUR RESPONSIBILITIES AS A CAT OWNER

CONTROL

Cats and people can get along together in the community, but there must be responsible ownership. When cats are neglected or uncontrolled, they quickly become a nuisance or, in the case of the wild species, a threat to public safety and welfare. In the negligent cat owner, we have the root of much of the hostility directed at cats in general by noncat owners. If your cat makes enemies instead of friends, then you can expect all kinds of trouble.

Actually, whether a cat is a pleasure or nuisance depends largely on the individual owner or family with whom the animal lives. If a cat is a nuisance, the prime offender is the irresponsible owner. He is the person who obtains a cat, gives it minimum care and, when the novelty of having the animal wears off, turns it loose to shift for itself, which probably means annoying the neighbors. Such a person ignores the rights of others. Permitting his cat to roam at large, he shrugs off the work that goes with keeping a cat. The list of offenses grows longer each day. Finally, this person's pet turns into the community pest. The result is an irate community, with individuals vowing to do something drastic to the cat.

Here is an actual letter which I received from an outraged and disgusted homeowner bothered by the uncontrolled cats of neighbors:

> This is an urgent plea for some sure-fire method to keep cats from wetting the doors of our house. The odor is indeed obnoxious and only with a twice-a-day application of a spray product are we able to keep these so-called "pets" of neighbors away. But if we once miss spraying—the cats return and wet the doors of the fine Victorian house in which we live. Nothing, absolutely nothing, seems to deter these cats—and the wetting on the same area seems to have become a tradition that has reached into the third generation of cats.
>
> I think the only thing is to use an air rifle to "educate" these pets. Help! help! help!

Here was an obvious situation in a community where irresponsible cat owners were at fault. The letter, despite the fact that it might seem amusing to some people, revealed the following facts: the letter writer had put up with the cat nuisance for a long time and was now fed up; she certainly was in no mood for a sermon on humanitarianism or a eulogy of cats as pets, and she was prepared to do violence to the offending animals. The owners of the cats showed a disregard not only for the rights of neighbors, but also for the safety and welfare of their pets. The loose cats annoyed a neighbor to the point of violence and were at the same time exposed to other hazards—traffic accidents, poisonings and pellets or bullets from guns. The lesson to be learned here is that your cat belongs at home under your control.

SANITATION

If you live in an apartment house or hotel with a cat, you will have to pay careful attention to sanitation. I would advise against keeping too many cats in an apartment or hotel suite. This may sound like unnecessary advice, but I can cite and document cases where people have kept as many as thirty cats in very small homes or apartments. When I was Manager of the Bide-A-Wee Home for Animals in New York City, I was called upon to take some cats that belonged to an old woman who had just died. Upon arriving at the small two-room apartment and opening the door, I was nearly knocked flat by the stench. Inside were twenty-five cats of all sexes, colors and dispositions! Granted, this may sound like a "tall cat tale" or bizarre situation, but it actually happened. There are many people in cities and suburbs who keep more cats than their facilities can handle. My advice is to keep no more than one, two or possibly three cats in the average-size home or large apartment. If you want more cats than that, find a place in the country and build a cattery.

Keep down cat odors—and complaints from neighbors—by cleaning the cat's sanitary pan daily. Dispose of the soiled part of the litter by wrapping it in newspaper and placing it in a metal can with a tight lid. If you have your own incinerator, burn the package. And if you live in the suburbs, see that your cat doesn't do its business on your neighbor's lawn or flower beds.

CATS AND BIRDS

Since nature made the cat a hunter, it is going to do what comes naturally and kill birds when it has the opportunity. Cats have fallen into disfavor with the increasing hordes of city and suburban bird lovers who maintain feeding stations. Here again, we have a situation that can lead to hard feelings between you and your neighbors.

There is no pat answer or sure-fire cure-all for preventing a cat from killing birds other than keeping the animal in the house. Bells on the cat's collar may work sometimes, although I have watched cats equipped with collars and bells stalk birds so quietly that the bells never rang or tinkled until it was too late and the birds were in the cats' claws.

Most bird-feeder stations have cat and other animal guards. The trouble comes when birds flutter to the ground to retrieve seeds that have fallen from the feeder. It is then that a cat can spring on its un-suspecting prey. If you have both a cat and bird-feeder station, my suggestion is to keep the cat indoors in the early morning and eve-ning, when the birds are most active feeding from the stations. Try belling the cat; it may work in your case and is worth a trial if it alerts even one of your neighbor's bird visitors. Also, you could suggest to your bird-feeding neighbors that they place wide trays around the bottoms of their feeders to prevent seeds from falling to the ground.

Keep your cat indoors as much as possible during the nesting season and when young birds are learning to fly. Many nestlings are caught by cats. (Nestlings are also lost by other means when they fall out of the nest and their parents are unable to rescue them, cat or no cat.) Avoid feeding raw meat to the cat in early spring when birds are active, since the meat may stimulate its appetite for birds.

Do everything you can to minimize the killing of birds by your cat. Songbirds are protected by law; so are game birds. In most states, anyone with a hunting license can legally shoot a cat caught molest-ing or killing game birds. Some laws even go as far as to state that a cat found with a dead bird that is on the protected list may be destroyed—even though no one actually saw the cat kill the bird. In these cases, you cannot recover damages; therefore, you will simply have to keep your cat out of such troubles.

FISH PONDS

Outdoor fish ponds are another source of trouble with cats. Gold-fish swimming in a garden pool will naturally attract a cat. Although no law can stop the cat from fishing, in most regions your neighbor may take steps to stop your cat from raiding his goldfish pond, including the drastic action of killing the cat. Often the law recognizes that cats are predatory animals and will not hold the owner responsible for fish caught by his cat. But the law also recognizes the right of a fish owner to protect his fish from a cat that is trespassing on his private property, even to the extent of destroying the cat. The legalities are quite complicated and the simplest thing to do is to keep your cat at home. If the animal fishes in *your* goldfish pond, well, that's a different situation altogether and you will have to settle the matter with your cat—at least the problem will be restricted to just you and your cat!

CAT BITES AND SCRATCHES

Some damage suits are brought against cat owners each year as a result of cat scratches or bites. Fortunately, they are not as common or numerous as cases involving dogs. Cats, before they will attack a person, usually try to escape, especially when outdoors. Most cases of cat bites and scratches occur indoors.

In many communities, cat owners are afforded the same protection concerning bite cases as owners of dogs. Under the common law, if a dog has never bitten anyone before, it is assumed the owner did not know the animal would do so or that it was vicious; therefore the dog is entitled to one bite before legal action is taken. If the same dog bites someone again, the owner will be held responsible because he failed to take effective precautions after the first instance.

The same legal reasoning applies to the cat in more enlightened regions of our country. In Buffalo, New York, for example, the State Supreme Court held that where bites are concerned, dogs and cats are equal in the eyes of the law. The Supreme Court jury found a cat owner innocent of negligence after her cat had bitten and scratched a house guest. The guest had sought $21,000 in damages. The jury agreed that, since the cat had never bitten anyone before, the owner did not know it was vicious and therefore could not be liable for the damages sought.

If you own a nervous or hostile cat, you should warn anyone coming into the house or yard that the animal might bite. But even this warning will not relieve you of responsibility for injuries should the cat live up to its reputation as a biter. Anyone bitten or scratched by a cat through no fault of his own can bring suit for damages. The verdict may be in your favor if you can prove that the person was bitten or scratched because of negligence in teasing or mistreating the cat. Again, these cases are complicated, and all that can be set down here are generalizations, but they will at least give you some idea of what to expect if your cat does bite or scratch someone.

Cat bites also introduce the possibility of rabies. Actually, rabies is relatively rare among cats, but it does occur. (See Chapter 10, Rabies.) Many communities have effective rabies control programs for dogs; few include the cat. Point Comfort, Texas, you will recall, does specify that *all* animals kept as pets must be vaccinated against rabies. You will be wise to check your state and local ordinances as to whether your cat must be vaccinated against rabies. Most states provide for the quarantine of all animals when a rabies epidemic strikes the region and usually stipulate what prophylactic measures, such as vaccinations, shall be taken during the epidemic or quarantine period. Whether you should have your cat vaccinated against rabies in the absence of a law requiring it depends on several factors, among them the question of whether your cat goes outside where it could come into contact with a rabid dog, fox, squirrel, skunk or other mammal. In any case, it is a good idea to talk the rabies vaccination matter over with your veterinarian. He is familiar with the rabies situation in your community.

YOUR CAT AND THE NEIGHBOR'S DOG

If there are cat-hating dogs in your neighborhood, you'll have to protect your cat. While most cats are quicker than dogs, some are occasionally caught and injured or killed. The best practice is to keep the cat indoors. Even though your property is fenced and will keep dogs out, your cat may very well go exploring over the fence and tangle with a neighbor's dog. I know of no way to provide complete protection from dogs other than keeping the cat indoors. It may be possible that your neighbor's dog will work out a truce with your cat. But I wouldn't count on it.

TRAVELING WITH THE CAT TO ANOTHER COMMUNITY, STATE OR COUNTRY

Some communities require certain precautionary measures for cats brought in from another region. In most cases a health certificate from a veterinarian, stating that the animal is free from communicable diseases, is all that is needed.

Interstate movement of cats is covered by more rigid laws. Again, a veterinarian's health certificate is usually required. Some states also require that a cat be vaccinated against rabies not less than thirty-nine days or more than five months before entering the state.

Similar requirements are mandatory when taking a cat into another country. Some countries have rather long quarantine periods. The British Isles, for instance, quarantines in-coming cats and dogs (especially from the United States) for as long as six months. Obviously, if you plan a trip to the British Isles for less than six months, you should leave the cat at home.

CONTROL OR RESTRAINT OF WILD CATS KEPT AS PETS

The trend toward keeping wild cats as pets presents some problems for the community, especially in the case of the greater cats. Even though these cats may be docile and manageable with their owners, the felines will not necessarily extend the same treatment to other people. Lion and puma cubs make cuddlesome pets, but when they mature it will take at least four strong men to control or restrain one of these cats, should it become frightened. A number of persons have been severely mauled, bitten and scratched by "tame" wild cats.

Serious and knowledgeable owners of big cats are aware that their unusual pets pose a threat to public safety and take measures to keep their animals under proper restraint. Unfortunately, some persons obtain wild cats without understanding at all the basics of animal behavior and the potential danger to members of the family or public should the animals go on a rampage.

What I am stressing is that wild cats, when forced into certain unfavorable situations, can be extremely dangerous. I further emphasize that one should not relax his vigilance because a lion or puma is "as tame as a kitten." Tame, the cat may very well be—but when faced with certain unfavorable stimuli, it can quickly turn into a raging, slashing beast.

This brings up the case of Leo, the lion mentioned in the previous chapter. It is a case in which I was a participant. Leo, a rickety and undersized specimen of *Panthera leo,* lived in Abington Township,

Pennsylvania. His owner, a garageman, had had the lion for about two years when fifty-five of his neighbors decided to sign a petition to oust Leo from the community. The lion, they complained, kept them awake at night with his roars. His jungle odors pervaded their homes. Also, they were afraid he might get out of his cage and hurt someone. Leo was animal non grata as far as they were concerned.

Abington Township had no ordinance against keeping wild animals, but hastily drafted one to pave the way for Leo's ouster. The law was vague, ambiguous and a quagmire of definitions as to what constituted a wild animal. In a very short time, the community was divided into two camps: the pro-Leos and the anti-Leos. Leo's owner contested the township's order to get rid of the lion and the fight was on. There were several hearings before a justice of the peace, ending in victory for Leo. The township solicitor appealed the case to a higher court.

Leo's case became a *cause célèbre* overnight, with people all over the country rallying to his defense. Newspaper reporters and editors, as well as television and radio commentators had a field day—all of them siding with Leo and chiding the township commissioners for trying to evict a poor, tired, sickly lion. *Life* magazine ran a two-page spread about Leo and the legal battle to oust him.

After the justice of the peace had dismissed the first case because, in his opinion, the township failed to prove that Leo was a wild animal, the township solicitor decided to call in some expert witnesses. Frederick A. Ulmer, Jr., Curator of Mammals at the Philadelphia Zoological Garden, and I appeared as witnesses for the township.

Now, I like all animals, including cats. I have had many cats of my own and have handled thousands at the Bide-A-Wee Home, including ocelots, margays and lynxes. My reason for appearing as a witness (and I made it a condition for appearing) was to clarify the term "wild animal," which both the township and defense attorneys were misusing. Instead of using "wild" to describe an animal that lives, in a natural state, independent of man, they were using it as a synonym for ferocious. In my opinion, this misuse of the term only clouded the issue and confused the public. Fred Ulmer's and my testimony as to what constituted a true wild animal finally convinced the justice of the peace that Leo was a wild animal. Nevertheless, he dismissed the case for other legal and technical reasons.

When I first saw Leo, he was lying in a patched-up old circus cage in his owner's garage. I could see at a glance that he was abnormal, moving with great difficulty, like an old man afflicted with rheumatism or arthritis. In fact, Leo suffered from a bone disease.

Leo, according to his owner and friends, was a friendly lion, not one of those nervous, snarling, pacing, tail-swishing types seen in zoos and circuses. He was simply a big, friendly, lovable cat.

As an observer of animal behavior in captivity, I had my reservations about how friendly and lovable Leo would be when put under stress or faced with an unpleasant situation.

Leo and his owner often played and romped together, engaging in wrestling matches (although it was apparent that the lion "pulled some of his punches"). But the fact that Leo and his owner played together did not mean the lion would extend the same willingness toward other people. Many animals have an affinity for some people and a strong antipathy for others. Also, animals often accept a human being as a member of their species. Thus, Leo's owner might stick his head in the lion's mouth and get a playful squeeze. I, or someone else, might try to do likewise and end up with a flattened skull. Fred Ulmer examined Leo and reported that the lion was "extremely dangerous"—sad, rickety and sickly though the lion seemed, he had strong jaws that were capable of severing an arm.

The legal battle continued, with Leo winning all the rounds. Fate, however, intervened and the lion died. His bereaved owner immediately obtained another lion, this time a young cub. By then the township had created a special Committee of Animal Experts to study the whole matter of wild animals in the community and ordinances to regulate them. Eventually, a sound, practical and fair wild animal ordinance was drafted and enacted. It has since become the model for other community wild animal laws.

I have told this much of Leo the lion's story because it illustrates some important points about keeping wild cats in a community. First, there was ample evidence that prior to receiving the summons to show cause why he should not be made to give up the lion the owner had been lax in the control of the big cat. Second, emotionalism, ignorance of animal behavior, publicity seeking, a biased press, and radio and television coverage distorted the case far out of its proper perspective. Yet those very same persons who charged the township with "picking on a sickly lion" might well be the first to accuse it of negligence if the lion had gone berserk and injured or killed someone.

To repeat: wild cats, particularly the larger species, are potentially dangerous and should be kept under adequate restraint. When goaded beyond endurance, or when not feeling well, any cat may turn on people, even the person with whom it lives.

In the past two years, there have been several cases where so-called tame lions or other large cats have turned on people and severely mauled them. One such case involved a two-year-old lion named Larry and a twenty-two-year-old model. The model was hired to pose with the lion for advertising purposes. While television cameras whirled, the first performance went well, with Larry behaving like a docile, playful kitten, and then the lion was ushered back into his cage. But a television crew wanted a retake and Larry was forced out of his cage. He didn't want to do an encore and balked, whereupon he was beaten with sticks, had his tail pulled and received a general goading.

When the model took her position alongside the reluctant Larry, the television cameras went to work and photographer's flashbulbs popped. Suddenly the lion turned on the pretty model and sunk his teeth into her left leg. She screamed and it took two men to force the lion's jaws apart and free her. The girl was rushed to the hospital, where an emergency operation was performed to save her leg. Surgeons said that she would need several more operations to repair the damage. This is only one of a number of cases where lions, leopards and other great cats have attacked human beings. It shows the folly of taking these animals lightly and of exploiting them in public.

The would-be owner of a wild cat should first consider his reasons for wanting to keep such a pet. An interest in and love for the unusual cats should be the paramount reason, of course. Exhibitionism and fashion fads are poor reasons for keeping an animal that will require time, patience, restraint and self-sacrifice, if there is to be a contented cat and happy owner. Finally, the owner of a wild cat should take every step, every precaution, to see to it that the animal does not become a threat or nuisance in the community.

I, for one, do not want to see more and more restrictive legislation regarding the keeping of cats and other pets in the community. But when irresponsibility and neglect are practiced on a wholesale basis, then the community has not only the right, but the obligation to enact laws for the protection of the public health, safety and welfare. Therefore, the owner of a wild or unusual cat must exercise more than ordinary judgment and care when it comes to his pet.

Part Three

CAT HEALTH

9. Your Cat's Health

Very few cats go through life without some kind of ailment or injury. Unfortunately, your cat cannot tell you when it is sick or injured. It will be up to you to detect when the animal is ailing, whether it is merely "off its feed" or is seriously ill or injured and in need of veterinary care.

THE HEALTHY CAT

Before you can decide whether your cat is injured or ill, or how severe its ailment may be, you should know the signs of a healthy cat. A cat in good health is alert, active, playful, bright-eyed and responsive. It will spend hours playing with its toys, chasing objects, climbing on high perches, running and leaping about. It will show considerable curiosity about everything around it. It will purr contentedly when you stroke its head or back. It will dance about you at feeding time, often standing on its hind feet and waving its forepaws. The aroma of food stimulates the cat's appetite and it will let you know in no uncertain terms that it is hungry and will attack its food with gusto.

When fed properly, a cat should be sleek and well-muscled, but not fat. Its coat should be glossy and soft to the touch, with no excessive shedding except in the spring. And, when groomed regularly, it will have no matted hair or parasites. The cat's skin also will be clear and free of sores, rashes and eczema.

The healthy cat's bowel movements are regular and formed. There should be at least one solid movement a day—more when a kitten. The normal rectal temperature will range from 101 to 102 degrees F. A well cat usually has no breath odor except after eating fish or other aromatic foods. It will be free of chronic coughs and sneezing, although it may cough and sneeze occasionally, especially when exposed to smoke, soot, dust or other foreign matter in the air.

The eyes of a healthy cat are bright and free of redness or discharge. Its nose also is clean and free of discharge, except for the normal colorless mucus. Its mouth will have no sores, ulcers or other irritations. Finally, the healthy cat has an air of contentment which shows through the animal's aloofness.

THE SICK OR INJURED CAT

Once you learn to recognize the signs of a healthy cat, those of the sick or injured cat will stand out by contrast, and, although you will have to train yourself to be observant, you will be armed with a standard of comparison.

The sick cat behaves in a manner markedly different from that of a healthy cat. It will lie around listlessly or sit in a hunched position, staring into space. Or it may slump down with its head hanging over the water pan. (See Chapter 10, Feline Enteritis.) Perhaps the cat will lie still with its head sunk on its chest, eyes closed. Illness or injury changes the cat from a bundle of energy into a dull, listless animal.

An ailing cat has a poor appetite or none at all. Remember, a refusal to eat one or two meals does not mean a cat is ill. It may not be hungry. But a prolonged fast does indicate that all is not well.

A dull, dry and listless coat also indicates that something is wrong. Metabolic dysfunctions, poor diet, internal or external parasites, skin diseases and allergies—all these affect the condition of the cat's skin and coat.

Soft bowel movements, diarrhea, or bloody stools are symptoms of disorders or disease, as is a straining movement while trying to urinate. Cats suffering from cystitis or urinary stones urinate frequently and with difficulty. The urine may be tinged with blood and the cat may cry out with pain. If the urinary tract is blocked, the cat's abdomen will be distended and painful. Cats with urinary trouble may vomit. Vomiting also is a sign of certain other diseases and of poisoning. (See Chapters 10, 11 and 16.)

A rise in temperature means that something is wrong. Although it isn't necessary to take a cat's temperature every day, it should be checked when you suspect that the cat is ill.

The sick cat may have an offensive breath. Mouth odors may be caused by certain foods, but urinary ailments and decayed teeth also cause bad breath. If your cat has a persistent breath odor and you have eliminated offensive foods as the cause, it is time to consult your veterinarian.

Chronic coughing and sneezing, particularly when accompanied with a heavy nasal or eye discharge, are symptoms of serious respiratory diseases. Continued redness of the eyeballs, conjunctiva or nictitating membrane all point to some ailment.

WHAT TO LOOK FOR IN THE AILING CAT

Refusal to eat or halfhearted eating for more than one or two meals. (See Chapters 10 and 11.)

Inactivity, listlessness or a tendency to lie around more than usual. (See Chapters 10 and 11.)

Dull, dry and lifeless coat. (See Chapters 12, 13 and 14.)

Excessive shedding of hair, bare spots and sores on skin. (See Chapters 13 and 14.)

Constipation, diarrhea, bloody stool or difficult bowel movements. (See Chapter 11.)

Frequent urination, straining while urinating and dark or blood-tinged urine. (See Chapter 11.)

Inability to urinate. (See Chapter 11.)

Temperature above or below the normal range. (See Chapters 10, 11 and 19.)

Persistent breath odor, after offensive foods have been eliminated. (See Chapters 11 and 20.)

Excessive sneezing and coughing. (See Chapter 10.)

Heavy, thick and discolored mucus from eyes and nose. (See Chapters 10 and 11.)

Bleeding. (See Chapter 15.)

Anemia or pale gums. (See Chapters 10 and 11.)

Pawing or scratching at the head and ears. (See Chapter 13.)

Vomiting between meals, especially a yellow fluid. Cats have a quick reverse action and may vomit for a variety of harmless reasons. But prolonged vomiting, with a yellowish discharge, is indicative of serious trouble. Vomiting may also be caused by poisoning. (See Chapters 10, 11, 15 and 20.)

Excessive intake of water. (See Chapters 10, 11 and 20.)

Sitting with the head hanging over the water bowl. (See Chapter 10.)

Swellings or abscesses on the face, legs, or tail. (See Chapter 11.)

Wounds, cuts or contusions. (See Chapter 15.)

Stiffness or inability to use a leg or paw. (See Chapter 15.)

Fractures. (See Chapter 15.)

WHAT SHOULD BE DONE ABOUT THE SICK OR INJURED CAT

The chances are your cat will need treatment some time during its lifetime. There will be minor ailments which you can treat at home, but more serious conditions should be referred to the veterinarian. It is your responsibility to learn to distinguish one from the other and to act accordingly.

Familiarize yourself with the causes, symptoms, mode of transmission and treatment of the various cat diseases (see Chapter 10), as well as the symptoms of injuries and first aid measures required. That is not to say that you should learn the technical terms, master the veterinary pharmacopeia or become an expert diagnostician, all of which are the province of the veterinarian. But you should have a working knowledge of the various cat diseases and injuries and be able to judge whether your cat should be taken to the veterinarian. You should also be able to describe the cat's condition intelligently—especially important when you talk to the veterinarian by telephone.

Another important reason for familiarizing yourself with cat diseases and injuries is that, in many cases, you will have to nurse the cat back to health. This will involve reporting symptoms and progress to the veterinarian, and you will be in a better position to make intelligent reports if you are well-informed. You will also better understand the veterinarian's objectives and be better able to follow his instructions.

Resist the temptation to doctor your cat when it is seriously ill or injured. As already stated, you should learn what conditions you can safety treat and do not attempt to go beyond them. When in doubt as to the severity of a disease or injury, or when a seemingly minor condition persists, always take the cat to the veterinarian. Don't risk your cat's life by trying to do more than you are trained to do.

HOW CAT DISEASES ARE TRANSMITTED

The major cat diseases are caused by bacteria, viruses, fungi and rickettsiae. (The latter are bacterialike organisms.) Before your cat can contract a disease, it must be exposed to the organism causing that disease. This exposure may consist of direct contact with an infected animal, eating infected food, or inhaling air infected by organisms. Also, minute droplets of water or mucus from a sick cat may contain types of viruses or bacteria which find their way into the respiratory system of another cat. Rabies, a virus disease, is transmitted through the bite of a rabid animal, and fungus infections are spread by direct contact, wind and water. Cats contract ringworm and favus, both fungus diseases, by rubbing against infected dogs, cats or human beings.

THE VETERINARIAN

A veterinarian should be selected with the same care used in choosing your own doctor. The veterinarian should be fond of cats and be able to inspire confidence in you.

Start your search for the right veterinarian before your cat becomes ill or meets with an accident. If you wait until an emergency arises, you will have to take the cat to the first available veterinarian. All veterinarians are competent in varying degrees to treat animals, but some of them do not treat cats.

Talk with other cat owners in your neighborhood and learn which veterinarians are considered responsible with cats and which are not. Evaluate these opinions with care. Many a fine veterinarian has had his reputation maligned by some disgruntled cat owner. Also, the veterinarian popular with your cat-owning friends and neighbors may not suit you—or your cat. Careful advance investigation, however, will give you leads to the veterinarians in your area who treat cats successfully.

Modern, up-to-the-minute hospital buildings and equipment are impressive, but are no substitutes for skill and knowledge. Don't condemn a veterinarian because he doesn't have a new building or fancy equipment. The care and sanitation of the building and equipment are important, however. Soiled cages, dirty runs, strong odors, filthy cats (or dogs), rough handlers and unsanitary instruments are all evidence which should lead you to decide that a veterinarian is unsuitable.

SOME SAFEGUARDS FOR YOUR CAT'S HEALTH

A knowledge of the causes and methods of transmission of the various cat diseases is valuable from the standpoint of prevention but should be augmented by active precautions. The most important is immunization against those diseases for which there are vaccines.

IMMUNIZATIONS

Fortunately, cats can be immunized against some of the major diseases. At the present time, there are vaccines for feline enteritis, rabies and pneumonitis. A cat may also achieve immunity from these diseases—*with the exception of rabies, which is always fatal*—if it recovers from an attack. In such cases the cat's body builds up defenses against diseases. White cells envelop disease organisms and destroy them, or the body manufactures antitoxins which work on the toxins given off by bacteria. But, while most cats can develop antibodies to attack specific organisms, it must be remembered that antibodies developed against a specific disease, such as pneumonia, are not effective against other diseases. For example, a cat recovering from feline enteritis is not immune to pneumonitis.

Natural immunity occurs only when medication does not interfere with the development of antibodies. Certain medicines and drugs destroy disease organisms in a very short time but, in doing so, interfere with the development of natural immunity. The buildup of natural immunity is a gradual process, and requires the presence of disease organisms. A cat that has been medicated, especially with antibiotics, may not develop sufficient antibodies to protect it against the same disease later on.

Most kittens have immunity from disease, inherited from the mother through the colostrum, or first milk. This inherited immunity wears off as the kitten grows older, usually within six weeks. This inherited immunity sometimes interferes with the development of antibodies when a young kitten is inoculated. You should keep this fact in mind. It may help explain why a vaccination fails to "take" on a young kitten.

INOCULATIONS

Since you have no way of knowing whether your cat has been exposed to and recovered from a disease, and thus established immunity, you should have it immunized against the major diseases. Also, since you have no way of knowing just when a kitten's inherited immunity will wear off, you should not delay its immunization. Your veterinarian will be happy to discuss your cat's immunization program and recommend those vaccinations which he feels are important.

10. Major Cat Diseases

Great strides have been made in the fight against major viral, bacterial, fungus and rickettsial diseases of cats. Inoculations have reduced mortality from the major cat diseases, and new drugs have also been effective in combatting bacterial, fungus and rickettsial diseases. Unfortunately, however, virus diseases continue to kill a large number of cats every year.

FELINE ENTERITIS

The most insidious of all the cat diseases is feline enterities, or panleukopenia. It is also called cat distemper. Feline enteritis is a highly infectious and quick-killing disease. Thousands of cats die every year from this dreaded virus disease. All breeds of cats are susceptible, including wild cats. While the disease appears to be more prevalent among kittens, it is not uncommon in older cats. However, the mortality is highest among kittens from four to six months of age. The death rate in a litter of kittens may reach 100 percent; among older cats mortality may reach 90 percent. An epidemic of feline enteritis can wipe out all the cats in entire neighborhoods.

Feline enteritis is caused by a filterable virus, one that is capable of passing through fine porcelain. Your cat can pick up the virus by coming into direct contact with infected cats or by entering a room, cage, box or other place where infected cats have been kept. Just how long the enteritis virus can live outside the cat's body has not been determined. When one cat dies from the disease, it is imperative that any new ones brought into the home be protected with enteritis serum or vaccine. All toys, dishes, pans, beds and other equipment used by a cat dead from enteritis should be discarded.

The incubation period for enteritis—the time elapsing between initial contact with the virus and appearance of the typical symptoms —is from four to ten days. This period may vary, of course. The disease comes on quickly and is dispersed throughout the cat's body, with few parts being spared. Very often, the symptoms of feline enteritis are mistaken for those of other diseases. For example, some of the symptoms, especially violent vomiting, resemble those of acute poisoning. The converse is also true: cats suffering from coccidiosis, an intestinal parasitic disease, often display symptoms similar to those of enteritis. It is not easy for the layman, or even the veterinarian, to diagnose feline enteritis in its early stages. If your cat has any of the symptoms listed here, waste no time getting it to the veterinarian.

One of most noticeable signs of feline enteritis is that of a cat sitting with its head hanging over the water pan. It may or may not attempt to drink. As the disease progresses, the cat becomes thin and emaciated. Its tail loses hair and the body fur becomes dull and lifeless, usually standing on end. The cat is listless and dull-eyed, with none of its usual animation, and has little or no appetite. All of these symptoms steadily increase in severity.

A cat with enteritis runs a high temperature, often as high as 104 degrees F. It may cry out in pain, vomit a yellowish or greenish fluid and have severe diarrhea. In the later stages of the disease, the cat becomes dehydrated and soon dies. Enteritis produces a marked decrease in the white blood cells.

The speed with which the disease progresses is amazing. A cat may be lively and playful one day and be dead a few days later. Death ensues within forty-eight hours of the appearance of the symptoms in some cases. Older cats may linger for a week or ten days, sitting with their heads over the water pan, until they finally give up the struggle.

Until effective drugs are developed to fight viruses, there is little that can be done for the cat with enteritis. Only a few recover from the disease, and these have a natural immunity. None of the known drugs are of much use against the enteritis virus. Antibiotics are useful, however, in preventing secondary infections, such as bacteria, fungi and rickettsiae. In large cities, where many stray cats roam the streets and alleys, the disease often reaches epidemic proportions.

When this occurs, prevention and control become major problems. Although early spring and summer bring a high incidence of feline enteritis, cats can contract it at any time.

IMMUNIZATIONS

Fortunately, your cat can be vaccinated against this scourge of catdom. However, it is important to understand that vaccines and immunization programs vary among different veterinarians. At any rate, discuss the immunization of your cat with the veterinarian; don't delay, your cat's life may be at stake.

ARE FELINE ENTERITIS VACCINATIONS PERMANENT?

It should be clearly understood that while high-quality feline enteritis vaccines confer long-lasting immunity, there is no such thing as a permanent vaccination. Therefore, it is best to consult with the veterinarian as to the frequency of any "booster" shots.

Unfortunately, some kittens and cats fail to respond to the vaccination and no antibodies are produced. There may be any one or a combination of reasons for the vaccination failure: (1) if a cat already has the virus in its body, the vaccine will not provide immunity (or cure); (2) cats in poor health, malnutritious or infested with internal parasites will have difficulty in building up immunity; (3) a young kitten may still have some inherited immunity from its mother, which interferes with the effects of the vaccine as the vaccination does not fortify any immunity present at the time of injection.

Most of the *Felidae* are susceptible to feline enteritis. Ocelots, margays, pumas, lions, tigers and other wild cats often contract and die from the disease. Enteritis is the scourge of zoos and menageries. Veterinarians usually vaccinate the larger wild cats by shooting into their bodies small syringelike darts containing the vaccine. Wild kittens usually can be handled and given inoculations in the same way that domestic cats receive their injections.

WHAT TO DO IF YOU SUSPECT YOUR CAT HAS FELINE ENTERITIS

Remember, enteritis works quickly. Get your cat to the veterinarian without delay. If he has an isolation ward in his clinic or hospital, he may hospitalize the cat. If not, he will instruct you how to treat the cat at home under his supervision. If the veterinarian is unwilling to keep the cat, it should not be held against him. Far from being callous or indifferent, he will have a good reason for this action. First of all, enteritis is very contagious and the possibility of an epidemic sweeping through his cattery is very great, and without isolation facilities he cannot afford to take the risk. Also, the treatment for enteritis in a veterinary hospital is often very costly, and the outcome is doubtful. The veterinarian often has this fact in mind when he insists upon home treatment for the cat.

HOME CARE

Your main objective in nursing a cat sick with enteritis is to stave off secondary infections and hope it will survive the main disease. But be prepared for the worst. Make the cat comfortable, try to build up its strength and keep it warm. Select a room with a constant temperature; fluctuating temperatures should be avoided. (See Chapter 16, Home Care of the Sick Cat.) If the temperature of the room must be kept low for some reason, cover the cat with a blanket. Affectionate pats now and then, and words of encouragement, will help the cat's morale.

The cat desperately ill with enteritis needs fluids; otherwise it swiftly becomes dehydrated. It may refuse to drink or be too weak, in which case you will have to feed it liquids by eyedropper or plastic bottle. Prepare a stock of the following formula: 4 tablespoons of corn syrup, ¼ teaspoon of bicarbonate of soda, ½ teaspoon of salt and 1 quart of water. Feed as much as you can of this liquid every two hours, warmed in advance.

If your cat survives and later shows signs of wanting to eat or drink by itself, switch to solid foods and warm milk or water. If diarrhea is present, control it by feeding small amounts of boiled milk, cottage cheese, cooked rice or macaroni. Should the cat vomit, eliminate the solid foods for a while and substitute boiled milk or beef broth. When the vomiting is under control, gradually feed small quantities of lean meat, such as chopped beef, lamb or chicken. Strained baby foods are excellent for the convalescent cat.

You may have to cater to your cat's tastes during the convalescent period, even to the extent of violating some of the general feeding rules. It must eat if it is to recover. Try a variety of foods, cooking them if necessary.

Nursing a cat sick with enteritis calls for considerable patience and devotion. It also demands work. But most cat owners will not hesitate to do anything they can to save the lives of their pets.

RABIES

Rabies is one of the oldest animal diseases known to man. It is mentioned in ancient writings, and Aristotle described it in great detail. Rabies is relatively rare in cats, chiefly because they usually manage to escape from rabid animals by climbing to places of safety.

Rabies is primarily a disease of dogs, wolves, coyotes, foxes, skunks and bats. It can be transmitted to cats and other animals, including man. The disease is caused by a virus which enters the central nervous system. The virus usually gains entry to the body through the bite of a rabid animal. It has recently been learned, however, that animals can contract rabies by mere exposure to the virus. As an experiment, dogs, cats, coyotes, foxes and skunks were placed in a bat-infested cave in Texas. They were all kept in screened, bat-proof cages; one of the cages was even insect proof. After a month, rabies appeared in all the foxes and coyotes, but not in the other animals. Foxes and coyotes, then, appear to be the most susceptible to the rabies virus. Both of these animals live on the fringes of civilization and may spread rabies by attacking dogs, cats and other domestic animals.

The incubation period for rabies ranges from fifteen to fifty days in animals. In the human being, rabies may incubate for as long as three months. Not every cat bitten by a rabid animal develops rabies. Several factors are involved, among them the depth of the wound, the amount of bleeding and the location of the bite. Wounds near the central nervous system (*e.g.,* on the face, legs and nose) present the greatest danger.

The symptoms of rabies are complex and its presence can be determined only by close observation. Rabid cats either run away or hide, and it is difficult to observe symptoms in them. A positive objective diagnosis of rabies can be accomplished only by a microscopic examination of the brain. When the rabies virus reaches the brain, small oval bodies known as Negri bodies are formed in the brain and nerve cells. These are visible under a microscope and are positive indication of rabies.

One of the first signs of rabies in a cat is a definite change in its behavior, but this symptom is not conclusive. A cat's disposition and behavior are changeable anyway, and you should not jump to the conclusion that your cat has rabies merely because it hisses or snarls. But be careful when an ordinarily friendly cat suddenly turns wild and ferocious, clawing and biting at everybody and everything in its path, or suddenly becomes very quiet and hides under a bureau or bed and refuses to come out. Another startling change in a cat infected with rabies is in its voice. A rabid cat usually cries in a deep-pitched hoarse voice entirely unlike its normal tone.

There are two kinds of rabies—a dumb, or paralytic, form and a furious one. While cats sometimes have the dumb or paralytic form, it is uncommon. A cat with the furious form of rabies becomes highly nervous and excited. Its pupils dilate, it experiences difficulty in swallowing and it runs about, biting and scratching. Cats stricken with the dumb form of rabies rarely try to attack a person or animal. Their throat muscles are paralyzed and they cannot swallow, although they drool profusely.

Later, as the disease progresses, the cat loses its appetite, becomes paralyzed, has difficulty drinking water and finally goes into convulsions. Once these symptoms appear, the course of the disease is rapid. The cat usually dies in from three to seven days after the symptoms appear. Rabies is also called hydrophobia, which means fear of water. Actually, this is a misnomer. A victim of rabies has no fear of water, but is merely unable to drink because of paralysis of the throat.

There is no cure for rabies, either in animals or human beings, but both can be immunized against the disease. The U.S. Public Health Service has developed a preexposure vaccine for the protection of veterinarians and others frequently exposed to rabies.

Since rabies can spread rapidly and reach epidemic proportions, most communities, states and countries have strict laws aimed at its prevention and control. Cats entering a state or country often must be accompanied by a certificate stating that they have been vaccinated against rabies, usually within a specified period of time. (See Chapter 8, Traveling to Another Community, State or Country.) Any cat that has bitten a human being is usually kept under observation for a period ranging from seven to fourteen days.

WHAT TO DO IF YOU SUSPECT YOUR CAT HAS RABIES

If you detect symptoms of rabies in your cat, don't panic; proceed with caution and keep out of its way. Call your veterinarian, police or health department, or local humane society. If possible, keep the cat confined to one room or escapeproof area, without endangering yourself.

If anyone is bitten by the cat, call a physician immediately, then report the bite to the police or health department. Surrender the cat to the proper authorities without argument—someone's life, perhaps your own, may depend on it. Give the authorities complete information about the cat, especially as to whether it has had a rabies vaccination, and when.

In the event you are bitten by a strange cat, regardless of whether you notice any symptoms of rabies, have the wound treated by a doctor. You can first wash the bite with warm water and strong soap. Tincture of green soap is good. Work up a good lather and keep it in the wound twenty or thirty minutes at least. While this first aid does not guarantee that you will not contract rabies if the animal was rabid, it may help. Next, go to a physician. He may cauterize the wound and prescribe a series of injections. The injections are usually begun after the attacking cat has been examined (the brain, in particular) and proved rabid by a microscopic examination for Negri bodies.

It is important to find the cat that bit you, so that it can be examined. If the offending cat belongs to you, or to a friend or neighbor, your search will be simplified. If not, give as complete a description of the cat as possible to the police, health department, humane society and other municipal organizations. Circulate the description in the newspapers, radio stations and other public communication media.

IMMUNIZATION OF THE CAT

Your cat can be immunized against rabies. The rabies vaccine usually is given when the cat is six months old. Currently, there are several kinds of rabies vaccines. Until recently, rabies vaccines were of the killed tissue type, but now there is a live virus vaccine developed exclusively for the prevention of feline rabies. Rabies Vaccine Avianized (Agricultural Division, American Cyanamid Company) is a specially prepared, modified live virus vaccine that is bolstered by an aluminum hydroxide adjuvant (an extra, helpful ingredient), which provides more effective immunizing power against rabies. Consult your veterinarian for the best rabies vaccination program for your cat. If the veterinarian advises a yearly vaccination, mark the date down and see to it that your cat is revaccinated each year, especially if the animal goes outdoors.

TOXOPLASMOSIS

Toxoplasmosis is a serious disease caused by the protozoan *Toxoplasma gondii*. It occurs in all parts of the world and may be acquired or congenital in cats and other small animals. Infection may be transmitted by eating contaminated food left by infected animals and by contact with infected nasal discharge, saliva and feces of carrier animals. Young cats are the most susceptible to toxoplasmosis.

The symptoms of toxoplasmosis include fever, loss of appetite, cough, jaundice, emaciation, difficult or labored breathing and nervous system disturbances; paralysis may occur. Positive diagnosis can be made only by a veterinarian after demonstration of antibodies and isolation of the toxoplasmosis organism.

PNEUMONITIS

Pneumonitis is a feline disease which resembles the common head cold in human beings. It is caused by a virus (*Miyagawanella felis*) and is highly contagious, often sweeping through a cattery or neighborhood with astonishing rapidity. The incubation period ranges from six to ten days. Pneumonitis is not usually fatal, although secondary infections may cause death. The course of the disease may run as long as six weeks.

The symptoms of pneumonitis include running eyes, nasal discharge, sneezing fits and salivation. The cat's temperature may or may not rise.

Though pneumonitis is rarely fatal, it is serious enough to warrant the attention of a veterinarian, who will probably prescribe an antihistamine and antibiotics. You can help by cleaning the cat's nose, bathing its eyes and applying an eye ointment. (See Chapter 11, Eye Ailments.)

A pneumonitis vaccine is available, but it is not highly effective. At most, it protects the cat for about six months. If there is an outbreak of pneumonitis in your neighborhood, however, an inoculation may protect your cat for the duration of the epidemic.

PNEUMONIA

Pneumonia (not to be confused with pneumonitis) may be caused by a virus or a bacteria. (There also is a type of pneumonia caused by foreign matter in the lungs.) The disease usually follows exposure to cold and dampness. Pneumonia takes various forms, but the one most commonly found in the cat is *bronchopneumonia*. It may occur as a primary infection or as the sequela of another disease, such as enteritis.

A heavy, harsh cough is perhaps the first noticeable symptom of pneumonia. As the disease progresses, the cat will have a thick nasal discharge, perhaps bloody, breathe abnormally, with labored, rasping sounds, and run a high temperature, well above the normal range.

Pneumonia is a serious disease. Keep the cat warm until you can get it to the veterinarian. Cover it with a blanket or sweater. Cats rarely survive an attack of viral or bacterial pneumonia without proper medication; uncomplicated cases usually respond quickly to antibiotic therapy.

On the other hand, complicated cases of pneumonia, such as those followed by pleurisy, may require a long time to cure. Pleurisy causes the lungs to break down into pockets, forcing the cat to breathe heavily and laboriously. This condition is known as *emphysema* or, in popular terminology, the "heaves." Cats with emphysema lack stamina and are short of breath. There is no cure for emphysema.

TUBERCULOSIS

Tuberculosis is rare in cats. In the few cases that do occur, the victims more often than not are farm cats which come into contact with cows, sheep, goats and pigs, any of which may be carriers of tuberculosis. Also, raw milk may be infected with tuberculosis bacilli and farm cats drinking it may contract the disease.

The diagnosis of tuberculosis calls for X rays and laboratory tests. These, of course, must be done by the veterinarian. There is no record thus far of cats transmitting tuberculosis to human beings.

FELINE VIRAL RHINOTRACHEITIS

Feline viral rhinotracheitis, or FVR, as it is called, is a respiratory disease with symptoms similar to those of pneumonitis. In fact, the two diseases were considered to be the same until the FVR virus was isolated about ten years ago. The diagnosis and treatment should be left to the veterinarian. Cats usually recover within a few weeks. Recovery from FVR, however, does not confer immunity.

CANCER

Almost all types of cancer are found in the cat. The most common are those of the skin, mammary glands, bones, blood and blood tissues. Leukemia and other blood cancers, which cause a very high mortality among cats, often go undetected until it is too late. As is the case with cancer in man, when detected early enough, some forms of cat cancer can be cured. Usually, however, the cancer is not discovered in time and treatment can give only a certain degree of relief from suffering.

Although the incidence of feline leukemia (FeLV) is low, it is a factor to be considered in areas of high cat populations. The leukemia virus can be transmitted to other animals, including human beings, according to researchers at the Sloan-Kettering Institute in New York. Feline leukemia can be transmitted in urine, feces, saliva, feeding bowls and litter pan. The virus can be detected by a laboratory test known as the Feluek test developed by Dr. William D. Hardy, Jr., chief of the veterinary cancer laboratory at the Sloan-Kettering Institute.

A cancer is an excessive growth of tissue. Lumps on the skin, bleeding from the rectum or reproductive organs (other than the usual bleeding during the female's heat period) should be regarded with suspicion. Internal cancers offer even fewer clues that might lead to early detection. Older cats should receive a regular examination by a veterinarian, who can watch for signs and symptoms of an early cancer.

11. Other Ailments

The major diseases discussed in the previous chapter all require immediate veterinary attention. In addition, cats are subject to other ailments, some acute, some chronic, all of which also require prompt care and most of which should be referred to the veterinarian. It is important to remember that prompt attention to all ailments, no matter how trivial they may seem, is your best method of preventing serious complications.

URINARY INFECTIONS AND STONES

Cats, like human beings, are often troubled with urinary infections and stones, or uroliths. Cystitis, an acute or chronic inflammation of the bladder, caused by stones or infection, is common in cats and can be very painful and debilitating. Cystitis may exist as a primary ailment or as a complication arising from another disease. Stones (uroliths) in the bladders of cats are usually composed of phosphate of ammonia, calcium, magnesium and xanthine. They vary in size and shape, often having sharp edges which irritate or tear the bladder.

The symptoms of cystitis include frequent urination, straining (sometimes the cat is able to void only a small trickle of urine), pain, bloody urine, vomiting, fever, loss of appetite and abnormal thirst.

Cats with cystitis often cry out with pain as they strain in an effort to urinate. Vomiting and bloating are other symptoms, and usually indicate a blockage of the urinary tract. When blockage occurs, the cat's abdomen becomes distended and sensitive to the touch.

Death may follow within forty-eight hours. Uremia, an accumulation of urinary substances in the blood, is a serious complication of complete blockage in the urinary system.

Prompt veterinary attention is imperative in such cases. Don't wait until the cat's bladder is blocked, but take it to the veterinarian at the first signs of continual straining while attempting to urinate. The veterinarian may be able to dissolve stones or treat infections before any complications set in. Surgical removal of the stones will be necessary when they cannot be dissolved.

Cystitis may recur. Some authorities believe that foods high in calcium and other minerals contribute to the formation of uroliths. However, there is some disagreement with this opinion. (Refer to Chapter 5, Nutrition.) A number of urologists believe that the retention of urine resulting from thickened tissues in the bladder and urethra (the canal which conveys urine from the bladder to the surface; in the male, it has a double curve) caused by disease, injury or scarring after an operation may be a major consideration in the formation of uroliths.

SWOLLEN OR INFECTED ANAL GLANDS

Cats frequently are bothered by swollen or infected anal glands. These glands are two baglike organs located inside the anus and on each side of it. Scientists are not certain just what purpose the cat's anal glands serve. Some think the glands are similar to the musk glands of the skunk, which have at least one obvious purpose—to drive enemies away. It has also been suggested that the cat's anal glands lubricate the anus and help void rough, undigestible materials, such as stones, seeds, bones, etc. The anal glands secrete a yellowish fluid.

When the anal glands become swollen they should be emptied. Occasionally, the glands become infected and cause great discomfort. The cat slides its rear along the floor in an effort to get relief. This sliding along the floor is also one of the symptoms of tapeworms. (See Chapter 12.)

EMPTYING THE ANAL GLANDS

The task of emptying the anal glands is a relatively simple one, although the struggles of the cat and resulting odor are so unpleasant that most cat owners prefer to let the veterinarian do the job. If you wish to do it yourself, here is the procedure:

First, place the cat on a table and have someone restrain it. Next, try to detect the swollen glands by examining the area around the anus on the outside. If the glands are swollen, you should be able to feel them. Also, you may be able to empty them by exerting pressure on the outside of the anus. Before you exert any pressure on the glands, cover the anal opening with several layers of gauze, cloth or absorbent cotton. Otherwise, you may be sprayed by the anal fluid when pressure is applied. Keep the cloth pressed against the anus with one hand, while you press on the glands with the other.

If external pressure fails to empty the glands, you will have to work inside the anus. Put on a rubber glove or finger covering and apply Vaseline or mineral oil on the finger to be inserted. The cat will be very sensitive, so someone will have to restrain it by force. Gently insert the greased finger into the cat's anus and feel to the left and right and downward from the anus, which should enable you to locate the anal glands. Hold the cloth or gauze around the inserted finger and the anus, and gently exert pressure on the glands, using a massaging motion.

The cat should feel better immediately, once the glands are emptied. But keep an eye on the animal for a few days. If the glands fill up again, the process will have to be repeated. If anal gland trouble persists, there is likely to be an abscess or other infection, and the cat should be taken to the veterinarian.

CONSTIPATION

Older cats are frequently troubled by constipation. The condition has a variety of causes, among them lack of exercise, faulty diet, hair balls, ingestion of foreign matter and tumors. Constipation is not a disease in itself, but an indication that something is wrong elsewhere.

Cats bothered with constipation usually are lethargic, have poor appetites and distended abdomens. Try adding more roughage to the cat's diet. A mild laxative, such as milk of magnesia, will relieve ordinary cases of constipation. In stubborn cases, you may have to give the cat an enema. (See Chapter 16, Giving the Cat an Enema.) If constipation persists, consult your veterinarian.

HAIR BALLS

All cats constantly lick themselves; consequently, they often ingest large quantities of hair, which accumulates in the digestive tract and is rolled into balls. These hair balls can cause constipation and severe intestinal blockage.

Most of the time, the cat regurgitates the hair ball in the form of a tight roll similar in appearance to the casts (feathers, bones, fur and other indigestible matter) coughed up by hawks and owls. When the hair ball manages to slip from the stomach into the cat's intestines, however, the cat may be unable to regurgitate it. If it doesn't pass through, it then causes intestinal stoppage. When intestinal stoppage occurs, the cat usually refuses to eat. You must get the cat to the veterinarian without delay. It may be necessary to remove the hair ball by surgery.

Intestinal blockage from hair balls can be prevented by feeding the cat a special preparation. Available in most pet shops, the preparation consists of a petroleum jelly, usually flavored with malt or other substance. Ordinary Vaseline may be used, but is not as palatable as the flavored preparations. Whichever you use, smear the cat's nose or paws with it. The cat will lick it off and ingest enough to lubricate its intestinal tract and cause a hair ball to slide through. A weekly treatment with the petroleum jelly will usually prevent hair balls from blocking the intestinal tract.

DIARRHEA

Diarrhea is not a disease but a symptom of a disease or a sign that the intestinal tract is infested with parasites or some foreign body. It may also be caused by malfunction of the intestinal tract, brought on by poor diet, excitement or chemical irritants. A true diarrhea is characterized by very loose bowel movements and is watery or bloody. A soft bowel movement does not constitute diarrhea.

If your cat has diarrhea, go over its diet. You may be feeding too much of a laxative food, such as liver or milk. Try to control the diarrhea by feeding starchy foods. Boiled milk, cooked rice, macaroni, barley or cottage cheese will help to solidify the bowel movements. A diarrhea preparation will also help. If diarrhea persists for more than a day or two in spite of your attempts to check it, take the cat to the veterinarian. Bloody diarrhea, however, should receive immediate veterinary attention. It may be caused by parasites, tumors, injuries or disease.

VOMITING

Cats can vomit almost at will and it is not always a sign of illness. It may be caused, however, by disease, excitement, obstruction (hair balls), worms, poor liver and kidney function and poisoning.

If your cat has persistent vomiting spells and you know it has not eaten poison, skip its regular meal. *If you know or suspect that it has been poisoned, get it to the veterinarian at once.* (See Chapter 15, Poisoning.) For ordinary vomiting, feed the cat warm beef bouillon and restrict its milk and water intake. Permit it to lick an ice cube instead. If the vomiting persists, consult your veterinarian. It may be caused by something more serious than an upset stomach.

BAD BREATH

Bad breath may be caused by certain foods, intestinal disturbances, urinary ailments or infections of the teeth and mouth. A meal of fish will leave an odor on the breath. A sour or acid breath indicates a digestive disturbance, and an odor of urine is a sign of trouble in the urinary tract. The treatment for bad breath depends upon the cause. If bad breath persists after you have eliminated odoriferous foods, consult a veterinarian.

TARTAR AND INFECTED TEETH

Cats are not as prone to tooth decay as human beings are. But, although the cat's teeth are apt to remain sound up to old age, infected teeth are not uncommon. Tartar accumulates on the teeth of older cats and must be removed. It sometimes builds up to a depth of ⅛ inch, pushing back the gums, interfering with mastication and causing bad breath.

Improper diet contributes to the formation of tartar. Wild cats rarely have accumulations of tartar, mainly because of their varied diet, but house cats fed mostly on canned foods or all-meat diets are susceptible to tartar deposits. If house cats were to eat feathers, bones and other coarse matter, they would rarely be troubled by tartar.

Tartar is not difficult to remove, provided it has not been permitted to become too thick. A metal pick will snap tartar off, but the process may frighten or irritate your cat, and it is best to let the veterinarian do the job. Heavy deposits of tartar require special dental tools. Also, veterinarians may have to anesthetize a nervous or unruly cat to remove the tartar.

An improper diet, especially one deficient in calcium and phosphorus, will lead to poor teeth. Loose and infected teeth should be removed by the veterinarian. Old cats with few teeth should be fed soft foods. (See Chapter 20, Care of the Old Cat.)

MOUTH ULCERS

Mouth ulcers, which appear on the upper lip or inside the gum line, may result from disease, injury or allergy. There may be diseased tissue and swelling of the lips and gums, and the cat may be in pain. Permanent disfigurement of the mouth may result, if treatment is not prompt. Mouth ulcers should be brought to the attention of the veterinarian.

EAR TROUBLES

Ear troubles can make your cat miserable and irritable. Infection of the outer ear, cankers, blood tumors (hematoma), parasites, and insect bites and stings are the more common ear ailments of cats.

CANKERS

An ear canker, or ulceration, may be caused by infection or parasites. It is characterized by an accumulation of foul-smelling wax in scabs or crusts, and the cat shakes its head and paws at its ears, all of which aggravate the condition.

You can relieve the itching and discomfort by washing the canker with mild soap and water. Use absorbent cotton and wash off the scabs or crusts. Next, dip a cotton swab into mineral or sesame oil and gently swab the affected parts of the ear. Do not penetrate too far into the ear canal or you may damage the eardrum. Apply the oil only to the parts of the ear canal that you can see. After the oil has been applied, dust the ear with an antiseptic powder. If the canker persists, consult your veterinarian.

HEMATOMAS

Blood tumors, or hematomas, can lead to serious ear troubles if neglected. A hematoma usually forms between the skin and the ear cartilage, and often follows injury. The symptoms include pawing at the ears, shaking the head, a soft swelling inside or outside the ear, pain or sensitivity when touched, and heat in the affected parts. The ear will actually feel hot. Hematomas cannot be adequately treated at home. They require surgical drainage. Take the cat to the veterinarian.

EAR MITES

Many cats become infested with small, barely visible ear mites, which get into the outer ear canal. They can lead to serious ear trouble and should be treated by the veterinarian. (See Chapter 13, Ear Mites.)

EYE AILMENTS

Cats are susceptible to various eye troubles. City cats that roam at large are subjected to dust, smoke, soot, oil fumes and other impurities from polluted air, any one of which can cause acute or chronic inflammation of the eyes. Respiratory diseases usually cause redness of the eyes, watering and sensitivity to light (photophobia).

CONJUNCTIVITIS

Conjunctivitis is an inflammation of the membrane lining the inner surface of the eyelids and the front part of the eyeball. It is distinguished by redness, watering and photophobia, or sensitivity to light. It may be caused by smoke, soot, dust, fumes, injury or disease. Should there be a foreign body in the eye, it must be removed. (See Chapter 6, Care of the Eyes.)

You can provide some relief for the cat by washing its eyes with warm water. Using an eyedropper, squeeze a few drops of the water into the corners of the eyes. The cat will wash the water over its eyes when it blinks. Apply a safe ophthalmic ointment, such as Neomycin ointment, inside the lower lid.

KERATITIS

Keratitis is an inflammation or ulceration of the cornea. The cornea may merely be inflamed or it may have a small ulcer or crater, which usually results from an injury. You may be able to see the ulceration. Sensitivity to light and, occasionally, a bluish-white clouding of the eye are signs of keratitis.

The treatment for ordinary inflammation of the cornea is similar to that for conjunctivitis. Ulcerative keratitis needs the attention of a veterinarian, although you can give the cat some relief by washing the eye with warm water and applying eye ointment.

FOREIGN OBJECT IN EYE

A foreign object in the eyes must be removed; otherwise an infection, often serious, will develop. (See Chapter 6 for technique of removing foreign object from the eye.)

CATARACTS

A cataract is an opacity of the lens of the eye. One or both eyes may be affected. Cataracts are most often found in old cats. (See Chapter 20, Eyes.)

ANEMIA

Anemia is commonly found in cats and may be caused by disease or nutritional deficiency. Other factors contributing to anemia are loss of blood from severe wounds and a destruction of the red blood cell structure.

The symptoms of anemia include listlessness, weakness, poor appetite and sometimes vomiting. Since these are also symptoms of other diseases, a positive diagnosis of anemia can be made only by a veterinarian.

FELINE INFECTIOUS ANEMIA

Cats are susceptible to a disease known as feline infectious anemia which is caused by a parasitic organism (*Haemobartonella felis*). The disease may be acute or chronic. In the acute phase, cats run a high temperature (103 to 106 degrees), have a loss of appetite, are depressed and show signs of jaundice. A chronic form of this disease is characterized by normal or *subnormal* temperature, weakness, depression and a gradual loss of weight. Positive diagnosis can be made only by a veterinarian.

CONVULSIONS

Convulsions are not a disease in themselves but are brought on by a variety of causes, including brain injury or disease, parasites, fright, constipation, poisoning and autointoxication, such as uremia. Extremely nervous cats may go into convulsions when alarmed or handled.

The symptoms include enlarged pupils, excitement, foaming at the mouth, running madly about and lying prostrate, with twitching legs. These also are symptoms of rabies and eclampsia. (See Chapter 10, Rabies, and Chapter 19, Eclampsia.)

The treatment, of course, depends upon the cause. Strychnine poisoning, for example, can be counteracted by an injection of Nembutal. Constipation-causing convulsions can be relieved by a laxative or enema or by a change in the diet. If your cat has convulsions, take precautions against its injuring itself. Move it to a safe distance from any sharp corners of furniture or other hazardous areas. Wrap a heavy blanket around the cat when moving it to a safe place. If you suspect the cat has eaten poison, take it to a veterinarian. Convulsions may recur. If your cat has repeated seizures of convulsions, consult a veterinarian.

DROPSY

Dropsy, or edema, is caused by an accumulation of fluids in the legs and abdomen. The distension of the abdomen is so great that the cat appears to be pregnant. The condition is more common in older cats. Faulty kidneys and heart trouble contribute to edema. Kidney involvement can be suspected if the cat drinks large amounts of water. However, the intake of too much water only aggravates the condition. A cat with dropsy should receive veterinary attention. You can help by restricting the cat's fluid intake to small amounts.

HEART TROUBLE

Old cats have various heart troubles, all of which need the attention of the veterinarian. (See Chapter 20, Care of the Old Cat.) Shortness of breath, gasping and fatigue are symptoms of heart trouble. Younger cats may have heart infections or infestations of heart worms. The diagnosis of heart troubles should be made by a veterinarian.

ABSCESSES

Abscesses are small swellings on the skin caused by an accumulation of blood, lymph or vaccination fluid. An abscess may result from an animal bite or scratch, an insect sting or a faulty vaccination. The symptoms include swelling, pain or sensitivity to touch, loss of appetite, irritability and a rise in temperature.

Ice packs or cold cloths sometimes help to reduce the swelling. Surgical drainage often is necessary. If the abscess persists for more than a day or two, take the cat to a veterinarian.

12. Internal Parasites

All animals harbor internal parasites at one time or other, and the cat is no exception. Some internal parasites are beneficial. Others, such as worms and protozoa, are harmful and cause considerable damage and sometimes death. Of these two major internal parasites which infest cats, worms are the more common and troublesome. Every cat owner should know something about the life cycles, method of entry, and control of intestinal parasites. There are specific drugs or vermicides for expelling worms and protozoa, but cats can be re-infected at any time. Only by destroying the life cycle of these pests can an effective control program be carried out.

WORMS

Worms are especially dangerous to young kittens. The parasites sap their strength, cause irritability and pave the way for more serious ailments by lowering the body resistance.

ASCARIDS

The ascarids, or roundworms, are the worms most frequently found in cats. Those infesting cats are *Toxocara canis, T. leonina* and *T. cati.* These ascarids also infest dogs, foxes and other mammals. They measure from one to seven inches in length and usually inhabit the small intestine, although they are frequently found in the stomach. Ascarids are widely distributed over the United States and present a particularly serious threat to cats and dogs in most sections of the country.

While the different ascarids vary in size and shape, they have fairly similar life cycles. They are passed from infected cats into the feces as eggs. Other cats pick up the eggs by contact with infected feces. The eggs enter the cat's body through the mouth. When the eggs reach the small intestine, they penetrate the intestinal wall and circulate in the bloodstream. Later, they are carried by the blood to the lungs, where they infiltrate the air passages and migrate up as far as the trachea and into the esophagus. From the esophagus, they make their way down into the intestines, where they mature. This migration from the small intestine to the lungs, trachea and esophagus and back to the intestines takes about ten days. The entire life cycle, from egg to mature worm, is from seventy-five to ninety days long.

Young kittens are the most frequent victims of ascarids, although older cats do become infested. Many kittens are infested with ascarids at birth, the parasites having been passed to the fetus by the mother. When a kitten is infected in the uterus, the worm larvae localize in its liver. Some may migrate to the lungs. Within twenty-four hours after the kitten is born, the immature ascarids migrate from the lungs to the intestines. Eggs of ascarids may appear in the kitten's feces within twenty-one to twenty-four days after birth.

Symptoms of ascarid infection include a distended abdomen, poor coat, diarrhea, thin body and a sweetish breath odor. Vomiting may occur, with mature worms expelled in the vomitus. Since the ascarids migrate to the lungs, pneumonia may be a result of a severe infestation. It causes the sudden death of many kittens infested with ascarids. Once the ascarids mature in the kitten's intestinal tract, they may produce various other complications, from severe diarrhea to a complete blockage of the intestinal tract.

Although ascarids do not ordinarily mature in the human intestinal tract, children have been known to become infected with these parasites. Research is under way to determine the extent of human infestation by animal ascarids.

Since ascarids can be passed to a kitten while in the uterus, it is wise to have your new kitten examined for possible infestation. A specimen of the kitten's stool should be taken to a veterinarian for microscopic examination.

However, the age at which the specimen is taken will have an important bearing on the diagnosis. Remember, the larvae may still be in the process of migrating to the lungs. If this is so, no sign of them will appear in the bowel movement. At four weeks of age, if the kitten is infested, the ascarids will have migrated to the intestinal tract.

If you suspect that your cat has ascarids or if you detect worms in the stool or vomitus, have a specimen examined by the veterinarian. From the specimen, he will be able to tell which species of ascarid infests your cat and will prescribe the proper vermicide. While many cat owners worm their own cats, the procedure has some risks, especially for the novice. Many kittens have been killed as a result of ignorance on the part of their owners as to how they should be wormed. A worm medicine or vermicide is a poison—that is why it kills the worms. An overdose can kill a kitten or cat, as well. Be safe —worm the cat under the supervision of a veterinarian.

HOOKWORMS

Hookworms are small worms which also live in the cat's intestinal tract. They fasten onto the intestinal wall with sets of hooklike teeth. Hookworms cause anemia and emaciation and are especially damaging to young kittens. A severe infestation of hookworms may terminate in death.

The hookworm infesting cats is not the same as that which infests human beings. The human hookworm is large; the animal hookworm rarely exceeds ⅝ inch in length. Several species of hookworms are found in cats and in other animals. The most common is *Ancylostoma caninum,* found throughout the United States. Another hookworm, *Ancylostoma braziliense,* is found in the southern states. A northern species, *Uncinaria stenocephala,* is not as common as the others.

Hundreds of hookworms may be found in a single cat. All of them will be firmly fastened onto the intestinal wall by their small hooklike teeth. The female hookworm may produce several thousand eggs each day. The eggs are passed in the cat's feces, but do not begin to mature until the incidence of certain favorable conditions. In order for the life cycle to begin, hookworm eggs need plenty of oxygen, moisture and warmth. They thrive in sandy soil and in damp, shady areas. Exposure to direct sunlight, wind or very cold temperatures inhibits growth and may kill the eggs.

When the favorable conditions needed for development are present, hookworm eggs grow into infectious larvae within five days. The larvae may be ingested by a cat when it is playing with infected toys. Hookworms also gain entrance to the body through cuts, scratches and other wounds. Prenatal infection of kittens may occur, and the hookworm eggs appear in a kitten's feces as early as thirteen days after birth.

After the hookworm larvae enter the cat's bloodstream, they move to the lungs, where they soon find their way to the trachea. From the trachea, the larvae are coughed up by the cat, swallowed and sent back to the intestinal tract, often in the cecum, or blind gut. Hookworm eggs will appear in the cat's feces in from three to six weeks after the larvae reach the intestines.

The migratory phase, from the initial entry into the bloodstream and thence to the lungs and trachea and back to the intestines, takes approximately three days. The complete life cycle, from egg to mature worm, is twenty-one days.

As in the case of ascarids, young kittens are the most frequent victims. Many kittens born with hookworm larvae have little chance of survival. Early symptoms of hookworm infestation include anemia, listlessness, diarrhea, bloody bowel movements and loss of weight. In the later stages of hookworm infestation, many symptoms resembling these of feline enteritis appear, such as thick nasal and eye discharges, coughing, poor coat and temperatures above 102 degrees F.

The treatment for hookworms may be prolonged. Furthermore, the outlook is often discouraging, since the kittens are in a poor state of nutrition and health. The logical step would be to try to build up the kittens, but this is difficult as long as the hookworms remain fastened to the intestinal walls, sucking blood and causing anemia.

There are patent vermicides for hookworms, but since hookworm infestation is serious, you would be wise to let a veterinarian take care of your cat. After a cure is effected, you should practice rigid sanitation around the premises to prevent reinfestation. This is particularly important if you live in a hookworm region, such as the southern states. If the cat roams at will, prevention becomes more of a problem. It is better to restrict the cat to a screened outdoor run. Sodium borate will kill hookworm eggs and larvae. Work the compound into the soil and rake it in; merely scattering it over the ground is not sufficient. Also, feed the cat a diet high in proteins, along with some iron and copper, which help to prevent anemia.

WHIPWORMS

Whipworms are small whip-shaped worms which infest the colon and cecum. They sometimes grow to a length of three inches, but the average length is about one and a half inches. The whiplike part of the worm's body, the long esophageal section which takes up three-quarters of the body, fastens itself onto the lining of the cat's colon or cecum, and can be withdrawn when the worm moves.

Whipworms are common throughout the United States. They are difficult to eradicate, mainly because of their habit of "sewing themselves" into the intestinal lining. Surgery is the usual method of removing them, although several whipworm compounds have been developed.

The eggs of the whipworm are passed in the feces of infected cats and start to divide within twenty-four hours. This division, or fission, is the initial step in the development of the larvae. No further change takes place until the larvae find their way into the colon or cecum, where they mature. The complete cycle takes from ninety to a hundred days. Since the life cycle is a long one, kittens under nine weeks of age rarely have mature whipworms. Although whipworms are sometimes found in the colon, they prefer to feed in the cecum. Inflammation of the colon and cecum, with pain or tenderness, loss of weight, diarrhea and occasional vomiting are symptoms of whipworm infestation.

Whipworms lower the cat's resistance to other diseases. Dual infestations of whipworms and ascarids are not uncommon. Since whipworm infestation is a serious condition, the diagnosis and treatment should be left to a veterinarian. You can help by practicing rigid sanitation to prevent reinfestation after a cure is effected.

TAPEWORMS

Tapeworms are common in cats and kittens. There are two kinds of tapeworms—armed and unarmed. Armed tapeworms have hooks or suckers which enable them to cling to the intestinal walls. The unarmed tapeworms are fitted with a pair of grooves or slits, which permit them to hold onto the intestinal lining.

Armed Tapeworms

There are two species of armed tapeworms which cat owners should know about. These are *Dipylidium caninum* and *Taenia taeniaformis*.

They are similar in size and shape and both have a head, neck and various body segments. Individual tapeworms vary in size, but those usually found in cats measure from one to two feet. Both species of armed tapeworm are widely distributed in the United States.

D. caninum, or the flea-host tapeworm, is carried by fleas, and possibly by other insects. Your cat takes this parasite into its body when it bites and eats fleas which harbor the tapeworm eggs. After gaining entry into the cat's intestinal tract, the tapeworm eggs mature in from three to four weeks. When mature, the segments of the tapeworm below the neck become larger and larger, with the last few segments containing eggs. When ripe, the eggs pass out of the cat's body with or without a bowel movement and cling to the hairs around the cat's anus, where they remain until dry. When dry, the eggs resemble small, brown rice kernels. Eventually, the eggs drop off and may be picked up by other cats; thus cats may become infected with *D. caninum* either by ingesting fleas which carry the eggs, or directly, by eating the castoff eggs themselves.

T. taeniaformis, or the rodent-host tapeworm, has a similar life cycle. Larger and coarser than *D. caninum,* the eggs of *T. taeniaformis* pass out through the cat's anus and are attached to weeds, grass and other vegetation. Rodents feeding on or near this infected vegetation ingest the eggs and the cycle starts. The tapeworm larvae work onto the rodent's liver and remain dormant until the liver is eaten by a cat or other animal.

Unarmed Tapeworms

There are three unarmed tapeworms which infest cats—*Diphyllobothrium latum* (fish-host tapeworm), *D. mansoni* and *D. mansonides.* The fish-host tapeworm is found in cats fed freshwater fish, usually in the Great Lakes region. *D. mansoni* is found in cats in Puerto Rico and nearby islands, while *D. mansonides* infests cats in the southern United States, mainly in Louisiana, although a few cases of *D. mansonides* infestation have been reported in New York.

The life cycle of the unarmed tapeworms is similar to that of the armed. Only the intermediate hosts differ. *D. latum* uses the human being as a host and its eggs are passed into sewers, which in turn empty into lakes. Small crayfish eat the eggs and in turn are eaten by fish. Cats eating the fish infected with the eggs then become infested with the larvae, which develop in the cat's intestinal tract.

Trout, whitefish, pike, salmon, and perch are known carriers of *D. latum* tapeworm eggs.

The eggs of the other two unarmed tapeworms also are passed into freshwater lakes and ponds and are eaten by small crustaceans which then become infected. The crustaceans are eaten by amphibians and reptiles. Cats catching and eating infected amphibians (frogs, for example) become infected with the larvae.

Tapeworms, like the ascarids and hookworms, feed on the intestinal walls, but the damage caused by tapeworms is not nearly as severe as that caused by ascarids, hookworms or whipworms. One distinctive symptom of tapeworm infestation in the cat is the dragging of its rear end over the floor or ground. This can also be a symptom of infected or swollen anal glands. (See Chapter 11, Anal Glands.) Other symptoms of tapeworm infestation include poor coat, vomiting, nervousness and possible convulsions. Occasionally, a heavy infestation of tapeworms causes a blockage in the intestinal tract.

A positive diagnosis of tapeworms can be made only when the eggs are seen on the anal hairs or in the bowel movement. Tapeworms are relatively easy to eliminate. Various patent vermicides are effective in eradicating tapeworms, but they must be used with care as there is always the danger of overdosing. For safety, have the veterinarian prescribe the kind and amount of tapeworm eradicator.

The prevention of reinfestations of tapeworms is largely a matter of sanitation. It may be difficult to prevent a cat from coming into contact with tapeworm hosts, such as rodents, fleas and amphibia, but if your pet is well fed it is less likely to hunt rodents and amphibia. Cook all fish thoroughly, particularly those species known to be carriers of tapeworm larvae. Eliminate fleas and other external parasites both from the cat and its sleeping quarters. (See Chapter 13, External Parasites.)

BLADDER WORMS

Cats are occasionally infected with bladder worms. The type infesting the cat is known as *Capillaria felis cati,* which is a white, hairlike worm from one to two inches long and related to the whipworm. Bladder worms cause inflammation of the bladder, and frequent and painful urination. Diagnosis and treatment should be left to the veterinarian.

INTESTINAL PROTOZOA

Another important group of intestinal parasites infecting the cat are the protozoa: small, microscopic organisms found in cats of all ages.

COCCIDIOSIS

There are four species of coccidia which produce the condition known as coccidiosis in cats, dogs and other animals. Each of the four species prefers one particular species of animal as a host. But cats sometimes become infected with poultry coccidia when they eat raw chicken viscera containing the organisms.

Coccidia fasten onto the cells lining the small intestine and the tissue under the lining. Here they reproduce and develop into oocysts, highly infective oval cells which subsequently are eliminated in the feces. Cats take in the oocysts by contact with infected feces.

Coccidiosis produces enteritislike symptoms: nasal and eye discharge, weakness, emaciation, bloody diarrhea and loss of weight and appetite. There may also be a rise in temperature. Kittens are very susceptible to coccidiosis, especially after they are weaned. Nursing kittens do not appear to be as badly affected by the disease as are weaned kittens.

Young kittens may pick up the oocysts from their mothers or from infected feces. The disease is the scourge of pet shops, especially those without proper sanitation. Kittens lick their paws after walking in infected feces, and take in the oocysts. Flies are also suspected of being carriers of the coccidia oocysts.

Cats and kittens usually recover from coccidiosis and it is more or less self-limiting. But neglected cases may terminate in death, since secondary infections may set in. Recovery from a specific type of coccidia usually confers immunity from that type, but a cat recovering from coccidiosis caused by the poultry species, for example, is not immune to the other species. Positive diagnosis of coccidiosis is made by a microscopic examination of the feces. Both the diagnosis and treatment should be left to the veterinarian. You can help guard against reinfestation by keeping the cat's sanitary pan clean. Keep stray cats away and promptly remove any feces from the house, pen or grounds.

GIARDIASIS

Giardiasis is an intestinal disease caused by another protozoan, *Giardia lamblia,* and found mostly in kittens and young cats. The disease is characterized by diarrhea or dysentery, often with a heavy flow of mucus and blood; emaciation; listlessness and loss of weight.

The parasite causing giardiasis lives in the cat's small intestine and passes through two stages of development. The parasitic form, known as a *trophozoite,* is pear-shaped. It is a very active organism and may be seen in loose or semiliquid stools under a microscope. An oval-shaped form, less active than the *trophozoite,* is found in formed stools. The organism is cystic and it is at this stage that it is transmissible. *Giardia lamblia* is frequently found in young ocelots and margays shipped to this country from compounds. Diagnosis and treatment should be entrusted to the veterinarian. Giardia are also found in human beings, although the protozoans are not known to be pathogenic. They do, however, cause diarrhea.

INTERNAL PARASITE CONTROL

It may not be possible for you to prevent your cat from becoming infected with worms and protozoa, but you can reduce the hazard by good sanitation. A periodic examination of the cat's stool by the veterinarian is another good preventive measure.

Internal parasites will cause less trouble and complications when infestations are detected early and treatment administered promptly.

13. External Parasites

In common with all other warm-blooded animals, cats are plagued with ectoparasites (external parasites). Fleas, lice, ticks, mites and fungi are among the parasites living on the cat. All of them, if left unchecked, can cause skin diseases, poor coat and loss of vitality, and some of them may be carriers of serious diseases or internal parasites.

Most external parasites are easily eliminated and controlled. As with worms and protozoa, prevention of infestations of external parasites depends largely upon interfering with or breaking up their life cycles. A knowledge of the life cycles, habits and effects of external parasites will enable you to eliminate these pests and prevent further infestations.

FLEAS

There are four species of fleas associated with animals or human beings—the human flea (*Pulex irritans*), the cat flea (*Ctenocephalides felis*), the dog flea (*C. canis*) and the sticktight flea (*Echidnophaga gallinacea*). Each of these fleas usually prefers a specific host, such as a dog or cat. But upon occasion a dog flea will infest a cat, or vice versa. Fleas are found on any part of the cat's body, although the sticktight fleas prefer the ears.

The flea has a simple life history. A female deposits her eggs in sand, dirt, rugs, furniture, blankets or cracks and crevices. After a few days, the eggs develop into larvae, which spin protective cocoons. During the cocoon phase, the larvae eventually turn into pupae, which feed on organic material incorporated into the cocoon. The adult flea emerges in from ten to fourteen days. The entire life cycle requires about thirty days. One female may lay as many as 500 eggs in her lifetime.

Flea pupae may remain dormant in the cocoon until favorable conditions appear. Usually the temperature must be above freezing or the adult flea will not emerge. While fleas can withstand cold weather, subzero weather (especially if prolonged) will reduce the flea population.

Fleas are small, hard-shelled, very active insects which spend their adult lives on cats or other animals. They can jump great distances despite their small size. Most adult fleas prefer the warmest parts of the cat's body—the chest, neck, ruff and root of the tail. Sticktight fleas are attracted to the less hairy parts, such as around the eyes and ears.

Fleas, as was pointed out in Chapter 12, are capable of carrying tapeworm eggs. They are also carriers of organisms causing bubonic plague and endemic typhus fever in man. Although all fleas do not carry these organisms, it is wise to safeguard your cat from these pests, both for your own and the cat's sake.

DEFLEAING THE CAT

Elimination of fleas is a simple process. There are various insecticides which are safe for cats. Do not use any insecticide, however, which contains DDT, lindane or chlordane, all of which are toxic to cats. Use a flea powder or spray which has rotenone or pyrethrum as the killing agent. These can be used safely if directions are carefully followed.

The easiest way to deflea a cat is to use a cat bag or heavy towel. Dust or spray the cat and place it in the bag or wrap it in the towel. Keep it there for fifteen minutes, with its head outside. The fleas will move to the cat's head. When they do so, carefully dust the head, avoiding the eyes. You can protect the eyes by coating them with Vaseline or eye ointment.

Remove the cat from the bag or towel, stand it on newspaper and comb out the dead and stunned fleas. Be careful to remove all the insecticide from the cat's hair. Wrap up the fleas and dead hair in the newspaper and burn them. Repeat the defleaing process at least once a week. Keep alert for new infestations.

The cat's sleeping place, whether bed, blanket or pillow, should be dusted or sprayed. Defleaing the cat itself is only part of the job; fleas and larvae, pupae or adult, hiding in the cat's equipment, rugs or furniture also must be destroyed. Dust and spray liberally and use a vacuum cleaner on rugs, carpets and blankets. Remember, it is important to break up the flea's life cycle.

LICE

Lice, although not found on cats as commonly as fleas, are just as much of a pest. Small, wingless insects, lice are of two types—biting and sucking. A biting louse, *Felicola subrostrata,* is the one most frequently found on cats. It spends its entire life, from egg to adult, on the cat. The life cycle is a simple one. The female lays her eggs on the cat's hair and these hatch in from two to three weeks.

Adult lice are dependent upon warm-blooded animals for their existence and will not voluntarily leave the host. They are transferred by direct contact with an infected cat or hair that contains the lice eggs or nits. Lice are not as active as fleas and cannot jump or leap from animal to animal. They will freely infest different animals, including man. If you have children and one or more pets, the chances are good that you will have to delouse all of them when an infestation is found in one.

Lice cause severe anemia in kittens by feeding on their blood. Kittens infested with lice usually acquire them through direct contact with an infected mother while nursing or climbing over her. In addition to being a pest to the cat, lice are carriers of organisms causing typhus fever, trench fever and relapsing fever in human beings.

CONTROL AND ERADICATION

Lice can easily be eradicated from the cat by the technique used in eliminating fleas. After dusting or spraying the cat, put it into a bag or wrap in a towel. Comb out dead lice and burn them. Be sure to use a safe insecticide.

TICKS

Ticks were once regarded as strictly rural parasites, but these hardy pests are now widely distributed in cities and suburbs. Together with the itching and irritation caused by ticks, there is always a possibility that they may be carriers of organisms causing piroplasmosis in animals and Rocky Mountain spotted fever and tularemia (rabbit fever) in man.

The tick is an eight-legged, hard-shelled parasite that burrows into the skin and feeds on blood. It is not an insect, but an arachnid. Ticks are very rugged and stubborn parasites, capable of fasting for long periods and withstanding extremes of weather and climate. In some respects, ticks are more dangerous than either the flea or louse.

One female tick may deposit as many as 5,000 eggs in her lifetime. The eggs are laid on the ground, usually in a sheltered site. After laying her eggs the female dies. When conditions are favorable, the larvae or seed ticks make their appearance, from three weeks to six months later. These seed ticks have six legs. When conditions are favorable they begin their search for food. Climbing to the top of weeds, grass or brush, the seed tick awaits an intermediate host, usually a meadow mouse or other rodent. When the mouse or rodent brushes against the weeds or grass, the seed tick moves onto the animal's hair and works its way down to the skin, where it digs in and gorges itself by puncturing the skin with its mouth and sucking blood from the opening. The seed tick feeds up to ten days, then drops off.

Back on the ground again, the seed tick undergoes a metamorphosis, changing into an eight-legged form known as a nymph. When conditions are favorable, the nymph in its turn climbs up on vegetation and waits for a small rodent upon which to fasten. The nymph remains on the rodent for from three to ten days. After it is gorged with blood, the nymph falls to the ground and molts into an eight-legged adult tick. The adult tick repeats the tactics of the seed and nymph ticks, climbing up on vegetation and awaiting a victim. This time the victim may be a cat, dog, sheep, cow or human being. As is apparent from the above description, the tick has a more elaborate life cycle than most other external parasites.

Cats infested with ticks are apt to be thin and anemic, since the tick feeds on blood. Some ticks inject a toxin into the cat which affects the neuromuscular system. Also, infections or abscesses may form at the point where the tick punctures the skin as it burrows into the cat's skin.

REMOVING TICKS FROM THE CAT

When there are only a few ticks on your cat, you can pull them out with blunt-end tweezers, not the sharp or pointed type. Do not attempt to pull ticks off the cat with your fingers. First of all, ticks burrow in deeply and you may pull out only the body, leaving the head imbedded in the skin. This head may later become a source of infection and irritation. Also, should the tick happen to be a carrier of Rocky Mountain spotted fever or tularemia, you are exposing yourself to one of these diseases when you pull ticks out by hand. Work carefully with the blunt tweezers and be sure to *slide* the entire body of the tick out of the cat's skin. After you've withdrawn the tick, apply antiseptic powder to the site of the skin puncture. Ticks may also be loosened by soaking them with vinegar, alcohol or acetone (nail polish remover).

When a cat is heavily infested with ticks, it must be dipped in a special tick solution. Dusting with powder is not as effective as a dip. But the dip must be a safe one. Use a commercial dip containing rotenone or pyrethrum. When dipping the cat, use the some procedure as for bathing. (See Chapter 6, Bathing the Cat.)

TICKS IN THE HOUSE

Once ticks are entrenched in a house or other building, they are difficult to eradicate. They work their way into crevices and remain indefinitely, whether or not the premises are heated. When eliminating ticks on the cat, therefore, it is obviously wise to spray the premises, as well. Since the spray will not ordinarily come into contact with the cat, you can use a commercial tick spray. Spray into all cracks and under rugs, in the corners of furniture and in other likely hiding places. Spare no effort in getting rid of ticks. Once you have them in the house and permit them to remain there, they can cause a great deal of misery and expense.

If you live in a tick-infested region, it is important to eradicate ticks from the surrounding area by breaking up their life cycle. When possible, eliminate all intermediate hosts, such as meadow mice and rabbits. Mow or cut tall weeds, grass and brush which might serve as feeding and observation posts for the seed, nymph and adult ticks.

A rigid tick control program is a must, if you are to keep your cat and house free from these parasites.

EAR MITES

Ear mites are small parasites which congregate in the cat's ears. They work their way down the outer ear canal and feed on the tissue juices. Ear mites cause a crumbly wax formation, which can be easily distinguished from normal wax. Actually, the wax formation caused by ear mites is composed partly of wax and partly of scabs. Ear mites are very irritating to a cat.

Cats infested with ear mites continually shake their heads or paw at their ears. This vigorous shaking of the head is one way by which these parasites are transmitted from one cat to another. When the cat shakes his head, some of the ear mites fly out. Also, cats sometimes scratch their ears so violently that they cause blood tumors or hematomas.

Ear mites are usually easy to eliminate when they have not been allowed to burrow deep into the cat's ears. It is best to let a veterinarian treat the cat. However, you can provide some relief by removing any serum or thick crusts on the cat's ears. Soak a cotton swab in dilute hydrogen peroxide and soften the crusts or exudate. Do not probe too deeply into the cat's ears; also, have someone help restrain the cat, since the ears are very sensitive to touch. Next, apply some light mineral or vegetable oil to the affected parts. Then take the cat to a veterinarian for further treatment.

Bear in mind that the cat may shake ear mites onto the floor, rugs or furniture and be reinfested. It is wise to treat the floor, rugs and furniture with a safe insecticide. It may be necessary to repeat the treatment both of the cat and the premises several times.

14. Skin Ailments

The various skin ailments of the cat may be divided into two groups —parasitic and nonparasitic. The parasitic skin diseases are caused by mites and fungi. The nonparasitic skin conditions have various causes, among them poor diet, faulty metabolism and allergy. While most skin diseases respond to treatment, the process may be long and expensive.

PARASITIC SKIN CONDITIONS

MANGE

Mange is a parasitic skin disease that may take one of two forms: demodectic and sarcoptic. Both are caused by mites which burrow into the skin.

Demodectic Mange

The feline demodectic mange mite is an elongated parasite (*Demodex cati*) that resembles a small worm with eight stubby legs. The mite causes two types of demodectic mange: (1) a *squamous* form, in which the skin is mildly inflamed, with a loss of hair and (2) a *pustular* form, which is associated with certain bacteria. In the pustular form of demodectic mange, the skin becomes very red, there is a bloody discharge and a very disagreeable odor. While the demodectic mange mites attack the skin primarily, they have also been found in the liver, spleen, lungs and other organs of the cat.

Demodectic mange is characterized by excessive shedding of the hair, reddening of the skin, bare spots around the eyes, a thickening of the skin and a bloody discharge. The lesions may be localized on the head, elbows, hocks and toes or they may spread over the entire body.

The squamous form of demodectic mange may be confused with other skin conditions, particularly eczema. The only way to find out whether your cat has demodectic mange is by having the veterinarian examine a skin scraping under the microscope. Demodectic mange is very persistent and should receive veterinary attention. Cats with the squamous form, as a rule, respond more readily to treatment, although some cats do not respond at all and when the mange is widespread, it is sometimes necessary to have a cat put to sleep.

You can give your cat emergency treatment by washing the affected parts with mild soap and warm water, then applying a salve composed of rotenone and cold cream or glycerin. Further treatment should be under the supervision of the veterinarian.

Sarcoptic Mange

The sarcoptic form of mange is caused by another mite called *Notoedres cati*. The condition is characterized by intense itching, thick and dry skin, scabs and loss of hair. The condition usually begins on the cat's head, around the eyes, ears and muzzle. However it may also appear on the lower abdomen, chest, under the front legs, and at the root of the tail. A positive diagnosis can be made only by examining a skin scraping under the microscope.

The treatment of sarcoptic mange should be left to the veterinarian, although you can provide emergency treatment by applying a rotenone and cold cream salve.

RINGWORM

Ringworm is a very contagious skin disease caused by a fungus. Two species of fungi are responsible for ringworm—*Trichophyton megalosporon* and *T. microsporon*. Ringworm is common in young kittens and can be transmitted to human beings, dogs and other animals.

The ringworm fungi limit their activity to the outer layer of the skin. They fasten onto the hair follicles and in between the hair sheaths, eventually destroying the coat and causing the hair to fall out. Ringworm usually begins on the head, neck, and legs, but may be found on other parts of the body.

Ringworm is characterized by round or oval lesions on the skin, bare spots and scabs and crust. The lesions may be well-defined scaly patches, forming irregular circles up to two inches in diameter, or they may appear as small, red, swollen areas on the hairless parts of the body. A third type is characterized by reddish pustules around the edges or rims of the affected parts.

Ringworm responds to treatment with tincture of iodine or iodine ointment. The disease is contagious, and you should therefore wear rubber gloves when handling the cat. Stand the cat on newspaper, clip away the hair around the lesions and remove scabs and crusts by washing with mild soap and warm water. Apply iodine or iodine ointment to the affected parts. Wrap up the hair and scabs carefully, and burn them. Oral medication for ringworms is also available, and if the disease persists, the cat should be taken to the veterinarian.

FAVUS

Favus is another skin disease caused by a fungus, *Anchorion schonleinii*. It is transmissible to human beings and other animals. The fungus causing favus grows into the hair follicles and penetrates more deeply between the layers of the epidermis than does the ringworm fungus. The disease is characterized by honeycombed crusts on the face, ears, head and paws. Stumps of broken hairs may be seen in the center of the honeycombs. A positive diagnosis can be made only by the veterinarian examining a skin scraping under a microscope.

Favus also responds to iodine or iodine ointment. Use the same precautions as for ringworm, and if the condition persists, take the cat to the veterinarian.

NONPARASITIC SKIN CONDITIONS

The nonparasitic skin conditions are very perplexing to the layman. Since one condition may have various causes, treatment often has to be experimental. The discovery of the cause of a nonparasitic skin condition may take a long time.

ECZEMA

Eczema may often be a symptom of a disorder, rather than a disease in itself. It has long been a controversial skin condition, affecting both human beings and animals, and has various causes—among them faulty diet, allergy, hormone imbalance, external parasites, kidney ailments and vitamin deficiencies. Still other factors may be involved. The symptoms of eczema include itching, pustules, bloody discharge, scabs and dandruff. These are also symptoms of other skin conditions and it is very easy to confuse eczema with mange and ringworm.

The treatment depends upon the cause, which may take some time to discover. The diagnosis and treatment should be left to the veterinarian, although you can give emergency treatment by washing off the scabs with soap and warm water, and applying a soothing agent, such as calamine solution.

DANDRUFF

Dandruff is another skin condition with many causes, among them excessive bathing, use of a caustic soap, faulty diet, parasites and exposure to dry heat. The most noticeable symptoms are dry skin and grayish-white scales.

Here, again, the treatment depends upon the cause. Go over your cat's diet to see whether it is getting enough fatty acids. A daily grooming will help to get rid of the scales or flakes, but it will not cure the dandruff. Take the cat to the veterinarian if the dandruff persists.

ALOPECIA (Baldness)

Some cats lose their hair without any apparent reason. However, among the suspected causes are the friction involved in lying on hard surfaces, functional disorders, chemical irritation, dietary deficiencies, disease and parasites. Kidney ailments and thyroid and pituitary gland disorders often produce loss of hair.

The symptoms of alopecia are obvious: either small, localized bald spots or large, irregular bald areas over the body.

The treatment depends upon the cause and it may take some time, plus various tests, to determine the source of the baldness. Alopecia, while unsightly, causes no great discomfort to the cat. However, since the hair helps insulate the cat's body and protect it from insects, large denuded areas may be bothersome. Consult the veterinarian for diagnosis and treatment.

IMPETIGO

Impetigo is an inflammatory skin condition and is highly contagious to other animals and human beings. It is characterized mainly by pustules. The pustules, which are not as deep as those encountered in mange and ringworm, break easily, causing the disease to spread rapidly over the body. Impetigo usually responds well to treatment. Dust the pustules with an antiseptic powder such as BFI. Avoid contact with the pustules by wearing rubber gloves. If the condition persists, consult the veterinarian.

DERMATITIS

Dermatitis is a generalized inflammation of the skin with vague or obscure causes. A thickened skin, scaling, loss of hair and intense itching are the most prominent symptoms. The itching is often so intense that the cat constantly licks the affected parts or rubs itself raw against tables, chairs and other hard surfaces.

Among the suspected causes of dermatitis are faulty diet, food allergies, intestinal parasites, metabolic disturbances, insect and animal bites, stings, blows, scratches, chemical irritations, burns, scalds, freezing and excessive sunlight.

Chronic dermatitis should be brought to the attention of the veterinarian. Some temporary relief can be given the cat by washing the affected areas with mild soap and warm water, then applying a soothing lotion such as calamine.

ALLERGY

Many cats are allergic to certain foods, plants and other substances. An allergy may reveal itself in various ways: it may be accompanied by dermatitis, swelling, itching or skin sores. Tracing the specific cause of an allergy is often a complicated process, making it necessary for the cat to undergo various tests. A skin condition of undetermined origin should be treated by the veterinarian.

THE ELIZABETHAN COLLAR

In treating skin diseases, it is necessary to cover the affected parts with oils, ointments or salves. Cats lick the medicines off, thus retarding treatment. To prevent this situation, it may be necessary to fasten an Elizabethan collar around the cat's neck. This collar can be made from a disk of ordinary carton cardboard eight inches in diameter, with a hole in the center large enough to fit over the cat's head. The collar will slip over the cat's head more easily if you slit the cardboard all the way from the circle in its center through the circumference of the disk. The collar can be padded with cloth or roller bandage.

15. First Aid for Your Cat

Your cat does not have nine lives. He has only one and, despite his speed and agility, that one can be endangered in many ways. Cats are curious animals and their curiosity often places them in perilous situations. As a cat owner, you should be prepared to render first aid when your cat meets with an accident. Here are some of the common cat accidents:

Falls from open windows or roof terraces
Automobile accidents
Scalds
Imprisonment in closets, drawers, trunks or boxes
Poisoning by licking paint cans and eating rodent and insect poisons
Electrocution by contact with live wires, overturned floor lamps, Christmas trees with lights and other electrical appliances
Strangulation by ribbons, collars or bones
Suffocation by catching head in cans, bottles or jars or plastic bags
Being stranded in trees
Drowning
Fights
Snake, insect and animal bites

WHEN ACCIDENTS HAPPEN

Prevention of accidents is always preferable, but when they do occur, you should know what to do and what not to do until you can get your cat to the veterinarian. In the initial stage you should do everything you can to save its life and ease its pain.

You yourself can treat some minor accidents, such as cuts and insect stings, but when you are in doubt, let the veterinarian take over. In rendering first aid, keep cool, work quietly and keep reassuring the cat. Remember that cats are apt to be very nervous and highly excited after an accident. Use the proper restraint and get someone to help you, if possible.

HANDLING THE INJURED CAT

Before you can examine or treat the cat, you will need to have it under control. A frightened or nervous cat will bite and scratch. You should, therefore, protect yourself, and at the same time protect the cat from injuring itself further by thrashing around.

LIFTING THE INJURED CAT

The easiest way to lift the cat is to grasp it by the scruff of the neck with one hand, with the other hand supporting its hind quarters. When picked up in this manner, it will do one of two things—go limp or stiffen its body. Hold the cat well away from you in order to avoid its claws and teeth. Do not pick a cat up if you suspect that any bones are broken until after you have applied splints. (See Fractures, this chapter.)

HOLDING THE CAT FOR EXAMINATION OR TREATMENT

When examining or treating head injuries, the best method of holding the cat is to wrap it in a heavy blanket with the head outside. When injuries are elsewhere, two persons are needed to restrain the cat. Your assistant should hold the cat's head, with the fingers of one hand under the chin, the thumb behind the head, and the other hand holding both forelegs firmly. You yourself should hold the hind legs with one hand and examine with the other. If both of you hold on firmly but gently, the cat will be restrained.

TRANSPORTING THE INJURED CAT

As veterinarians rarely visit homes or go to the scene of an accident, you will probably have to take the cat to the veterinarian. If there are no broken bones, the cat can be carried in a blanket, cat bag or carrier. When there are fractures, apply splints and carry the cat in a blanket.

BLEEDING

Jagged cuts or gashes, caused by contact with sharp objects on fences or walls or by animal bites, are responsible for most serious loss of blood by cat.

ARTERIAL BLEEDING

Arterial bleeding may be recognized by the bright red blood which gushes or pumps out of the wound.

VENOUS BLEEDING

Venous blood is dark red or purplish, and either flows in a steady stream or oozes out.

FIRST AID

Apply pressure at once! Most arterial and venous bleeding can be stopped by applying pressure directly to the wound. Take a sterile pad, clean handkerchief or towel and place it on the wound; press down firmly.

If you cannot stop the bleeding by applying pressure, apply a tourniquet if the wound is on the cat's leg. Use a belt, necktie, roller bandage or strip of strong cloth. A tourniquet about two inches wide is preferable. Apply the tourniquet close to the wound and between it and the cat's heart. Tighten the tourniquet sufficiently to check the bleeding. Wrap it around the cat's leg several times, knot it, and let it remain until the veterinarian takes it off. Get the cat to the veterinarian as soon as possible.

MINOR CUTS AND SCRATCHES

Most of the time, the cat can treat itself by licking minor cuts and scratches. When it cannot reach cuts or scratches with its tongue, you can treat them.

Trim away any matted or bloody hair from around the wounds. Wash with mild soap and warm water. Apply an antiseptic powder or spray to the cuts or scratches.

NAIL PUNCTURES

Nail punctures (or any punctures) are dangerous and should be treated by the veterinarian. Punctures close up quickly, thus permitting tetanus bacteria to go to work.

If a veterinarian is available, take the cat to him right away. If not, you must clean the punctures. Restrain the cat. Wash the punctures with soap and warm water. Open up the punctures in order to soak the wounds with soap and water. Apply an antiseptic, working it into the punctures. Get the cat to the veterinarian as soon as possible.

BULLET OR SHOTGUN PELLET WOUNDS

Some persons shoot cats on sight. If your cat has been shot, restrain the animal and check bleeding. Do not probe for bullets or pellets. Apply antiseptic and bandage. Get the cat to the veterinarian as soon as possible.

SHOCK

Shock usually follows an accident involving severe injury. It is caused by an interference in the blood supply to the brain. Look for shock after auto accidents, burns, snakebite, etc. In case of severe injury, treat for shock as a matter of routine, *but only after you have checked serious bleeding or applied artificial respiration,* as the case demands.

A cat in shock may or may not be conscious. Its eyes will be glassy and it will have a vacant stare. It will shiver or tremble, its breathing will be shallow and irregular, often with long breaths alternating with short gasps. It may also vomit.

A cat in shock loses heat rapidly, and should be kept warm by covering it with a blanket, coat or sweater. If possible, slide a rug or newspaper under its body. Lower its head to assist the flow of blood to the brain. You can do this by placing a rolled coat or blanket under the front part of its body, with its head hanging down. If the cat is conscious, keep it quiet. Get it to the veterinarian as soon as possible.

WHEN THE CAT IS STRUCK BY A CAR OR TRUCK

Fractures and internal injuries caused by automobiles and other vehicles need the immediate attention of the veterinarian.

First, remove the cat from the path of traffic. Slide it onto a blanket or coat and drag it to the side of the road or street. Remember, the animal may try to bite or scratch, so take precautions.

First control the bleeding and then examine the cat carefully for possible fractures.

FRACTURES

Fractures are roughly classified as simple, compound and "green stick." A simple fracture is one in which the bone is snapped. In a compound fracture the broken bone protrudes through the skin. In a "green stick" fracture the bone splinters and twists, but does not snap entirely through. It resembles a broken green twig, in that some of the bone still remains intact. In the case of a simple fracture, a large swelling and inability to move the broken part are the most obvious symptoms. The compound fracture can be distinguished by the bone protruding through the skin. A "green stick" break is also characterized by a swelling or lump.

APPLYING SPLINTS

Use stiff cardboard, folded newspaper or wire mesh for emergency splints. Place the improvised splint carefully against the broken parts, with the upper and lower ends of the splint extending beyond the broken parts. Fasten the splints to the legs or tail with strips of roller bandage or adhesive tape. Tie above and below the break.

If the cat seems to be paralyzed in the hind quarters, it may have a fractured pelvis. You cannot put a splint on this part. Place the cat gently on a board and have someone hold it motionless. Rush it to the veterinarian.

After the bleeding and fractures have been taken care of, treat the cat for shock.

STOPPAGE OF BREATH

Cats may stop breathing when exposed to excessive smoke, water or gas, or to electric or lightning shock. In such cases speed is essential in reviving the cat.

SYMPTOMS

Short of obvious failure of the cat to breathe at all, the symptoms of breath stoppage include unconsciousness, weak or absent pulse, irregular heartbeats.

FIRST AID FOR SMOKE OR GAS EXPOSURE

Remove the cat from the area filled with gas or smoke. Work quickly, taking precautions that you are not overcome. Keep low to the floor or ground. Once the cat is in the fresh air, start applying artificial respiration. Place the cat on its side, with forelegs stretched out in front, hindlegs out in back. Take your handkerchief and pull out its tongue to prevent it from interfering with breathing. Next, place your hands on the cat's chest: press down, release, wait. Repeat this sequence rhythmically. Don't give up too quickly. If the cat responds, it will begin to breathe slowly and shallowly, and then gradually increase its respiration rate and depth. Treat for shock when the cat revives and get it to a veterinarian.

FIRST AID FOR DROWNING

Although most cats dislike water, they can swim for a certain length of time. But they can also drown. After a cat has been rescued from the water, hold it upside down to drain out any remaining water. Then place it on its side and use artificial respiration. Treat for shock when it revives and then take it to the veterinarian.

FIRST AID FOR ELECTRIC SHOCK OR LIGHTNING

Cats are often electrocuted by live wires and electrical appliances. Although they are rarely struck by lightning, it is a potential hazard. The symptoms for electric shock are the same as for stoppage of breath due to smoke, gas or drowning. There may also be burns. Treat first for breath stoppage.

Should the cat lie across a live wire, lift it off the wire with a dry board or broom. Be careful not to push or slide it, and thus cause more burns. Get the board or stick under the cat and lift it off the wire with a scooping motion. If the wire is on top of the cat, take the stick or board and flip it off. If possible, shut off the current.

Next, use artificial respiration. When the cat revives, treat for shock. If there are burns, they should be treated. (See Burns and Scalds, below.) Take the cat to a veterinarian.

BURNS AND SCALDS

Cats may be severely burned by lightning, electric shock, chemicals, open flames or hot ashes. Many cats are scalded by hot liquids in busy kitchens. In cases of first-degree burns, the skin is red or blistered. The hair may also be singed. In more severe burns, the hair may be burned off and the skin charred or blackened.

When a cat has first-degree burns localized in one area, trim away hair from around the burned area. Wash the burns with mild soap and warm water. Apply a thick grease, such as Vaseline, axle grease, butter, lard or commercial burn ointment. *Do not apply any anti-septic.* Tea leaves may be helpful. A teabag soaked in warm water will serve. Tea leaves contain tannic acid, which helps reduce pain and loss of fluids, which must be controlled. Tea leaves should not be used on large burns or scalds, however, since too much tannic acid may be toxic to cell tissues.

When a cat is severely burned or scalded, try to get it to a veterinarian at once. If a veterinarian is not readily available, however, first aid measures should be taken at once. Trim away singed hair from around the burned areas. Cover the burns or scalds with a thick grease and cover with a sterile pad or cloth. Next, wrap a clean cloth over this dressing and bandage the whole area with roller bandage or strips of cloth. Treat for shock, then get the cat to a veterinarian as soon as possible.

In treating burns or scalds of any degree, avoid touching them with your fingers or unsterile instruments. Do not breathe on the burns. Most important, do not use any antiseptic. Simply apply a thick grease and dressing to exclude the air.

INSECT STINGS

Insect stings can be painful and dangerous, especially if the cat is allergic. When a cat is bitten or stung by an insect it usually cries out in pain, leaps into the air and dashes off, possibly to climb a tree or post. An examination of the cat will reveal a swelling or lump.

If you can see the sting, remove it with tweezers. It will be visible as a small black spot in the center of the swelling. Cold packs of crushed ice or cold wet cloths will help relieve the pain and swelling. Calamine solution can be applied to ease itching. Treat for shock. If the swelling persists beyond a day or two, take the cat to a veterinarian. There may be an abscess or allergic reaction.

DOG BITES

Before you can treat a cat for dog bites, you may have to break up a fight. When given the opportunity, the cat will try to escape. If the cat doesn't escape, you will have to resort to one of the methods suggested below.

If the cat is on the dog's back, take a broomstick or pole and try to slide it under the cat and propel the animal off the dog's back, at the same time shouting to distract the cat's attention. Don't try to lift it off with your hands, as you will be scratched by the cat or bitten by the dog.

If a hose is handy, you may be able to separate the combatants by spraying them with water.

As a last resort, try frightening them with a loud noise, such as that caused by banging pots and pans together. Occasionally, this will send dog and cat scurrying off in opposite directions.

Dogs usually rip or tear as they bite, sometimes leaving gaping wounds, which may bleed profusely.

First, control all bleeding and wash wounds with mild soap and water. Apply antiseptic to wounds. If the wounds are minor, they may need no further attention, but severe ones should be treated by a veterinarian. The rips or wounds may have to be sutured. Treat for shock after all wounds are treated. Large wounds should receive the attention of a veterinarian.

CAT BITES

Cats fight each other, especially during mating. Cat fights are more easily broken up than those between cats and dogs. Turn a hose on the cats or make a loud noise. Cat bites are usually more dangerous than those of dogs because they are smaller and close up more rapidly. The wounds can easily become infected and possibly develop into painful abscesses.

Cat bites are visible as small holes. An abscess starts a swelling at the site of the wound and later erupts, exuding a thick yellowish discharge. The cat may run a high temperature (above 102 degree F.), lose its appetite and become inactive and listless.

Wash all cat bites with hydrogen peroxide, working it into each wound. If the bite wounds abscess, take the cat to the veterinarian.

SNAKEBITE

Although cats rarely are bitten by snakes, poisonous snakes are a potential hazard. There are four poisonous snakes in the United States —rattlesnake, copperhead, water moccasin and coral snake. How dangerous are the poisonous snakes? Herpetologists agree that they vary in the toxicity of their venom, and this variation applies to individuals within a given species. Thus, the bites of two rattlesnakes may have different toxicity, depending upon such factors as age, quantity of venom ejected, state of health, length of fangs, etc.

Snakebites usually appear as two small punctures. The symptoms include swelling, intense pain, weakness, shortness of breath, vomiting, poor vision and eventual paralysis.

If your cat is bitten by a poisonous snake and you are within an hour's drive of a veterinarian, get the cat to him right away. If not, treat it as follows:

First, try to keep the cat still; wrap it in a blanket or coat. Motion tends to increase the movement of the venom toward the heart.

Next, put these measures into practice:

Constriction. If the bite is on the leg, tie a belt or strip of cloth around the leg two inches above the snakebite and swelling. This is not a tourniquet, but a constriction band. It is to prevent the venom from flowing toward the heart. Loosen this band if the cat's leg gets cold. Remove for one minute in every fifteen.

Incision. If you have a long-haired cat, trim away the hair from around the bite zone. Sterilize a sharp knife over a flame. Make a ¼ inch crosscut or X through each bite. Don't be squeamish about this procedure—your cat's life may depend upon it. When you have made the incisions, press the lips of the wounds together to promote bleeding.

Suction. Now apply suction to the cuts. If you have a snakebite kit handy, use the suction apparatus. If not, you will have to improvise. *But do not suck the venom out with your mouth.* This is a dangerous procedure, especially if you have any cuts, ulcers or cavities.

Light a match or piece of paper and insert it into a whisky glass, canteen top, vial or other small vessel. The flame will use up the oxygen and reduce the atmospheric pressure in the vessel, thus producing a vacuum. Quickly place the open end of the vessel firmly on the snakebite so that no air can enter, and leave it there until it falls off with a suction action. This suction will not be as strong as that produced with a syringe, but it will serve in an emergency. Repeat this technique at least a dozen times.

If the swelling begins to spread more than two inches above the snakebite, move the constriction band higher and make a new incision at the new swelling and apply suction as before. Try to get the cat to drink water. Treat for shock. Get it to a veterinarian as soon as possible.

SKUNK SPRAY

Although older cats usually are cautious with skunks, inexperienced kittens may get sprayed by them.

An overpowering odor is the most obvious symptom. The cat's eyes may also be inflamed from the skunk spray and the animal may paw at them in an attempt to get rid of the pain.

Skunk odor is difficult to eliminate. Although there are various treatments and home remedies, none is 100 percent effective. The best you can hope for is to reduce the strength of the odor and ease the cat's discomfort. One standard treatment consists of washing the cat in tomato juice, which will dilute most of the odor. Avoid getting the tomato juice in the cat's eyes. In the case of inflamed eyes, wash with warm water, then apply an eye ointment. Badly inflamed eyes should receive the attention of a veterinarian.

POISONING

Cats may be either accidentally or deliberately poisoned. Irrespective of how the cat was poisoned, you must act swiftly if you are to save the animal's life.

Your cat may be poisoned by eating anything from rat baits to garbage. The symptoms of poisoning include pain, trembling, vomiting, panting, burned mouth (from an alkali or acid), convulsions and eventual coma.

Most city and suburban homes, farms and ranches have on hand various substances that are poisonous to cats. For example, insect and rat poisons or baits, lye (cleansers), herbicides, etc., are now commonly kept in city, suburban and rural homes. It is also possible for your cat to be poisoned by spoiled food in discarded cans or garbage dump.

Don't waste time! If the cat does not have a burned mouth, force the animal to vomit. Have someone call a veterinarian, giving the cat's symptoms and the kind of poison, if known. Many cities now have poison control centers and these may be utilized for help in cases of poisoning.

If you know what poison your cat ingested and have the can, jar or bottle, follow the directions on the label. Antidotes usually are listed. If you do not know what kind of poison was eaten or are doubtful, proceed as follows. Produce vomiting by giving the cat equal parts of hydrogen peroxide (3%) and water. Administer the same way as for liquid medicines. A strong solution of mustard can be substituted if you have no hydrogen peroxide. Salt water may also be used to induce vomiting; even one or two teaspoonsful of salt placed on the back of the tongue will make the cat vomit. After the cat has vomited, give the animal beaten egg whites or milk. Cats that have eaten lye or acids usually have burned mouths; therefore vomiting aggravates the situation. In such cases give the cat milk or beaten egg whites.

In all cases of actual or suspected poisoning, render first aid and get the cat to a veterinarian as quickly as possible. Speed is imperative. Keep in mind that cats are highly sensitive to all insecticides and herbicides (plant-killers). Untold numbers of cats have been killed by insect and plant sprays. The late Rachel Carson in her book *Silent Spring* mentioned that antimalarial spraying in western Java killed off thousands of cats. Insect and plant sprays used in Venezuela were also lethal to native cats, reducing them to the status of a rare species! It is also important to remember that in some cases of poisoning—strychnine, for instance—the cat may have to spend many hours under a veterinarian's care even though you have administered an antidote.

CHOKING

Choking may be caused by a bone or other foreign object in the mouth or throat.

The cat with something stuck in its mouth or throat will try to cough or vomit it up. He may gasp or gag. There may be a bloody and foamy saliva. In serious cases, breathing may be stopped.

If breathing has stopped, apply artificial respiration. Try to get the cat to a veterinarian for removal of the foreign object. If this is not possible, you will have to remove it. Have someone hold the cat, wrapped in a blanket or coat. Grasp the cat's lower jaw with your left hand, pushing its upper lips down over his teeth and holding them there with your fingers. Then tilt its head upward, so that the lower jaw hangs open. With the fingers of your right hand try to dislodge the bone or object. Work quickly and hold the cat's mouth open during the entire procedure. Reverse the directions if you are left-handed. Treat for shock. Get the cat to a veterinarian.

HEAT EXHAUSTION

Cats suffer from excessive heat and should not be left in hot rooms or automobiles. Symptoms of heat exhaustion in a cat are heavy and labored breathing, vomiting, prostration and eventually coma.

Remove the cat to a cool place. Wet it thoroughly with cold water, especially its head. When it regains consciousness, give it a teaspoonful of black coffee. Do not give it any liquids while it is unconscious. When it is revived, take it to a veterinarian.

LAMENESS, LIMPING AND SORE FEET

Lameness may be caused by a sprain, fracture, rheumatism, a bruise or foreign object in the toes or pads, or by a nail that may be ripped loose.

The cat with a sore foot, paw or leg will limp, hop on three legs, hold up the sore member and meow. There may be swelling or bleeding.

Have someone restrain the cat while you examine it. Look for thorns, glass, nails, etc. Check the leg for possible fractures. Remove any foreign object from the pads or toes. Wash with soap and warm water and apply an antiseptic to any wounds. If a nail is torn loose, check the bleeding, apply antiseptic to the site and wrap loosely with a roller bandage. Take the cat to the veterinarian.

FIRST AID KIT OR MEDICINE CHEST

Every cat owner should keep a first aid kit or medicine chest equipped with the following:

Tweezers, blunt ends
Rectal thermometer
Alcohol
Absorbent cotton
Roller bandages, 2- and 3-inch widths
Sterile pads
Adhesive tape, 1- and ½-inch widths
Small scissors, blunt ends (bandage scissors, if possible)
Nail clippers
Sandpaper sticks
Brush and comb
Eyedropper
Spoon
Small medicine bottle or baby syringe (for administering liquid medicines)
Mineral oil, light
Vaseline or commercial ointment for burns
Eye ointment (Neomycin ophthalmic ointment)
Cotton swabs
Glycerin
Insect powder (rotenone and pyrethrum only, for ticks, fleas and lice)
Antiseptic powder or spray
Milk of magnesia
Calamine lotion

Epsom salts
Bicarbonate of soda
Diarrhea medicine
Malt-flavored petrolatum for hair balls
Hydrogen peroxide
Snakebite suction apparatus, if in poisonous snake region

Note: Do not include aspirin in the cat's medicine chest as a pain-killer. Aspirin is toxic for most cats. The reaction of a cat to aspirin is similar to that of a child who gets an overdose. At first, the cat shows signs of abdominal pain, with labored breathing. Its pupils dilate to the point where the animal is almost blind; there is delirium and the cat may die. Researchers have found that cats fail to eliminate aspirin from their systems as fast as other animals; hence, there is a tendency to accumulate or store up aspirin in the body.

16. Home Care of the Sick or Injured Cat

Intelligent home nursing under the supervision of a veterinarian is the best means of speeding your cat's recovery from a serious disease or injury. When your cat is discharged from the hospital you should provide good home care until it is completely well.

Cats can be difficult patients. Their nervousness and tendency to bite and scratch when confronted with an unfamiliar situation often make treatment hazardous, and you must learn how to handle the cat under all kinds of conditions. Always resort to proper restraint, such as placing the cat in a cat bag or wrapping it in a towel, if it is nervous or highly excitable. As you become more proficient in handling the sick or injured cat, home care will be less burdensome.

SICK AREA

The very sick or badly injured cat should be kept away from all traffic in the home, although it is not necessary to isolate it altogether. In fact, it will probably convalesce much more quickly if it can see familiar people. Therefore, select a corner of the room that is not right in the middle of the family activities. The site should be comfortable, well ventilated (but not drafty) and easily cleaned.

After you have chosen the area for the sick cat, remove rugs or carpets and replace with several thicknesses of newspapers. Windows should be covered to exclude bright light. This is especially important to the cat with photophobia.

The sick bed may be a box with clean litter or a washable blanket. Hang a room thermometer near the cat's bed, about a foot off the floor and maintain a temperature of from 70 to 72 degrees F. Avoid drafts and dampness.

EQUIPMENT

Provide yourself with a work area near the cat. A small table or bench will prove useful. On it you can store all medicines, instruments, food and water pans, etc. Keep labels on all medicine jars and bottles. If there are small children in the house, it is wise to lock all medicines and sharp instruments in a cabinet or box. All instruments and pans should be washed and sterilized after use. Use a germicidal detergent (but no *phenol*) and rinse in boiling water. Also be sure to wash your hands before and after handling the cat.

DAILY RECORD OF PROGRESS

It is up to you to keep the veterinarian informed of the cat's progress. Since he will not telephone you or come to the house, a daily record of the cat's progress will be helpful in reporting to the veterinarian. Use either a simple notebook or a chart for recording the cat's temperature, dosage of medicines, symptoms and any other information which you think may assist the veterinarian in evaluating the cat's progress.

TAKING THE CAT'S TEMPERATURE

It is important to take the cat's temperature at least twice a day. The degree of temperature is an indication of the animal's progress in fighting disease or infection, and is thus an important diagnostic aid for the veterinarian. The cat's temperature will fluctuate during the day; usually it is low in the morning and high in the afternoon and evening. The temperature should be taken in the morning and in the evening.

Hold the cat on your lap or table. Coat the bulb end of a rectal thermometer with Vaseline and insert it about one inch into the cat's rectum. Keep it there for three to five minutes. Remove the thermometer, wipe it clean with absorbent cotton and take your reading. Remember, a grown cat's normal temperature range is from 101 to 102 degrees F. Kittens may have a slightly higher normal temperature.

MEDICATING THE CAT

Cats, like children, dislike medicine, but must not be humored. Administering medicine to the cat can be easy and simple once you have mastered a few fundamental techniques. Until you have acquired this skill, however, it is better to have an assistant hold the cat while you administer the medicine.

LIQUID MEDICINES

Liquids may be given by spoon, plastic bottle or rubber syringe. A plastic bottle or rubber syringe is best. First prepare the medicine, then have your assistant hold the cat on the table. Keep its head level. Now take the loose skin on one side of the mouth near the corner, and pull it away from the teeth. When you pull the skin away from the teeth, a pouch will be formed. Pour the medicine into the pouch, taking care not to pour too quickly, as this may result in some liquid getting into the windpipe or lungs. After you have poured all the medicine into the cat's pouch, release the skin and it will go back to its former position. Hold the cat's mouth closed until it swallows.

PILLS, CAPSULES AND TABLETS

It is not difficult to administer pills, capsules or tablets, once you have mastered the trick. First, place the cat on a table, one side toward you. Put your thumb at one corner of its mouth and the index finger on the other. Now tilt the head backward, so that the cat's nose is pointing upward. This will make it open its mouth slightly. Hold the pill or capsule between the thumb and index finger of your free hand, then press the mouth open wider with your middle finger acting as a lever on the cat's lower lip.

While the mouth is open, quickly drop the pill or capsule as far back as possible and then release the lower jaw and your grip on the head. Hold the mouth closed. Natural swallowing should follow. If it does not, wet a finger and rub it across the cat's lips. This stimulus usually causes a cat to swallow.

You may not succeed on the first trial. The cat may cough up or spit out the pill. In this case, immediately repeat the process. Make sure to get the pill well back into the mouth, near the throat. If necessary, try pushing it with the eraser end of a long pencil.

Some cats will drool after taking medicine. This is nothing to be alarmed about; it is merely a sensory reaction and will stop after a short time.

KEEPING THE SICK CAT CLEAN

If your cat is seriously sick, injured or paralyzed, it will not be able to move about and attend to nature's calls and will soil its bed and itself. The cleaning task will be easier if you place a washable blanket or heavy cloth under it. While shredded newspapers make a good bed, they will get wet and soiled and will cling to the hair. You can put a diaper on a very sick or injured cat. This may sound ridiculous, but it will help to keep the cat and its surroundings clean.

Remove all soiled material from the sick area as often as necessary. Keep the cat's body clean. Wash soiled places with warm water and mild soap. If the hair is matted, which may occur around the anal region, soften it with water or mineral oil and comb it out. If the hair is hopelessly matted, clip it off. Wash the cat's eyes with warm water and apply eye ointment if the eyes are inflamed. Should the cat vomit, wipe its mouth with a solution of table salt and warm water. A gentle brushing will make the cat feel and look better.

If the cat is unable to move, you will have to turn it over several times a day to help prevent strain, discomfort and bedsores.

GIVING THE CAT AN ENEMA

Cats unable to stand or walk may become constipated. If the veterinarian so prescribes, you can give the cat a laxative, such as milk of magnesia. But the veterinarian may forbid a laxative and prescribe an enema instead.

A very weak or paralyzed cat will offer little resistance to an enema. But one that is up and around may struggle. Have someone assist you.

An enema causes less trouble when administered in a laundry tub or bathtub. First of all, the feces and enema solution can be washed down the drain. Also, a tub is a safer place in which to work, as it helps confine the cat.

Use a regular quart enema bag with a small nozzle. A rubber syringe may be used in giving kittens an enema. The enema solution may consist of mild soap, warm water and a tablespoon of corn syrup. It should be warmed to the cat's body temperature.

Fill the enema bag with the solution, then dip the end of the nozzle into Vaseline or mineral oil, but be sure not to plug up the opening in the nozzle.

Open the clamp on the rubber tube and permit a little of the solution to run out. This will clear out any air.

Close the clamp and gently insert the nozzle about two inches into the cat's rectum.

Hold or hang the enema bag about one foot higher than the cat's body. (Your assistant can do this or you can hook the bag on a nail.)

Open the clamp, allowing the solution to flow slowly into the cat's rectum. Keep the pressure low, by lowering the enema bag or partially closing the clamp if necessary. If the cat gets very uneasy and squirms about, it may have all the solution it can take.

To stop the flow of the solution, close the clamp.

Allow the solution to remain in the cat's colon a few minutes, then quickly remove the nozzle and the cat will expel the solution and feces.

FEEDING THE SICK CAT

The sick or injured cat must eat if it is to have a rapid recovery. If the veterinarian places the cat on a special diet, follow it meticulously. Cats recuperating from injuries can usually be fed the regular diet.

If the cat refuses to eat, try catering to its taste. Cook the food, if necessary, and try tempting the cat with a variety of foods. Beef liver, kidneys and hearts, cooked or raw, may be appetizing. Experiment with the diet—the results are worth the trouble. Tomato juice, egg yolks and brandy have all been used to stimulate a sick cat's appetite.

The very weak cat will have to be hand-fed. Feed liquid or soft foods. Put liquids into a plastic bottle and feed by taking the loose skin on one side of the mouth near the corner and pulling it away from the teeth to make a pouch, slowly pouring in liquid foods such as broth, baby cereal and warm milk. Soft foods, such as liver paste, can be placed on the cat's tongue.

Switch to a liquid diet, also, whenever the cat has difficulty in keeping down solid foods. Feed the liquids in small quantities several times a day. Once the cat is able to retain liquid and soft foods, you can gradually change to more solid foods.

Should diarrhea be present, eliminate the regular solid foods and change to a starch diet. Boiled rice, macaroni or cottage cheese will help bring the diarrhea under control. In severe cases of diarrhea, give the cat a tablespoonful of diarrhea medicine; such as Kaopectate, or one prescribed by the veterinarian.

In general, do everything you can to get the cat to eat, even if you have to violate some of the rules of cat feeding mentioned in Chapter 5.

DRESSINGS AND BANDAGES

Don't change bandages unless the veterinarian has instructed you to do so. Most animals resent bandages and dressings and will try to pull them off. Cats treated with skin disease medicines will also lick these off, thus interfering with healing. You can forestall some of this damage by putting an Elizabethan collar on the cat. This device usually keeps it from pulling off bandages or dressings and from licking ointments, salves and oils. (See Chapter 14, Elizabethan collar.)

Part Four

REPRODUCTION

17. Sexual Behavior and Mating

Unless you have your male cat altered or the female spayed, you will have to contend with the vigorous sex life of your cat. Females possess great sexual energy and will copulate with more than one tomcat during a heat period. Courtships are short but noisy, with both male and female yowling until the mating is over. There is a good reason for the yowling of the female, which will be discussed a little further on.

HEAT PERIOD OR ESTRUS OF THE FEMALE

Sexual maturity occurs in the female, or queen, at a much earlier age than in the male. On the average, females have their first heat period or estrous cycle when they are between six and eight months of age. A determining factor in the appearance of the heat period is the length of the days. Just why this is so has never been determined, although it may be that nature intends that kittens be born during the warm seasons.

The female has several estrous cycles in succession in both summer and fall. When mating takes place, the cycle stops. If the female is not mated, the cycle may repeat until she has been mated. Three or four heat periods a year are not uncommon.

PHASES OF THE HEAT PERIOD

There are four phases or stages to the heat period.

Proestrus: In the initial or proestrus phase, the cat's uterus and vulva are preparing for a possible mating. The vulva swell, although the swelling may not be prominent. A discharge occurs during the proestrus phase.

Estrus: The second phase of the heat period is the time when mating can take place. This phase lasts from four to seven days. The uterus continues to undergo changes and the swelling of the vulva is very noticeable. During this phase, the cat is extremely affectionate, rolling on the floor, meowing and going through all sorts of antics. She often lies on the floor, with all four feet outstretched. She usually loses her appetite during this phase.

Metestrus: This third phase occurs when the cat is not mated. During this phase, the uterus and vulva lose their activity and enter the fourth phase.

Anestrus: In the fourth phase, the reproductive system has more or less returned to its normal condition. If the cat was not mated, ovulation will not have taken place and the cat can repeat the heat cycle.

SIMILARITY OF CATNIP BEHAVIOR AND ESTRUS OF FEMALE

The rolling behavior pattern seen in cats responsive to catnip is very similar to the behavior of the female cat in heat. In fact, the similarity is so remarkable that the average person can easily mistake a catnip reaction for a heat period. The cat's reaction to catnip has suggested the possibility of some relation to the estrous state. A basis for this possibility is that cats do not normally include rolling over as part of their behavior pattern, *except during the estrous period and the postreaction following copulation.* (Some males will roll over when in contact with catnip and their behavior along these lines is under investigation.) Further study of the neurophysiological basis of catnip response and the relationship of catnip to sex odor is necessary to obtain data on the similarity of the male and female cat nervous systems.

SPAYING

The female's heat periods can be eliminated by having her ovaries removed. This operation is called spaying. It is a simple operation when done early, and the cat is hospitalized for only a few days.

You may wonder about the advisability of having your female spayed. If, like many people, you have listened to false information about the operation, you may be set against it.

First of all, the operation is relatively safe. The cat is anesthetized and feels no pain. Spaying eliminates the heat periods and prevents the cat from having unwanted kittens. Basically, it is an easy way of ridding the cat of most of the sexual behavior symptoms. Usually a spayed female has no interest in tomcats. Furthermore, she tends to be gentler and more apt to remain at home.

Many people regard spaying as being "against nature." Some may feel the operation, which prevents reproduction, to be against their religious laws. However, most religions have a lenient attitude toward spaying animals. The Catholic Church, for example, does not prohibit the spaying of animals. Other people believe that spaying a female will make her fat and lazy. There is no ground for this belief —any cat will become fat and lazy if overfed.

Aside from the pros and cons of the operation itself, there is a practical argument in its favor. There are too many unwanted kittens in the world. Our cities abound with stray and homeless cats. Yet many people allow their female cats to mate and produce kittens for which there are no homes. Producing purebred kittens for sale as pets or breeding stock is an entirely different matter, of course.

Spaying also eliminates certain diseased conditions, such as cystic ovaries. Diseased ovaries often cause a condition known as nymphomania, in which the cat seems to be constantly in heat. Spaying will not make your cat mean or vicious. On the contrary, most spayed females become very docile and gentle. Spaying should be done at an early age, preferably before the cat first comes into heat.

SEXUAL BEHAVIOR OF THE TOMCAT

The male, or tomcat, may be considered sexually active all year round. Sexual maturity may occur in the tom when he is between six and twelve months of age, the average being from ten to eleven months. Toms under six months of age may show sexual interest. They will tussle with a female or male kitten, mounting their backs and perhaps simulating the sexual motions. These actions do not mean your tom is abnormal or oversexed. It is just nature's way of preparing the cat for his future role as a procreator of his species.

As the tomcat matures, he will show more and more interest in females. He will carefully examine their external genitals, mount them and go through the sexual motions. If a female in heat is nearby, the tom will cry and try to get out. He may spray urine around the room or house. There is nothing abnormal in this expression of his sexual prowess and advertisement of his availability.

ALTERING OR NEUTERING THE TOM

Tomcats can be neutered (castrated) to prevent them from roaming and to eliminate the strong odor of the urine. Neutering also tends to make the male more docile and "softens" his appearance. If done early enough, at from five to six months of age, altering eliminates the coarse features of the tomcat.

The operation is safe and simple. The veterinarian anesthetizes the tom and removes the testicles. Usually, the cat spends only a day or two in the hospital, and there are ordinarily no complications after the operation.

CRYPTORCHIDS

A cryptorchid is a male cat in which both testicles have failed to descend from the body into the scrotum. Cryptorchids are sterile. Usually, the undescended testicles have either atrophied (wasted away or decreased in size) or the body heat has destroyed the sperm. The condition may be hereditary or a result of disease or injury.

MONORCHIDS

Another abnormal sexual condition of male cats is monorchidism, in which only one testicle has descended into the scrotum. Monorchids are not sterile. They can mate and produce offspring. However, the condition is regarded as a fault by cat-show standards. Some geneticists regard the condition as inherited.

MATING

Unless one has a purebred cat and is mating it to another purebred, mating usually takes place unobserved by human beings, but it is often heard. As mentioned before, mating can be very noisy. There is a ritual connected with the mating of cats roaming at large. The queen sits in the center of a ring of tomcats, each of which awaits the chance to mate with her. When the opportunity arrives, one of the toms leaps on the female and catches her by the scruff of the neck. Toms usually fight over the queen.

COPULATION

If you have a purebred female and want to mate her, you probably will have to take her to the male. You will be wise to arrange for the mating in advance. Keep a record of your female's heat periods, so you will know when to take her to be mated.

If there is a purebred tom of the same breed in your neighborhood, your problem will be simplified. Make sure that he is in good health and is not sterile. Also, have a written agreement with the owner of the tom as to method of payment for the stud service.

Some owners of purebred tomcats advertise stud services in the classified advertisement section of the newspapers. Others list "toms at stud" in the cat and pet magazines. (See Appendix.) When breeding your female to one of the professional studs, you will have to observe certain rules. First, all arrangements are usually formal. You will have to produce the female's registration papers and a veterinarian's health certificate. You also may be required to send a photo of your cat.

Some professional breeders stipulate that their studs are available only to "approved" females. Usually, these breeders have high-grade stock and a reputation which they wish to maintain; therefore, they are particular as to which queens they allow to mate with their studs.

It is your responsibility to get the female to the tom. If you have to ship the cat, be sure to make all arrangements in time. This is particularly important to insure getting the female to the tom in the right stage of heat. If she arrives too early, you will have to pay a boarding bill. If she arrives too late, you will have had the trouble and expense of shipping her to and from the breeder all for nothing.

If you own a purebred tom and wish to mate him, shop around for a desirable female. Advertise in the local newspapers that your tom is "at stud." When you get a response, work out the arrangements and put them into writing.

Matings usually are carried out at the home of the tomcat. There is a good reason for this: the tom performs better in familiar surroundings. Also, if he has to travel too far, the tom may be tired, nervous and excited, and fail to mate.

Select a secluded room, basement or garage for the mating. Make certain there are places to which the tomcat can escape after mating. After the tomcat withdraws his penis, the female will be in pain and may strike out at him with her claws. Males have had their eyes injured by females after coition. If there are no other places of escape, put up a shelf upon which the tomcat can jump after mating.

When mating is about to take place, the female crouches down, her pelvis raised in the air. The tomcat sniffs her genitals, and cries out, and then moves onto the female from the rear and to the side. The female obliges by lifting her tail. After the tom mounts the female, he begins to knead her sides with his front paws, while performing a treading movement with his hind feet. He next thrusts several times, then remains motionless as he ejaculates. Finally, he withdraws his penis and the female cries out in pain because the tom's penis is covered with small horns or barbs, which rip the lining of the vagina.

When the male withdraws his penis, the female ovulates. When ovulation takes place, the follicles of the ovaries are sealed with blood. These plugs of blood are the start of a yellowish mass which forms over the ovarian follicles. The mass is called the *corpus luteum*. It produces hormone which puts an end to the estrous cycle.

To make certain of conception (assuming both cats are not sterile and the female is in the right stage of heat), it is well to arrange for another mating a day later.

18. Elements of Cat Breeding

Cat breeders have gone to great lengths and heavy expense to develop the fine specimens of purebred cats seen today. Selective breeding has played an important role in this development. By selective breeding, we mean the careful choice of cats to be mated with a view to producing desirable characteristics.

BREEDING SYSTEMS

Purebred cat fanciers follow certain established breeding principles. First of all, a purebred cat is one having both parents of the same breed. The breed is a group of cats with common characteristics which distinguish them from others. For example, the fawn coat, blue or seal points and blue eyes of the Siamese are breed characteristics. So are the absence of a tail in the Manx, the rabbitlike fur of the Abyssinian and the blue or mauve coat of the Russian Blue.

INBREEDING

Inbreeding is the mating of very closely related cats, such as father and daughter, mother and son, brother and sister. It is practiced when it is desired to perpetuate certain characteristics in concentrated form —for example, an exceptionally thick neck ruff on a long-haired cat or a particular color shade or shape of the head. Inbreeding is not recommended for the novice cat breeder, since many undesirable traits may be produced. Contrary to popular belief, however, inbreeding does not always produce monstrosities.

LINE BREEDING

Line breeding is the most common and reliable system of breeding cats and other animals. It consists of mating animals that are related, but not as closely related as those used for inbreeding. Mating cousin with cousin is an example of line breeding. You can distinguish line breeding in a cat's pedigree by the appearance of the same cat's name in different generations.

OUTBREEDING

Outbreeding is the practice of mating unrelated or remotely related cats within a breed.

CROSSBREEDING

Crossbreeding is the practice of mating a purebred cat with a purebred cat of a different breed.

GRADE BREEDING

Grade breeding is the practice of mating a purebred cat with a mongrel or mixed-breed.

CHOOSING A MATE FOR YOUR CAT

If you own a purebred cat, you will probably want to breed it with a purebred cat of the same breed. If you plan to exhibit any of the kittens in the various cat shows, study the breed standards. Each breed has a standard of perfection—that is, a set of requirements which would add up to the perfect cat for the particular breed. This perfection is rarely achieved, but cat fanciers keep trying. Many of them have come very close to the standard of perfection.

If you are not interested in cat shows or breed standards, mate your cat with one that closely resembles yours in size, color and disposition.

GENETICS

Genetics plays a major role in animal breathing. Briefly, genetics is the science of heredity. The primary concern is the transmission of heredity units from generation to generation, as well as the assertion of these heredity units during the growth and life of the cat.

An in-depth discussion of genetics is beyond the scope of this book. Those who wish a more technical treatment may find a number of books on genetics in the library. However, the average cat owner who may want to mate his or her cat should know some basic genetics.

Genes

The basic units of heredity are called *genes*. They are found along the chromosomes (rod-shaped bodies) of cells. A specific gene occupies a certain spot on a particular chromosome. Theoretically, every mature reproductive cell (*e.g.,* sperm and ovum) contains a gene for every inheritable characteristic. An individual resulting from the union of two such reproductive cells is endowed with a set of genes from each of its parents. Inheritable characteristics include shape and height of the body, color, length and texture of hair, etc.

Genes allow certain enzymes to be formed, which in turn allow specific chemical reactions to occur. These reactions ultimately determine the specific patterns of growth and development. Genes may also reproduce themselves. Geneticists tell us that genes are made up of deoxyribonucleic acid, or DNA. However, some protein must be on hand for the genes to function. Occasionally, a gene will produce a new hereditary trait through a change in its chemical structure (it is estimated that such a change will occur 1 time in 100,000). This spontaneous change is known as a *mutation*. Genes will mutate more frequently under irradiation or in the presence of certain chemicals. Finally, genes may be dominant or recessive.

Dominant characteristics

A dominant characteristic is one of any pair of opposite characters (for example, tallness and shortness) which, when genes for both are present in the germ plasma, rules or dominates over the other and appears in offspring. Or, to put it another way, one gene in a pair may hide or prevent the expression of the other one.

Recessive characteristics

A recessive characteristics is the opposite of a dominant one. It remains latent or unexpressed.

Incomplete dominance

Genes are not always completely dominant or recessive. The alternative forms of a gene are known as *alleles*. In some characteristics, both alleles of a pair may be expressed. For example, the color of Shorthorn cattle is a good illustration of incomplete dominance. A homozygous red Shorthorn (*i.e.*, when the paired genes for a particular trait are the same, the animal is *homozygous* for that trait) mated with a homozygous white Shorthorn produces an offspring with a blend of red and white, or a *roan color*. The lack of a tail in the Manx cat is another example of incomplete dominance.

Purebred cat

A purebred cat is one that has recognized characteristics which have been preserved through generations of unmixed descent or breeding. (Abyssinian, Burmese, Manx, Siamese, etc.)

BREEDING FOR COLOR

You may want to breed your cat to produce various colors or color combinations. Color breeding can become complicated, and it is therefore better to limit yourself to the simpler examples. Suppose, for instance, you have a white long-haired cat and would like some white kittens, but have been unable to find another white long hair to mate with your cat. A friend has a red long-haired cat. If you breed your white cat to this red one, what can be expected in the way of color in the kittens?

White is dominant over red if the white cat is a natural white and not an albino, so the chances are good that at least some of the kittens from such a mating will turn out to be whites. Whether there can be red kittens will depend on whether your cat inherited a gene for another color besides white.

Black and tabby belong to the same color group and neither is dominant over the other. Years ago, when the modern house cat's ancestors lived in the wild, the banded tabby was the natural color scheme for cats. It afforded excellent camouflage. Through evolution, the tabby has given way to solid black. Therefore, you can breed tabbies with black cats and expect to have some tabby and some black kittens in the litter.

If you were to breed a Siamese cat with a solid black short-haired cat, the kittens probably would turn out to be blacks with gray undercoats. The reason for this is that black is dominant over all other colors except natural white, red and tabby. (Bear in mind that white usually predominates over all other colors.)

LENGTH OF HAIR

Should you want to breed your cat for length of hair, remember that short hair is dominant over long hair. Two short-haired cats may produce long-haired kittens, but two long-haired cats may never produce short-haired kittens.

ABSENCE OF TAIL

The tailless feature of the Manx cat is inherited and is due to the presence of dominant genes for this trait. Actually, it is only imperfectly dominant and might be considered a deformity. When two Manx cats are mated, some of the kittens may be crippled. Harelips are another example of this kind of inheritance. Occasionally, a pure Manx, when mated to a cat with a normal tail, will produce all tailless kittens, but usually the kittens have tails or stubs.

EYE COLOR

Breeding for eye color has not received the study accorded to the production of coat color. Thus, obtaining a specific eye color is still a matter of luck.

DEAFNESS

Deafness in cats (barring disease and accidents) is generally associated with blue eyes, although all cats with blue eyes are not deaf.

POLYDACTYLISM

Polydactylism, or extra toes, is an inherited trait stemming from a dominant gene. A cat with a pair of genes dominant for this trait will have kittens with extra toes. A cat with one of these genes mated to a normal cat may have half her kittens with extra toes· and half with normal toes. A pair of cats with inherited extra toes, each with only one gene for the trait, probably would produce approximately 25 percent of their kittens with normal toes.

BREEDING FOR OTHER TRAITS

Other traits are transmitted, of course, including size, shape of the head, neck ruffs and general appearance. Do not expect to obtain all the characteristics you are seeking from the first few matings. It will take time and experimentation. Breeders have spent years trying to produce one trait.

Suppose you have a seal-point, straight-tailed Siamese female on the small side and would like her kittens to be like her. If you try mating her with a small, seal-point, straight-tailed tomcat, you will probably get some kittens closely resembling her. But don't be surprised if a kinky-tailed kitten appears in the litter, as there may be a crooked or kinky-tailed ancestor somewhere in the family tree of the father or mother.

Breeding cats for disposition is not reliable. First of all, environment plays an important part in the cat's disposition, as does its state of health. Even so, some cats are born with a highly nervous and excitable temperament. Mating two calm and docile cats in itself does not insure that the kittens will not be nervous or excitable.

The science of genetics is a fascinating study. For sources of more detailed and advanced information on breeding see the Suggested Reading list at the end of the book. For a general idea of breeding, however, keep the following in mind:

Decide which of your cat's characteristics you want to see transmitted to kittens.

Locate a mate with similar characteristics.

Do not expect to become an expert breeder at once.

Avoid trying to breed for unusual or abnormal features.

Use line breeding whenever possible; otherwise use outbreeding or crossbreeding.

Remember that white, red, black and tabby are dominant over all other colors.

Keep in mind that long hair is recessive and that short hair is dominant.

In general, try to mate your cat with one that possesses as nearly as possible the qualities you would like transmitted to kittens.

BREEDING ARRANGEMENTS

If you own a purebred male or female, you may want to breed it. Breeding fees and the rights of both owners can become the subject of violent arguments and possible litigation. If you own a purebred male and want to offer him for stud service, get a written agreement with the owner of any female using this service. The owner of the male usually sets the price for the stud service, which may be paid for in cash or by one or more kittens from the ensuing litter. If you have a female cat, get a written agreement setting down the terms of the mating.

The written agreement should state the fee and method of payment, whether cash at mating, partial payments or the pick of the litter. Also, when the payment is to be in the form of a kitten, specify at what age the owner of the male is to claim the kitten, and whether it is to be a male or female.

The owner of the male should stipulate in the agreement that he cannot guarantee conception and that a return service is not mandatory. He merely agrees to permit his male to copulate with the female. Needless to say, both the male and female should be in good health and free from communicable diseases. You should ask for a health certificate before allowing your cat to mate with another.

Should your tomcat roam about and mate with a female belonging to someone with whom you have no stud service agreement, you cannot, of course, demand a stud fee or kitten from the litter. Under common law, the kittens are the property of the owner of the female. This is so even if the female trespasses on your property and is bred by your tomcat. The law considers the owner of the female the loser. Where before he had only one cat, he now has a whole litter to feed and shelter. In all probability, however, your neighbor will be glad to give you a kitten.

SHIPPING A BREEDING CAT BY PUBLIC CARRIER

You may find it necessary to ship your cat on a train, boat or plane. These are considered semipublic agencies. They cannot refuse to ship your cat, provided you present a veterinarian's health certificate and otherwise meet all their requirements for transporting animals.

The transportation agencies are obligated to feed and water your cat during a trip and to take precautions against injury, suffocation, drowning, etc. They may or may not provide a shipping crate or carrier. If no crate is provided by the company, you must provide one. Check with the transportation company as to what kind of crate is acceptable to them, for the company can refuse to transport your cat if it is sent to it in a poorly constructed or easily breakable crate.

While the agency is responsible for the cat as long as it is in their hands, it is not responsible for acts beyond its control. For example, if your cat chews its way out of the crate, the transportation agency cannot be held liable for its escape. It is your responsibility to provide an escapeproof carrier.

The rates for shipping animals from state to state are regulated by federal laws. Within a state, the rates are set by the state itself. You should inquire about shipping requirements, rates, insurance, food, water and crates well in advance.

19. Care of the Pregnant Cat and Kittens

Nothing contributes more toward a healthy litter of kittens than good care during the mother's pregnancy. If she is in good health at the time of mating, her pregnancy should pose no special problems. Early in her pregnancy begin to feed her a nourishing diet, clear up any skin conditions, eliminate parasites and in general prepare the cat for motherhood.

The average period of gestation in the cat is from sixty-one to sixty-three days. It is not unusual for a cat to deliver her kittens a few days before or after this period. On the other hand, should your cat go three or four days beyond this time—and you are certain of the breeding date—you should consult a veterinarian. She may be having delivery trouble or undergoing a false pregnancy.

FALSE PREGNANCY (PSEUDOCYESIS)

A false pregnancy is a condition in which the female displays physical and emotional signs of pregnancy but is not carrying kittens. The cat's breasts swell and produce milk, her abdomen is distended, she gains weight, eats more and continually works at preparing a nest for the kittens she expects, but is not to have. The cat need not have been mated to have a false pregnancy. The symptoms usually appear after the cat has gone out of heat and may persist for several months.

You will have to wait a month or so before you can determine whether the cat is pregnant or having a false pregnancy. After a month, you can palpate for signs of kittens by gently feeling through her abdominal wall for lumps. As a true pregnancy progresses and the kittens increase in size, the lumps become larger. The cat with a false pregnancy will not have any lumps, although she will manifest most other signs of pregnancy.

If your cat has a false pregnancy, you will have to cater to her idiosyncrasies. Tranquilizers and sedatives will help calm a cat that is constantly meowing, working on a nest or mothering old shoes or other objects. False pregnancies can recur. While the cat can be mated and bear kittens, there is no telling when another false pregnancy may occur. Spaying, of course, will eliminate the condition.

PRENATAL CARE

The cat should be given a health examination early in her pregnancy. Examine her for fleas, lice and ticks and keep her free from these pests. Have the veterinarian examine a stool specimen for signs of worms or other internal parasites. Remember, ascarids and hookworms can be transmitted to the fetuses. Worming is not advisable after the second week of pregnancy, however, since there is danger of aborting the fetuses. If your cat shows signs of worms later in the pregnancy, do not worm her until after the kittens are born.

The pregnant cat is hungry most of the time, especially in the later stages. Feed her well, but do not overfeed her. After the first month of pregnancy, two or three meals a day will be all right. She should be fed her regular ration, plus milk, vitamins and minerals. It is very important that the pregnant cat receive a vitamin and mineral supplement, preferably one high in calcium, to guard against a postnatal condition known as eclampsia. (See Eclampsia, this chapter.)

As her pregnancy progresses, the cat will become more and more inactive and will lie about, basking in the sun. Leave her alone—this is perfectly normal.

At about the eighth week, milk usually appears in the pregnant cat's breasts, although it may be produced earlier in some cases. The breasts will swell and may become hard and caked, and the cat will show signs of discomfort. She will constantly lick her breasts in an effort to relieve the pressure. You can offer her some relief by milking a few drops out of each breast by gently squeezing each nipple with a downward pressure. This will not harm the cat or "dry her up." If her breasts are dry or caked, apply olive or mineral oil.

As the time for her delivery draws near, the cat will become very restless, wandering around and scratching in her bed. Keep an eye on her, as she may decide to have her kittens in some secluded place, such as a cellar, garage, attic or other place where they may be difficult to find. Some mother cats try to hide their kittens in old barrels, boxes, drawers and other out-of-the-way places.

The cat may lose her appetite from twelve to twenty-four hours before the kittens are due. Also, her temperature will drop a degree at that stage.

PREPARING FOR THE ARRIVAL OF THE KITTENS

You can make some preparations for the big event. If your cat is long-haired, trim away the hair around her breasts. This will help the kittens find the breasts. Also trim the hair around the anus and vagina. If the cat is constipated, *do not give her any laxatives,* but consult a veterinarian.

Hundreds of thousands of cats give birth every year with little or no help from human beings. Occasionally there are some difficulties and these will be discussed a bit further on. While the chances are you will not have to assist at the birth of the kittens, you should be prepared to help. Keep the following materials handy:

clean hand towels	Vaseline	baby bottle
blunt-end scissors	hot-water bottle	eyedropper
newspapers	absorbent cotton	thermometer

thin rubber tubing (⅛-inch in diameter and 6 inches in length) with syringe attached

BIRTH

In a normal birth, all of the kittens will usually be delivered within two hours, although some cats take three or four hours and others may take as long as seven or eight hours. If a cat labors more than eight hours without delivering a kitten, something is wrong. Call the veterinarian for instructions. Similarly, if there is an interval of more than three hours between kittens, the cat is in some difficulty and you should seek veterinary advice.

When the cat first begins labor, let her alone. The labor contractions will start slowly, with long intervals of no activity. During the contractions, the cat will pant, move around and perhaps even leave her bed. Bring her back to the bed and watch from the sidelines.

The first kitten should be born within two hours after the contractions have speeded up. In a normal delivery, the kitten emerges head first. If the kitten appears with the hind legs first, it is a breech delivery. The cat may have some trouble with breech deliveries, in which case you can help by holding onto the kitten's rear legs with a clean towel and pulling gently as the cat labors. Time your tugs with her contractions, pulling lightly as she tries to expel the kitten. If this is not successful, call the veterinarian.

Each kitten is born encased in a transparent sac or membrane (a grayish, bulky mass) with the kitten visible inside. The membrane is attached by a cord to the placenta or afterbirth, which should come out immediately after the kitten. The placenta, the lifeline from the mother cat, is the means by which the kitten is fed while in the uterus.

The fetal membrane may rupture as the kitten is expelled. When this happens, pick up the membrane and kitten in a clean towel and place them in front of the mother. Normally, the mother will break the membrane, chew off the navel cord and lick the kitten clean. If she fails to do so, you will have to assist. If you have to break the membrane, pick up the membrane and kitten with a clean towel, gently stretch the membrane near the kitten's head, hook your finger into it and carefully rip it open, remove the kitten and sever the navel cord.

When the membrane is broken, the kitten should gasp for air. Let the mother lick the kitten clean. If she refuses, wipe the kitten with a clean towel. In some cases, breathing may be blocked by mucus in the kitten's nose, throat or lungs. This mucus must be removed. Open the kitten's mouth, insert a medicine dropper or eyedropper and draw out any mucus. Then rub the kitten vigorously with a clean towel, both with and against the lie of the hair. This will stimulate circulation.

If the kitten still does not breathe, take more drastic steps. Wrap the kitten in a towel, hold it cupped firmly in your hands, with the head toward your fingers, and swing the kitten downward in an arc in front of you, holding on tightly. Stop the swing suddenly. The centrifugal force should dislodge any mucus from the throat and lungs.

Should this procedure still fail to start the kitten breathing, attach one end of the rubber tube (listed previously as needed obstetric equipment) to the syringe. Squeeze the syringe firmly and then insert the loose end of the tubing into the kitten's mouth, well down into the throat. Release the syringe, thus sucking any mucus upward into the syringe. Keep working and do not allow the kitten to become chilled. A hot-water bottle wrapped in a towel will provide heat.

If the kitten still does not breathe, remove the syringe, insert the rubber tubing into the kitten's throat, and try forcing your own breath through the tube. First breathe air into the tube, then stop and press gently on the kitten's rib cage with your fingers. Do not press too hard or you may break the ribs. Keep trying and do not give up too soon.

THE PLACENTA

Cat owners sometimes become alarmed when their cat eats the placenta, or afterbirth, but this is a normal action. There are various theories as to why animals eat the placenta. One of them is that the animal does so to remove traces of the birth. This is important to wild animals, which must guard against other predatory animals lurking nearby, many of which will eat the young. Another theory is that the mother eats the placenta to provide a temporary source of nourishment, since she will be unable to leave the newborn animals for some time.

Try to keep a count of the placentas as each one is expelled. A placenta should follow the birth of each kitten. Sometimes a placenta is retained when the cord between the fetal membrane and the placenta breaks. If the cat does not expel the placenta, it must be removed in another way. Grasp the broken cord hanging out of the vagina with a clean towel and gently and slowly pull out the placenta. A retained placenta may interfere with the birth of the next kitten, and, if retained after the last kitten is born, will decompose and cause infection.

AS THE CAT CONTINUES TO LABOR

Even after the first kitten is born, there is no assurance that the others will follow quickly. Remain near the cat, and if her labor continues for more than three hours between kittens, call the veterinarian. Be prepared to tell him when the first kitten was born, whether it was a normal or breech delivery, how long the cat has been in labor with the present kitten and other pertinent information.

If all goes well, the kittens should be delivered and nursing within two hours. The mother will stop laboring and panting shortly after delivering the kittens and, unless there is a kitten left inside, will settle down to taking care of her new family. To check whether there is a kitten remaining in the birth canal, place your fingers on the cat's abdomen, on the underside of the pelvic region. If there is a kitten in the canal, you should be able to feel it, in which event leave the cat alone for a few hours. She may expel it. If she does not, call the veterinarian.

The mother cat may become so absorbed in her kittens that she will refuse to eat. Some mothers have been known to go as long as twenty-four hours without eating. Place a saucer of warm milk near the cat. She may drink some of it. When she does want to eat, however, she will let you know in unmistakable ways. Then feed her regular rations fortified with vitamins and minerals. Canned or whole milk is an excellent food for the nursing cat and may be fed freely during the nursing period. Keep fresh water near the cat at all times.

SOME POSSIBLE OBSTETRIC DIFFICULTIES

As mentioned before, most cats have no difficulty in delivering kittens. Obstetric troubles, when they do occur, may be caused by disease or malfunctioning of the reproductive system.

BREECH DELIVERY

As already stated, in a breech delivery the kitten arrives hind feet first. Usually the head of a breech kitten is large and the cat has difficulty in expelling the kitten.

CAESARIAN SECTION

When kittens cannot be born in a normal manner (that is, through the birth canal) they must be delievered through an incision in the cat's abdominal wall and into the uterus. This operation is called a caesarian section.

Caesarian sections can sometimes be anticipated early in pregnancy when the veterinarian determines either by X rays or palpation that the kittens are going to be too large to be delivered normallly. Sometimes the veterinarian must perform a caesarian to remove the remaining kittens after one or two kittens are born. The cat's uterine muscles may become fatigued, making her unable to expel the kittens. This is one reason for calling the veterinarian if your cat labors for more than eight hours without producing a kitten.

ECLAMPSIA

Eclampsia is a serious condition that often follows the birth of kittens. It is brought about by a depletion of the blood calcium. The symptoms include excessive panting, restlessness, loss of appetite, a temperature above 103 degrees F., a stilted walk and convulsions, eventually followed by collapse and coma. There is nothing you can do for the cat. Call the veterinarian immediately or rush the cat over to him. He can revive the cat quickly by injecting calcium gluconate into her bloodstream.

POSTNATAL PERIOD

The cat will have a discharge for a week or ten days. This discharge should be red or dark red in color. If it is green or greenish-yellow, there is something wrong. A placenta may have been retained despite your vigilance and serious infection may result. Such an infection may cause the cat's milk to dry up and eventually lead to her death, and that of her kittens. Do not delay when you see a green or greenish-yellow discharge. Get the cat to the veterinarian immediately.

CARE OF THE NEWBORN KITTENS

The mother and kittens should be left strictly alone for the first two or three days. Nursing kittens are very delicate, so avoid unnecessary handling. Caution children not to pick up the baby cats.

During the first ten days of life, the physical activities of the newborn kittens are very limited. They cannot see or hear; their legs are to weak to support their bodies and they must get around by crawling on their abdomens with a swimming motion. Baby cats will cry when they are hungry and sometimes stray from the warmth of their mother's body. Provide some barricade to prevent the kittens from getting too far from the mother.

Watch the kittens closely for the first week to make certain they are getting enough to eat. The mother's rear breasts contain the most milk and the more vigorous kittens will monopolize them. Keep rotating the kittens on the rear breasts, so that all get enough nourishment. You can tie different colored ribbons to one leg of each kitten as identification markers to help you keep track of which kittens have been fed on the rear breasts.

Excessive leanness, weakness and constant crying are signs that a kitten is not getting enough milk. Such kittens quickly become dehydrated. You can check for dehydration by pinching the skin at the back of the kitten's neck with your thumb and forefinger and quickly releasing it. If the kitten is dehydrated, the skin will not snap back to its former position, but will remain pinched.

In spite of good prenatal care, the mother may not have enough milk to feed all her kittens, especially when the litter is very large. Occasionally a mother cat dies while the kittens are still nursing. If either of these situations arises, you will have to bottle-feed the kittens.

BOTTLE FEEDING

You should have little difficulty in getting the kittens to feed from a bottle or eyedropper. Kittens have a natural urge to suck. Use an eyedropper or baby doll bottle for the first few days, and later switch to a larger bottle. Two- or three-day-old kittens do not consume much milk at a feeding, even though they seem to be eating all the time. The actual quantity that an average newborn kitten drinks at a feeding is from about five to twenty-five drops.

Newborn kittens should be fed five times a day. Your best gauge as to whether the kittens are getting enough of the formula is to apply the dehydration test already described.

If the kittens are dehydrated, increase the amount of formula for each kitten. You may make your own formula or use one of the commercial preparations. Here is a formula that has proved successful:

$\frac{1}{2}$ cup of evaporated milk
$\frac{1}{2}$ cup of water
$\frac{1}{10}$ cup of light cream
2 drops of water-soluble vitamins

This is a stock supply and should be kept in the refrigerator; warm any portion you feed to the kittens. If you use a commercial formula, follow the directions of the manufacturer. Clean and sterilize all utensils and bottles after each feeding.

WEANING THE KITTENS

The mother will begin to wean the kittens somewhere around the fourth or fifth week. First she will reduce the number of feedings each day by spending more time away from the kittens. Then she will bring food to the kittens and teach them how to eat it. When she begins weaning the kittens, take up the feeding yourself. Remember to introduce the new foods gradually and avoid overfeeding.

Finely chopped beef, baby cereals with milk, and strained baby vegetables are all excellent weaning foods. Feed the meat raw and serve all food at room temperature.

By the time the kittens are six weeks old they should be weaned from the mother. Put them on the feeding schedule for young kittens listed in Chapter 5. Once the kittens are weaned, they should not be allowed to nurse on the mother. She will usually get away from them when they try. You can help to dry up her milk supply by eliminating milk from her diet and cutting down on the number of her feedings. If the milk supply persists, consult the veterinarian. He can give the cat a hormone injection which will dry up the milk.

SLEEPING QUARTERS

Until they are weaned (and sometimes afterward), kittens will sleep nestled against their mother for the comfort of her body heat. You can provide the kittens with their own bed in the form of a large box placed where it is free from drafts and away from a hot radiator. Unless the room is very cold it is not necessary to provide additional warmth. Nature has provided the kittens with a fur coat and a metabolism which regulates body heat. You can determine when the kittens are cold by the positions in which they sleep. The colder they are, the closer they will snuggle up to each other. On the contrary, if the kittens are too warm they will sleep alone. Shred some newspapers and put the strips in the bottom of the sleeping box.

HOUSEBREAKING

By the time the kittens are weaned, they are ready to use the sanitary pan. Until that time, the mother will clean up after them. Place the sanitary pan near the sleeping box for a few days, then gradually move it away, a short distance at a time. If the mother uses the same pan it will help train the kittens. In any event they will eventually learn to use it by themselves.

To avoid confusing the cats, do not use the same litter both in the sanitary pan and in the sleeping box. If you use shredded newspapers in the sleeping box, use something else, such as shavings or commercial cat litter, in the sanitary pan.

EXERCISE

You will not have to worry about whether the kittens are getting enough exercise. After the tenth day they will become very active. Their eyes will open and they will push, shove, wrestle and play all day long. You can add to their fun by providing them with safe toys, such as hard balls, polished bones, paper tied to a string and whatnot.

HANDLING THE KITTENS

It is all right to handle the kittens after they are weaned. In fact, they should get accustomed to being handled and groomed. Start their grooming early. The nails of young kittens need to be trimmed more frequently than those of older cats. Most kittens have needle-sharp claws which can scratch or get snagged in rugs, carpets and curtains. Trim off the tips of the nails and file them with a sandpaper strip. (See Chapter 6, Care of the Claws.)

GENERAL HEALTH

The kittens should be alert, sleek, bright-eyed and full of energy. Watch them closely for signs of ill health. Examine them for parasites. Have a stool specimen from each kitten examined by the veterinarian for worms and protozoa. Start their immunization early. Consult the veterinarian for a vaccination program.

REGISTERING PUREBRED KITTENS

If the kittens are purebred, they should be registered in one of the cat registry organizations. (See list in Appendix.)

DISPOSING OF MIXED-BREED KITTENS

If the kittens are mixed-breeds, you may have difficulty in finding homes for them. Purebred kittens sell more easily than mixed-breeds. Make every effort to find new homes for mixed-breed kittens, however, as soon as they are weaned. Do not wait until they are three or four months old. If you cannot find homes for them, call your local humane society or take the kittens to the shelter. Do not abandon them or turn them loose. Remember, this is both inhumane and illegal.

Part Five

OLD AGE

20. Care of the Old Cat

Modern veterinary medicine has added years to your cat's life-span. With reasonably good care, it may live twelve years or more. In fact, today it is not unusual to see cats that are more than fifteen years of age.

At what age is a cat old? Most veterinarians agree that chronological age is not as important as the *degree* and *effects* of aging. These are related to many factors, among them the loss of tissue vitality and organic failure.

THE AGING PROCESS

The rate of aging varies with individual cats and is usually slower in females. Technically, the aging process begins at birth and continues through life. But aging is also a gradual process, with no visible signs until the stage of later life, or old age, is reached. Although the point at which a cat reaches old age varies in individual cats, veterinary gerontologists have fixed an arbitrary period at which a cat may be regarded as passing into active old age. Generally speaking, this age is considered to be from six to eight years.

Old cats have much in common with old people. Their eyesight fails, their sense of hearing diminishes or is lost altogether and they are plagued with various and possibly progressive diseases. Both in old cats and people memory lapses, intellectual abilities decline and orientation is sometimes confused. Senile people develop paralysis or other evidences of heart and nerve impairment. Old cats rarely become paralyzed, but many do develop weakness in the hind quarters. Aging also brings on behavioral changes in both man and cat.

How old age affects your cat depends upon many factors, among them how well it has withstood the years. If you have given it good care and a balanced diet during its younger days, the chances are that it will remain fairly robust and alert when it reaches old age. Conversely, if it has been neglected, it may show its age early and have many signs of senility, including poor teeth, failing heart, faulty digestion and other physical disorders.

PHYSIOLOGICAL CHANGES

The physiological changes in the aging cat are not unlike those encountered in a person who is getting along in years. An early sign of age in the cat is the graying of the hair around the nose or muzzle. The hair also loses its gloss and soft texture and becomes dull and dry. It may also fall out in bunches, leaving bald spots, especially on the abdomen. There is a noticeable change in the skin texture also. It tends to thicken with age and become drier, often scaly. This happens because the skin glands, which normally keep the skin and hair soft and pliable, lose their customary activity.

SKIN TUMORS

When the cat reaches old age, skin tumors make their appearance. Tumors may be localized or may show up on various parts of the body. Callosities may form on the hocks, elbows and other bony parts which come into contact with floors and other hard surfaces.

EYES

Old cats are subject to cataracts, which appear as cloudy spots seen through the pupils of the eyes. Not all old cats develop cataracts, but the condition is more or less associated with old age. Cataracts impair the vision and, if neglected, can lead to blindness. Surgical techniques for the removal of cataracts have been greatly improved over the past few years, and you should consult the veterinarian when cataracts first appear.

Other eye conditions may appear in old age, but none is as damaging as cataracts. Degenerative changes in the eyes are to be expected with advancing years.

Some cats become totally blind, but nature compensates for the loss of sight by sharpening other senses, especially those of scent and hearing. It is truly remarkable the way a blind cat makes its way around a room or yard. It walks with caution, but rarely bumps into obstacles, so keen are its other senses. Although the blind cat can find its way around, it is wise to take precautions. It should not be allowed outside alone. Should it wander out onto a busy street, it may become confused and expose itself to danger. Always keep an eye on the blind cat.

TEETH

Old cats often have tooth trouble. Decayed teeth interfere with chewing and digestion and should be removed by a veterinarian. Avoid giving the old cat with bad teeth hard toys, bones or other objects which may break its teeth. Accumulations of tartar should be scaled off the teeth by the veterinarian. (Teeth, Chapter 4.)

EARS

Old cats often suffer from ear infections. Some become deaf, while others retain their hearing to a ripe old age.

Deafness

Deafness may be caused by disease, injury or atrophy of the hearing mechanism. If an examination by the veterinarian reveals no disease or injury, the deafness can be attributed to old age and there is little that can be done about it. Although a deaf cat manages to get along very well without its hearing, you should recognize that it is handicapped and treat it accordingly. Avoid surprising it by moving slowly until it sees you.

Otitis

Otitis is an acute or chronic inflammation of the external, middle and inner ear. The condition can be very painful and often makes an old cat irritable. A cat with otitis may also refuse to eat. Upon examination, the ear will be found to be inflamed and there may be a discharge. The cat continually paws or scratches at its ears. Do not try to treat this condition yourself, as it can lead to deafness. Take the cat to the veterinarian.

OTHER AILMENTS OF OLD AGE

NEPHRITIS

Nephritis, or inflammation of the kidneys, is a common ailment in older cats. Some degree of nephritis is almost always present after a cat has passed its prime. The condition may range from the nonuremic type of nephritis, characterized by excessive thirst and frequent urination, to the more dangerous uremic form. Both types of nephritis require veterinary attention. A cat with chronic nephritis requires a special diet for the rest of its life.

DIABETES

Diabetes, a chronic disorder involving the function of the pancreas, sometimes occurs in older cats. *Diabetes mellitus* is the form most common in cats. The symptoms include excessive thirst, heavy and frequent urination, weakness, emaciation and eventually coma. Diabetes requires veterinary attention. The usual treatment consists of injection of insulin and a special diet.

PANCREATITIS

Old cats sometimes have an inflammation of the pancreas. The symptoms include pain in the abdomen, little or no appetite, a rise in temperature and possibly emaciation. The condition should be treated by the veterinarian. Old cats with pancreatitis should be fed a low-starch diet.

METRITIS

Metritis is an acute or chronic inflammation of the uterus. It may result from injury or infection during the delivery of kittens. The disease is sometimes seen in cats more than five years of age. It may also be a symptom of another disease. Metritis is characterized by a vaginal discharge (which may contain blood or pus), increased thirst, vomiting, abdominal pain and little or no appetite. The cat should receive immediate veterinary attention.

PYOMETRA

Pyometra is another disease of the older female. It is caused by an accumulation of pus in the uterus. The symptoms are loss of appetite, increased thirst, vomiting after drinking water, distended abdomen and pain in the abdominal region. There is a rise in temperature during the early stage of the disease, then a drop as the disease progresses. A cat with pyometra has a peculiar sweetish odor. The cat should be treated by the veterinarian.

ASCITES, OR DROPSY

Dropsy, or ascites, is another ailment of old cats. It is discussed in Chapter 11.

BEHAVORIAL CHANGES

Behavioral changes in the cat may take various forms. Old cats are creatures of habit. They have been accustomed to eating, sleeping and exercising in familiar surroundings for years. Drastic or sudden changes may upset them. For instance, old cats may react violently to extremes of heat or cold. Also, since the old cat may be suffering from some ailment, it may become irritable, often spitting and scratching when touched or handled.

The older cat may become jealous of the attention paid to children or other pets. As with old people who complain that they are no longer wanted, the old cat needs reassurance that it is still important. Affection in an old cat's waning years will help make its remaining days happier; make liberal use of it.

NUTRITION

Proper nutrition is essential for the health and longevity of the old cat. The food it eats will have a definite bearing on its lifespan, vigor and well-being. Unfortunately, even when it is fed a good diet, certain nutritional deficiencies may still appear. Various factors contribute to these deficiencies, among them poor absorption, loss of teeth, and disease.

The old cat—because of decreased activity—does not need a large quantity of food, but it does need food of high quality. Nutritional tests have revealed that those animals fed a high-quality diet live longer than those fed a large quantity of medium- or low-quality food. The caloric needs of old cats are considerably less than those of younger cats. This fact can be appreciated when one stops to think that the old cat's metabolic rate has slowed down and that it is not as active as it once was. Therefore, *overfeeding* should be avoided. Obesity in an old cat can be just as dangerous as it is in a human being.

You may continue to feed the old cat its regular diet, making allowances for its age. If it begins to put on weight, reduce the amount of food. If its teeth are bad or missing, grind the food or chop it up. If it has a kidney condition, it should be put on a low-protein diet. Actually, it is better to have the veterinarian prescribe a diet for your old cat, and you should then see to it that the diet is carefully followed.

GROOMING

The old cat will benefit from regular grooming. Oil its skin and hair if these are dry and scaly. Above all, keep the old cat free from parasites. Remember, the animal cannot stand too much stress, and an infestation of fleas, lice, ticks, worms or protozoa will sap its vitality. Avoid bathing the old cat except when it is absolutely necessary, in which case see that it is thoroughly dried. Trim the claws when they get too long. If the old cat has running eyes, wash them with warm water and apply eye ointment. In general, do everything you can to make the old cat comfortable and help it appear as young as possible.

THE END OF THE CAT'S LIFE

Sooner or later, every cat owner must face the fact that a cat must die. The death of a pet cat is often a serious blow to its owner. Unless the old cat dies from injury or heart failure, you may have to make the decision whether or not to have it put to sleep when it becomes seriously infirm or is in pain. It takes courage to make such a decision. There will be doubts, misgivings and recriminations. But in the case of terminal cancer or some other progressive disease there is a point beyond which you should not prolong the cat's misery.

The old cat can be put to sleep with no pain. The veterinarian simply injects an overdose of anesthesia and the cat closes its eyes, relaxes and slips off into a deep sleep from which it does not awaken. It is quick, painless, and humane.

POST MORTEM

Many people shudder at the thought of a post mortem. In the event your veterinarian requests permission to conduct a post mortem on your cat, should you consent or refuse? The decision is yours, of course. The veterinarian will not conduct a post mortem without your permission. But remember that your cat is dead and free from pain, and that nothing done to it now will hurt it, and that the medical knowledge gained by the post mortem may help save other cats. Remember, your own old cat's lifespan was increased by knowledge gleaned from the study of the dead bodies of other cats. Once again, the decision is yours. But think it over carefully and do not base your decision on ignorance or stubbornness.

BURIAL

If you live in the country, your cat can be buried near the house, provided the grave is dug deep and is covered with stones to protect it from other animals. Most cities have health ordinances against burying animals in back yards and vacant lots. Before you bury your pet be sure to check the local ordinances.

There are various pet cemeteries in which you can bury your cat. Consult your local newspapers, pet magazines or telephone directory. Your veterinarian will also be glad to help you find a cemetery. You may want to have your pet cat cremated and this is permitted in most areas. Sometimes a crematorium for human beings will oblige by cremating an animal. Finally, you can ask your local humane shelter to take care of the matter for you.

Appendix

CAT SHOWS

Cat shows are held by the many and various clubs throughout the United States. The shows are under the aegis of one of the cat registry associations or agencies. Information on cat shows—*i.e.,* dates, time, place, etc.—is usually listed in the several cat and pet magazines, as well as club newsletters or publications. Detailed information on what cat shows are all about can be obtained from local cat clubs or one of the cat registry associations.

CAT REGISTRY ASSOCIATIONS OR AGENCIES

American Cat Association, Inc.
American Cat Fanciers' Association
Cat Fanciers' Association, Inc. (has more than fifty affiliated cat
    clubs)
Cat Fanciers' Federation, Inc.
National Cat Fanciers' Association, Inc.
United Cat Federation, Inc.
(See cat and pet magazines for names and addresses of the secre-
    taries of these organizations)

MAGAZINES SPECIALIZING IN CATS

All Pets Magazine, Fond du Lac, Wisconsin
Cats Magazine, 4 Smithfield Street, Pittsburgh, Pennsylvania
Pet Fair, 3900 Diamond Circle, Jacksonville, Florida 32205

Suggested Reading

EVOLUTION AND DOMESTICATION OF THE CATS

Darwin, Charles, *The Variation of Plants and Animals Under Domestication*. London, 1868

McCoy, J. J., *Animal Servants of Man* (Chapter 5). New York, Lothrop, Lee and Shepard Co., 1963

Vesey-Fitzgerald, Brian, *Cats*. New York, Penguin Books, 1957

NATURAL HISTORY OF THE CATS OR *FELIDAE*

Walter, Ernest P., *Mammals of the World*. Baltimore, Johns Hopkins Press, 1965

UNUSUAL OR EXOTIC CATS AS PETS

Cisin, Catherine, *Especially Ocelots*. New York, Harry Cisin Publisher, 1967 (includes margay, puma, lynx, etc.)

CATS IN ART, HISTORY, LITERATURE, MAGIC, ETC.

Howey, M. O., *The Cat in the Mysteries of Religion and Magic*. London, Rider & Co., 1931

Langton, Neville, *The Cats in Ancient Egypt*. Cambridge, 1940.

Mellen, Ida, *The Science and Mystery of the Cat*. New York, Chas. Scribner, 1940

Mivart, St. George, *The Cat*. London, Murray, 1881

Neill, W. M., "Witch Cats in Scotland," *Occult Review*, Vol. 40, 1924

Simmons, Eleanor Booth, *Cats*. New York, McGraw-Hill, 1935

CAT BREEDING AND GENETICS

Jude, A. C., *Cat Genetics*, All Pets, 1955

ANIMAL BEHAVIOR

Hediger, H., *Wild Animals in Captivity*. New York, Dover, 1964 (paperback)

Scott, J. P., *Animal Behavior*. Chicago, University of Chicago Press, 1958 (paperback edition, New York, Doubleday, 1963)

CAT PERSONALITY

Aymar, Brandt, *The Personality of the Cat*. New York, Crown, 1958

Gay, Margaret Cooper, *How to Live with Your Cat*. New York, Berkeley, 1966 (paperback)

Index